A CULTURAL HISTORY OF OBJECTS

OBJECTS

VOLUME 1

A Cultural History of Objects
General Editors: Dan Hicks and William Whyte

Volume 1
A Cultural History of Objects in Antiquity
Edited by Robin Osborne

Volume 2
A Cultural History of Objects in the Medieval Age
Edited by Julie Lund and Sarah Semple

Volume 3
A Cultural History of Objects in the Renaissance
Edited by James Symonds

Volume 4
A Cultural History of Objects in the Age of Enlightenment
Edited by Audrey Horning

Volume 5
A Cultural History of Objects in the Age of Industry
Edited by Carolyn L. White

Volume 6
A Cultural History of Objects in the Modern Age
Edited by Laurie A. Wilkie and John M. Chenoweth

A CULTURAL HISTORY
OF OBJECTS

IN
ANTIQUITY
VOLUME 1

Edited by Robin Osborne

BLOOMSBURY ACADEMIC
LONDON • NEW YORK • OXFORD • NEW DELHI • SYDNEY

BLOOMSBURY ACADEMIC
Bloomsbury Publishing Plc
50 Bedford Square, London, WC1B 3DP, UK
1385 Broadway, New York, NY 10018, USA
29 Earlsfort Terrace, Dublin 2, Ireland

BLOOMSBURY, BLOOMSBURY ACADEMIC and the Diana logo are
trademarks of Bloomsbury Publishing Plc

First published in Great Britain 2021
This paperback edition published in 2024

Series design by Raven Design
Cover image: Wall painting of a kitchen, House of Julia Felix, Pompeii,
Italy, 2007 © Bridgeman Images

A catalogue record for this book is available from the British Library.

A catalog record for this book is available from the Library of Congress.

ISBN: HB: 978-1-4742-9865-0
        PB: 978-1-3504-6334-9
        Pack: 978-1-4742-9881-0

Series: The Cultural Histories Series

Typeset by Integra Software Services Pvt. Ltd.
Printed and bound in Great Britain

To find out more about our authors and books visit www.bloomsbury.com
and sign up for our newsletters.

CONTENTS

LIST OF ILLUSTRATIONS

SERIES PREFACE

Our lives are lived with and through and surrounded by objects. We shape them, we use them, and they shape us, too. Small wonder that scholars study them: not just those in disciplines like anthropology, archaeology, or science and technology studies that have long led the way in such research, but also—increasingly—historians, social scientists, literary theorists, and others. This six-volume *Cultural History of Objects* is a response to the growing appreciation of the subject's significance: both an authoritative summing up of the state of the art and a provocation for future work in the field.

A *Cultural History of Objects* explores how objects were created, the changing ways in which they have been used and understood, and their ongoing and cumulative consequences. Stretching from antiquity to the contemporary period, it is a chronologically wide-ranging but culturally specific project, one that focuses quite deliberately on the experience of the Western world.

Over the past three thousand years, Europe has seen the creation, maintenance, and development of a series of particular attitudes to the material world. These attitudes have been worked out through the creation and use of artifacts. These practices have involved expanding scales of production, commodification, industry, technology, and networks of distribution. At the center of this process is the idea of the object: a thing distinct from the subject who owns or uses it. This Western history of objects stands in contrast to non-Western and prehistoric attitudes to material culture in which distinctions between subjects and objects are often less clearly drawn.

For that reason, these volumes do not present a history of technology, a history of artifacts, or of material culture in which the geographic scope would necessarily be global and cross-cultural. Rather, the focus of the exercise is specifically the cultural history of objects.

This assumption shapes the periodization of the project, in which each volume deals with a recognizably Western epoch:

1. *A Cultural History of Objects in Antiquity* (c. 1000 BCE–500 CE)
2. *A Cultural History of Objects in the Medieval Age* (500–1400 CE)
3. *A Cultural History of Objects in the Renaissance* (1400–1600 CE)
4. *A Cultural History of Objects in the Age of Enlightenment* (1600–1760 CE)
5. *A Cultural History of Objects in the Age of Industry* (1760–1900 CE)
6. *A Cultural History of Objects in the Modern Age* (1900 CE–present)

Each volume shares the same structure. After an introduction, which places the period in a broader context, considering wider issues of cross-cultural exchanges with the non-Western world and the legacy of previous periods, the first chapter explores the critical question of how objecthood was understood and experienced. Successive chapters then uncover aspects of objecthood, tracing developments in technology, economic objects, everyday objects, art objects, architecture, and bodily objects. The final chapter goes further, opening up the volume and the subject more generally by using a particular object or class of objects to consider the "object worlds" of the period: the ways in which objects shaped human life in the past and shape scholarship in the present.

This approach enables readers to trace the story chronologically or thematically, reading each volume to explore a particular moment in time or reading the same chapter across all volumes to understand how particular types of object changed through time. Either way, *A Cultural History of Objects* offers an authoritative, provocative, and original account of this subject, whose importance can only grow.

General Editors: Dan Hicks and William Whyte

PREFACE

No one has ever tried to write a cultural history of objects before. Indeed, it is not entirely clear what a cultural history of objects would be. For that reason, the invitation to edit this volume was irresistible. Here was uncharted territory. And the news that five other editors were going to be assembling five other teams to do the same job, but that they would be doing so simultaneously, so that there was no possibility of our attack on this virgin territory being corrupted by influence from what anyone else was doing or thinking, made it only more attractive.

What you are about to read is, therefore, what happens if you take half a dozen distinguished academic cultural historians and throw them a minimal task description—the title of the volume, a chapter title, and a few thoughts from the general editors as to what might appear under each chapter title. The general editors adopted a policy of exercising supportive oversight and complete noninterference. We shared our drafts with each other, and I as editor gently nudged my authors in directions I thought might prove particularly productive.

The object that is this book has, of course, its own cultural history. It is a product in the first instance of a world where there are sufficient well-resourced libraries to make it practical for publishers to launch a series in the knowledge that the tag "A cultural history of ..." will itself attract sufficient sales to justify the enterprise, even before the merit of any individual volume or chapter has been assessed. It is a product, too, of a publishing world where small numbers of pictures are thought to improve the attractiveness of a book, but where even if the book is about objects, that number remains small. As readers will discover, this particular volume is somewhat subversive. I have used my picture budget unevenly. For some authors, situating objects culturally did not demand engaging with any particular object visually, but engaging with everyday objects—objects that almost by definition make little impact on written discourse while leaving a very significant material trace—demands seeing those objects before us.

More broadly, the willingness of colleagues in the USA and Europe as well as in the UK to write for this volume says something about the international academic culture. Across the Western world, at least, academics are being urged in various ways to cooperate across both national and subject boundaries. It is good to be "inter-"—whether that means being international or interdisciplinary. Academic culture fears accusations of insularity, and money is poured into the new highways of a "road and belt" policy.

Unlike the road and belt policy of the new Silk Road, the expectations that revenue will roll along these newly constructed highways are minimal. What the contributing authors trade in is ideas, and it is in the hope that by pushing out into new territory in company with a group of congenial minds—starting from virtually, but not actually, the same place—they will arrive at unknown destinations by routes never traveled before they embarked on this enterprise. They have done here what, as academic teachers, they take every opportunity to do—construct a course on a topic that they have not themselves ever properly explored, in the knowledge that as they seek the best way to educate others, they will succeed also in educating themselves.

But why choose the cultural history of objects as the topic, when there are so many other topics never properly explored? Quite apart from the fact that this was the bird in the hand, the cultural history of objects has particular attractions. Ever since Foucault insisted that "*Les mots et les choses*" needed to be thought of together—or, as his translators had it, that to do the archaeology of the human sciences one had to sort out the order of things[1]—scholars have been acutely aware of what cultural ordering does to the world of objects and what the world of objects does to cultural ordering. The naive descriptions that once dominated textbooks of archaeology and art history have been displaced by discussions that focus on human experience of objects and objects' shaping of human experience. Understanding the agency of the object and how that agency is shaped by the world of cultural expectations into which it is delivered is no simple matter, but it is an urgent matter. Unless we understand the pressures that objects have applied to people and the ways in which people have delimited objects, we will not understand any aspect of past lives, or of present lives. For all that the social sciences are keen to tell us that human behavior follows rules, that all human decisions are gaming strategies that can be described in mathematical formulae, getting those gaming strategies off the ground depends upon prior classification of objects—as food or inedible, as desirable or foul, and so on. And what we desire, we desire because of the cultures in which we have been educated.

The cultural history of objects is foundational. Forget politics or economics; forget studies of inequality or imperialism. If you want to understand the world—as it was in antiquity, as it is now—you need to start here.

March 25, 2019

LIST OF ABBREVIATIONS

IG   *Inscriptiones Graecae*
OR   Osborne, R. and Rhodes P. J. (eds.) *Greek Historical Inscriptions 478–404 BC* (Oxford: Oxford University Press, 2017)
RIC   *Roman Imperial Coinage*
RO   Rhodes, P. J. and Osborne R. (eds.) *Greek Historical Inscriptions 404–323 BC* (Oxford: Oxford University Press, 2003)

Introduction

ROBIN OSBORNE

> Whatever different detailed paths we have taken since we emerged as humans, we have as a species become more and more entangled in things.
>
> (Hodder 2012: 220)

The aim of this book, as of all six volumes of *A Cultural History of Objects*, is to offer an account of the increasing entanglement of humans and things, not simply assessing the changing extent of the entanglement, but revealing important shifts in the nature of that entanglement. In the thirty years since Arjan Appadurai drew attention to what he described, in a phrase that has proved wonderful to think with, as "the social life of things" (Appadurai 1986), scholars across the whole range of humanities and social sciences have taken a "material turn." Objects – that is, things made by human hands – and how their material presence impinges on human life have been the focus of attention of French theorists, above all Baudrillard and Latour, of anthropologists, led by Alfred Gell, of literary critics, in the wake of Bill Brown's "Thing Theory," and of sociologists, seeking a sociological theory of things, as well as of archaeologists, who, although they had always dealt with the material traces of the past, have become increasingly keen to explore "the engagement of mind with the material world" (to cite the title of one collection of papers).[1]

Historians have not been immune to this material turn. Alongside various works on the material culture of particular periods, they have attempted to survey the range of ways in which material objects shape history. The popular imagination was captured when the then Director of the British Museum claimed to be able to give a history of the world in 100 objects.[2] But just as successive scholars in other fields have complained that the vaunted material turn has not been material enough, and so too in the case of historians, materializing history has regularly been a matter of focusing on the history of patterns of consumer choice, rather than of thinking more broadly about the changing place of material objects within human history.

This volume and the series to which it belongs aim to be something more than a massive history of consumption, or indeed of production. The question which is variously investigated from different angles in the separate chapters is the question of how objects shape cultural possibilities, and how people's expectations of the material world shape what objects they make and what they make of objects. We pursue this question alike for everyday objects (Chapter 4) and for objects that lay claim to attention because of their aesthetic qualities (Chapter 5), for buildings and the built environment (Chapter 6), for objects with which people choose to be physically intimate and where there are often affective bonds between people and things (Chapter 7), and for objects prized above all for their value in exchange (Chapter 3). But we pursue, too, the question of how objects have been thought about—the human understanding of the physical world and the part that objects have played in human reconstruction of their past, present, and future place in that world. The volume concludes by taking a particular set of objects and using those to understand the world from which they come.

In this Introduction, I attempt to place the "Classical Antiquity" (that is, the Greek and Roman worlds in the millennium from around 500 BCE to around 500 CE) with which this volume is concerned into its wider natural and cultural environment, to assess its material inheritance from prehistory, and to offer a broad sketch of the ways in which the history of the political and intellectual cultures with which this volume deals is also a history of the changing place of objects in relation to knowledge, to power and to material and immaterial values. But I start by outlining the case for a cultural history of objects in antiquity by tracing some ways in which Greek and Roman authors continually revised their understanding of the appropriate status of objects and of the place that objects should occupy in the human world.

DID OBJECTS MATTER TO THE GREEKS AND THE ROMANS?

When the Roman poet Horace published three books of *Odes* together in 23 BCE, he declared at the start of the final poem in the third book, "I have finished off a monument longer-lasting than bronze" (*exegi monumentum aere perennius*, *Odes* 3.30). Other poets had compared their carefully crafted words to buildings, and Herodotus had suggested in the very opening sentences of his *Histories* that the task he was setting himself as a historian was to prevent the past works of Greeks and non-Greeks from being rubbed out by time, but

Horace takes the boast one step further: his verbal constructions will not serve to preserve the memory of monuments; they will be what is left when monuments of metal have perished (Nisbet and Rudd 2004: 364–9). His words will be impervious to the effects of wind and weather, and of time itself, dependent only on the persistence of a cultural context in which the words can be understood, a cultural context alluded to by reference to the religious rituals of Rome: "as long as the priest climbs the Capitol with the silent maiden [i.e. Vestal Virgin]" (*dum Capitolium | scandet cum tacita virgine pontifex*). Yet in formulating the condition for the survival of his words through the years in this way, Horace acknowledges that his cultural context is also a material one: were the Capitol not there to be climbed, the world in which his words made sense would have vanished.

This competition between the world of ideas and the world of things, and this acknowledgment of their mutual dependence, is present from the very earliest surviving Greek poetry. Hesiod, whose hexameter poems, the *Theogony* and the *Works and Days*, are earlier than or contemporary with the Homeric epics, the *Iliad* and the *Odyssey*, begins the *Theogony* by recounting his encounter with the Muses while he was looking after sheep on Mount Helicon in Boeotia. They addressed him, he says, accusing him of being a "mere belly," announced that they "know how to say many false things as though they were real, but we know, when we wish, how to proclaim true things," and then cut him a scepter from a laurel branch and told him to sing about the eternal blessed ones, but to start by singing of them. Hesiod then remarks: "But what is this to me, about an oak or a rock?" (*Theogony* 26–35)—a puzzling phrase, but one that starkly contrasts the world of the gods with the physical reality of Hesiod's environment. Throughout this passage there is play with the material and the immaterial—Hesiod is addressed by the immaterial Muses as if someone who conceived his own needs in material terms only ("mere belly"); the Muses claim to be able to talk about the immaterial in a way that makes it appear material, as well as talking about material reality; Hesiod is given a material token of the favor that will shape his immaterial words; and he treats this incident as not apt for telling by likening it, in what is likely to be an already proverbial expression, to talking about everyday material objects— wood or stone. The question of what matters (for we cannot ourselves get away from language that situates the important in the material), the world of "real" things or the world constructed in words, and of what tokens we can have of the status of words (Hesiod's immaterial "vision," or the laurel scepter he is left with?) is central here (Clay 2003: 57–66).

What Hesiod plays out in the abstract, the *Iliad* plays out concretely, bringing out the moral burden of things. The epic is, on the one hand, the story of Achilles' wrath toward Agamemnon after Agamemnon took back from Achilles the captive girl, Briseis, whom Achilles had earlier been given from the spoils of war as a reward for his part in that war. On the other hand, it is the story of the greatest of the Trojan warriors, Hector, facing up to the greatest of the Greek warriors, Patroclus, while Achilles is refusing to fight, and then Achilles himself after Hector's killing of Patroclus draws Achilles back into battle. Repeatedly, Achilles rejects material compensation for the loss of Briseis; it is only the immaterial costs of the loss of his comrade Patroclus that spur Achilles into battle once more, battle from which he returns with the corpse of Hector, which he despoils, dragging it around Troy and keeping it from burial. In the final book of the poem, Hector's father, Priam, secretly visits Achilles, bringing abundant material goods to secure the corpse of his son. Priam's supplication succeeds, not because of the goods that he has brought, though these are accepted, but because he reminds Achilles of his own father, Peleus, and of the human loss that Peleus and Priam will share (Taplin 1992: 251–84). From beginning to end of this poem material goods and human relations are weighed out against each other, and always it is the human relationships that win. Yet material goods are not irrelevant: Achilles' success against Hector would not have been possible without the new set of armor forged by the god Hephaistos for Achilles—a set of armor that includes a shield on which the worlds of the city at war and the city at peace are materially represented. Nor can we imagine the same reception had Priam come empty-handed.

When, almost 700 years later, Virgil constructed his *Aeneid* in dialogue with the Homeric epics, he chose to include no equivalent of *Iliad* 24. More particularly he chose to end his poem with the killing by Aeneas of the opposing champion Turnus, a killing that not only involves rejecting a suppliant's plea that explicitly refers to Aeneas' father, but that is signaled as an act fueled by terrible anger and burning fury (Tarrant 2012: 16–30). Poignantly, that fury is brought on by the sight of a particular object: the sword belt that Turnus had taken from the young Pallas when he had slain him in battle. In reacting to this object, Aeneas is of course reacting to the emotions evoked by the loss of the young prince, but the contrast between this reaction to an object and Achilles' reaction to Priam's person remains striking.

It is in strong contrast to all these earlier poetic explorations of human interaction with the world of things that in the 370s CE the imperial official Ausonius writes a poem that displaces both humans and things from the center to put there instead a force of nature, the river Moselle. Ausonius' poem, at almost 500 lines long, is unlike any earlier Greek or Latin poem. For while extended literary description of objects of various sorts, and particularly works of art, had been a feature of Greek and Latin literature from *Iliad* book 18's description of the shield made by Hephaistos for Achilles onward, descriptions of natural scenery had not.[3] Central to this poem is the juxtaposition not of the material objects to human passions, but of the world of nature to the world of human skill. For Ausonius the works of men work with nature, rather than competing against it, whether the river offers playful challenges to those in boats (199–239) or yields up its fish to the youthful angler (240–82), or whether the elaborate constructions of men on its banks embellish the riverscape (298–348). The fame of the Moselle is enhanced by the sophistication of human artifice just as it is also enhanced by the words of the poet, who will ensure even that other rivers know its glory (469–83).

Ausonius' poem builds on a poetic tradition that is distinctively Roman and manifests itself first in works of the first century CE, most notably in the letters of the Younger Pliny and the poetry of Statius, to whose verses Ausonius repeatedly alludes.[4] This tradition presents human capacity to alter and enhance the environment in a very positive way, stressing not so much the skill that the making of particular objects requires as the way in which those objects improve a natural setting. This stands in contrast to the persistent concern of earlier writers with the *un*natural effects of human constructions and the consistent preference for the simpler rather than the more technologically enhanced life. The objects that in Homer can never themselves satisfy, and that in Virgil act as provocation to destructive passions, now appear instead to work together with natural resources to create something greater than either nature or artifice alone can produce. That conceit embraces, too, the poet's own construction of his poem, which no longer competes with monuments, as Horace's had done, but itself works with the combined world of nature and artifice, which is the river that is praised, to ensure its greater fame. What Horace acknowledges obliquely (that his words depend upon the persistence of the culture to which they belong), Ausonius embraces wholeheartedly.

Together these poetic examples show the centrality of objects to the cultural history of antiquity. The object world, the universe of human-made things, provided Greeks and Romans not merely with the materials that made human life practically possible, but with the materials with which both to construct and to consider human relations not only with other humans, but also with the wider natural—and indeed supernatural—world. But what these examples also show is that the place of objects in Greek and Roman culture was neither single nor simple. For all that objects always fundamentally shaped what Greeks and Romans could achieve and how they related to one another, their moral and political uses were far from constant. To understand why that is, we must situate the cultural history of objects against a wider historical framework.

THE ENVIRONMENT OF GREEK AND ROMAN ANTIQUITY

Sustaining human life is not easy, and sustaining human social life is even harder. Hesiod blames divine punishment of attempted trickery by Prometheus for the fact that men cannot live off wild nature but have to undergo the labors of agriculture. Agriculture demanded not simply human labor, it demanded tools: not for nothing is the description of how to make a plow central to Hesiod's *Works and Days* (414–36). And cutting the wood for the plow required tools made of iron (*Works and Days* 420), a resource itself available only in some particular locations. But even equipped with a plow (and the oxen to pull it), the farmer was not guaranteed a livelihood: in the Greek peninsula and all around the Mediterranean, there were few places where agricultural labor could reliably yield the food required for survival. Massive interannual variability in rainfall rendered uncertain the cereal crops that were staple to men whom the Homeric epics already identify as "eaters of bread" (*Iliad* 5.341; *Odyssey* 9.89; Horden and Purcell 2000: 201–9). Communities of men could not survive unless they collaborated with one another. Life alone demanded this, let alone the good life. But collaboration not only demanded means of transport; it demanded ways of creating obligation beyond merely the supply of natural produce.

Extreme topographic fragmentation into geographically distinct regions combines in the Mediterranean region with the potential for connectivity enabled by the sea itself, as if nature had both ensured maximum diversity of circumstances and given the means to cope with—and indeed exploit—that diversity.[5] Climatic variability encouraged communities to diversify their agricultural production so as to grow a variety of crops with different demands for water and differently timed demands for human intervention. At the same time, topographic diversity encouraged communities to maximize their production of what their particular environment could produce easily or in quantity so as to have the wherewithal to engage in exchange to procure what their environment could not produce. Sensible decisions about how best to exploit the local environment demanded knowledge of others' situation, as well as an understanding of the possibilities and limits of one's own environment. Sensible decisions also looked beyond the immediate season and took thought for what could be effectively stored for future use. Where cows, sheep, or goats could flourish, turning milk into cheese converted a highly perishable asset into one that could be much more widely exchanged. Fish, too, that were in excess of local consumption needs were useful only if salted and dried (cf. Horden and Purcell 2000: 200).

The networks that enabled communities to survive in places where agricultural production was unpredictable also enabled the exploitation of resources that were locally abundant but generally scarce. There were some plant resources of which this was true (including the slightly mysterious silphium, which grew only in Cyrenaica), but it was much more generally true of stone and metal, and indeed of clay suitable for pottery. Fully to exploit mineral resources frequently involved investment in infrastructure that went far beyond what local demand could justify, but that yielded handsome profits, both material and in terms of contacts, when made available to places that themselves lacked those resources.

The distribution of Melian obsidian in prehistory shows how extensive the networks were that might be created in this way, even well before the period discussed in this volume (Torrence 1986); the exceptional insistence by Athens of controlling the movement of ruddle (*miltos* in Greek, a fine red clay) from the island of Kea shows equally how peculiar resources might attract peculiar political interference (Rhodes and Osborne 2003: no. 40).

If the Mediterranean environment required creating the means to establish contact with others elsewhere and encouraged turning primary products into secondary products, it also led to widespread awareness of diversity. The knowledge that was required for survival in one place could elsewhere be reutilized not simply for economic profit, but for purposes of emulation and distinction. Objects that were essential to survival in one place might be adopted for purposes of elite entertainment in another, as the water-lifting devices of Egypt became the means of producing the pleasures of running water in a Roman villa garden (Pliny *Natural Histories*: 19.60). At the same time, awareness of difference might encourage local pride.

THE INHERITANCE OF PREHISTORY

The period of antiquity with which this volume is concerned, for all that it followed a "Dark Age," enjoyed a very significant inheritance. The Bronze Age had seen dense networks of connections across the central and eastern Mediterranean, manifest in the distribution of distinctive objects and skills. Although the loss of skills is what has given the "Dark Age" its name (skills of writing—the loss of Linear B; skills of painting—the loss of Minoan and Mycenaean fresco technique; skills of building—such as those displayed in Mycenaean tholos tombs; skills in metalwork—such as those that went into elaborate Cypriot stands), much of the network of connections across the Mediterranean seems to have been preserved, and objects and knowledge continued to flow through those networks.

The current understanding of what happened at the end of the Bronze Age is not that invasion or natural disaster brought about catastrophic destruction of the preexisting order, but that the heavy degree of central organization that marked the Late Bronze Age, particularly in the Greek world where it is symbolized by the Mycenaean palaces with their Linear B archives, was fatally undermined, perhaps by a combination internal and external forces. What followed was a period of high mobility by groups that generally lacked the ability to muster great resources, but that maintained connections at a relatively low level (Broodbank 2013: 460–72). What has been thought of as the "emergence" of the Greek world from the Dark Ages is in effect the product of state formation, of the consolidation of political power. It was not so much that a new network had to be formed as that the Greek nodes of the network needed to generate significantly greater demand to create a significant and steady level of flow across the network. The entangled worlds of the late Bronze Age never became fully disentangled, and the expectations that objects could equally create links between people, as gifts, and set some people apart from others, as luxuries, were never lost, but with the formation of more complex political units, the range of ways in which material objects might be visibly deployed was greatly increased.[6]

The central Mediterranean inherited from prehistory both a set of geographic links and a set of expectations about what objects might do. Those expectations were partly formed by the physical presence of the past—the "Cyclopean" walls of Mycenaean citadels, for instance—and partly by the preservation within oral traditions. We can trace this particularly in the tradition of oral epic, of which the Homeric *Iliad* and *Odyssey* are products, where descriptions of particular objects play an important role. Some of these objects, like the boar's tusk helmet worn at one point by Odysseus or the mighty shield consistently carried by Aias, are objects that we have good reason to think were part of late Bronze Age reality; other objects, like various treasures that are said to come from Sidon, are elaborations on the types of objects that we know were moving around the Mediterranean at the end of the Dark Age. All of them fed the expectations and aspirations of those who heard poems from this oral tradition performed at festivals of the gods or on other occasions (Grethlein 2008).

OBJECTS AND KNOWLEDGE

One of the roles played by objects in the Homeric poems is to secure knowledge. In book 7 of the *Iliad* when the Greek build a wall in front of their ships, Poseidon, who in general is something of a complainer, complains to Zeus that the consequence will be that men therefore forget the wall that he and Apollo had built for Laomedon. Zeus responds by promising that, when the Greeks depart from Troy, Poseidon can come and break up and obliterate the wall that they built (*Iliad* 7.443–63; cf. 12.9–37; see Bassi 2016: 40–63). Here, right at the beginning of the Greek poetic tradition, we already see a consciousness that history and archaeology—the linguistic representation of the past and the continued existence of objects that bear witness to the past—are in constant negotiation: objects required linguistic representation in order to claim a place in history, but historical claims that have no objective correlate are thereby rendered fragile.

The fifth-century historians Herodotus and Thucydides variously revisit the relationship between objects and historical knowledge. Herodotus likes to confirm a story with a surviving object that adds plausibility to the story. So after telling of the rescue of a musician named Arion by a dolphin after he had been thrown overboard, he notes the existence of a statuette of a man on the back of a dolphin in a sanctuary at Cape Taenarum (Ht. 1.23–4). Both he and Thucydides use objects as evidence for what was the case in the past; both cite inscriptions, and Thucydides draws conclusions from what amount to archaeological excavations when he concludes from observations made when old graves were dug up on the island of Delos as part of its "purification" that the inhabitants of the graves were Carians (Thuc. 1.8). But Thucydides is also aware that material remains can mislead. Famously he observes that the material manifestation of Sparta is so paltry that anyone judging by that alone would reckon Sparta far inferior to Athens (Thuc. 1.10). He is therefore reluctant to draw any conclusions from the size of Mycenae about the truth or otherwise of the epic tradition on the size of the Greek army that went to Troy. Drawing historical conclusions from the nature, and even from the mere existence, of objects is not straightforward—these objects need to be contextualized.

Objects play a much smaller part in the evidence base deployed by later historians. This is partly because they are dealing with questions that do not lend themselves to illumination by the existence or nonexistence, or even the nature, of surviving objects. It is partly because the periods in which later historians are primarily interested were periods from which texts survived or about which there were texts on which later historians could rely. Political history dominates ancient history, and those who reached back into the history of early periods, such as the Roman historian Livy, came to do so on the basis of only one peculiar kind of object—earlier historical writings. The knowledge that mute objects give is now not so much evidence for past events as evidence for attitudes. It is the extent of his new palace, the "Golden House," and the ambition of his plans that reveal, as far as Tacitus is concerned, the audacious and unconstrained ambition of Nero (*Annals* 15.42–4). Ammianus finds evidence for corruption in Rome in gold statues, high carriages, and ostentatious dress (Ammianus Marcellinus 6.8–9).

In drawing attention to objects as telling of moral values, these historians were writing in a long tradition of mockery of men and women for their material display that has roots in Homeric epic and was a prominent feature of such archaic Greek writers as Hipponax. Such satire is particularly prominent and particularly well developed in early imperial Rome, as manifested in the *Satires* of Juvenal and the *Satyrica* of Petronius. In these works, the fictionalized individuals on whom the satirist's attention rests acquire substance from the objects that they create and with which they surround themselves. The satirist relies upon the distinctive ways in which individuals of different sorts relate to the world of objects to make persuasive his fictionalized portraits. Characteristically, the distinctions concern bodily objects (dress and jewelry), objects of personal consumption (food and drink, perfume), household furnishings and the immediate physical environment more generally, and modes of transport. Juvenal's *Satire* 10.36–46 (trans. Green) illustrates this well as the poet wonders how the laughing philosopher Democritus would have reacted:

> Suppose he had seen the praetor
> Borne in his lofty carriage through the midst of the dusty
> Circus, and wearing full ceremonial dress—
> The tunic with palm-leaves, the heavy Tyrian toga
> Draped in great folds round his shoulders; crown so enormous
> That no neck can bear its weight, and instead it's carried
> By a sweating public slave, who, to stop the Consul
> Getting above himself, rides in the carriage beside him.
> Then there's the ivory staff, crowned with an eagle,
> A posse of trumpeters, the imposing procession
> Of white-robed citizens marching so dutifully beside
> His bridle rein, retainers whose friendship was bought
> With the meal-ticket stashed in their wallets.

Objects were never, however, merely witnesses to events or characters. They also provided the evidence to confirm how the world worked. For Plato, objects give the best idea we can acquire of what the world is really like, by instantiating—albeit in qualified form—the ideas behind them. So in *Republic* 10 (596a–598d) he is critical of visual artists because they simply copy objects (a couch, in his classic discussion), when those objects are themselves already copies (on actual couches, see Chapter 4). The best sense of what the true object in question is like is gained not by the artist who represents the object, nor even by the craftsman who makes the object, but by the user who discovers whether the object does what is required of it (*Republic* 601c–602a). As we deploy objects to do things for us, we acquire both a sense of what an ideal world would be like and a sense of the deficiencies of the objects we are obliged to make do with.

Plato's idealism was only one model of knowledge in the Greek and Roman world. But Aristotle, too, thought that to have knowledge of something was to know its cause or essence, and he argued that not all knowledge could be deductive and that knowledge of principles could only be had by induction (*Nicomachean Ethics* 6.3; Bolton 2012: 57). Aristotle's own inquiries focused on knowledge of the natural world (in particular of animals), but succeeding thinkers not only extended inquiries to plants, but to the world of objects. Objects in fact provided the best example of the epistemological primacy of theory: what objects did was confirm the theories on which they were based. The best mechanicians were held to be those who had both theoretical skills in geometry, arithmetic, astronomy, and physics and practical skills in metalworking, building, carpentry, and painting (Pappas *Mathematical*

Collection 8.1). Many texts regard the objects themselves as very much inferior by-products of theoretical work—as Archimedes' military work is presented as a by-product of his theoretical inquiries by Plutarch (*Life of Marcellus* 14, 18). But there are also texts that recognize that some things can only be learned from doing the practical work itself and engaging in some trial-and-error investigations, as exemplified very nicely by the description by Philo of Byzantium of how Ptolemaic engineers perfected their artillery: Philo concludes that "it is evident that it is not possible to arrive at a complete solution of the problems involved merely by reason and by the methods of mechanics, and that many discoveries can be made only as a result of trial" (*Belopoiika* 3.50.40–5).[7]

The history of architecture shows how profound was the sense that theory was prior and that objects instantiate theory. As J. J. Coulton demonstrated, Greek temple architecture was based on rules of proportion, not on using scale drawing to allow a sense of what was aesthetically right.[8] And although such drawings were part of the architect's armory by the time Vitruvius wrote in the reign of Augustus, he still begins by insisting that the expertise of the architect is borne of both practice and reasoning, with reasoning explaining the proportions of buildings and practice allowing the building to be completed: buildings built without reason are forgotten; reasoning alone results in architects who chase after a shadow (Vitruvius 1.1.1–2). It is to the education of the architect that he devotes his first chapter, insisting on the need for knowledge of geometry, arithmetic, history, philosophy, music, medicine, law, and astronomy, as well as of draughtsmanship, and he proceeds from there to introduce the terms in which the principles of architecture are described—design, shapeliness, symmetry, correctness, and economy. When in the second book he turns to the materials of building, he again begins with theory—the Greek philosophers' identification of earth, air, fire, and water as the material elements of the world; on this basis he starts his discussion with mud bricks. Similarly, in the third book, when he turns to temples, he begins with the first principles of symmetry and with perfect numbers.

The dominant understanding of things was not that they allowed theories about the world to be tested—even Philo does not quite commit himself to that—but that they were best made in accordance with existing theory. Of course, our knowledge of attitudes is heavily biased, since it is from technical treatises composed by those with a stake in the priority of theory that we derive our knowledge. But the evidence for dialogue between theory and practice is very limited.

OBJECTS AND POWER

At the very end of antiquity, Procopius of Caesarea wrote a substantial work in six books called *On Buildings*. This was not a guide for architects, but an account of the buildings for which the Emperor Justinian was responsible "so that it may not come to pass in the future that those who see them refuse, by reason of their great number and magnitude, to believe that they are in truth the works of one man" (*On Buildings* 1.1.17, trans. Dewing). Procopius starts in Constantinople and with Hagia Sophia, which he describes in rather abstract terms, with selective treatment of only some aspects of the construction techniques and anecdotes to illustrate the role not simply of the architect but of the emperor in building decisions. Since Procopius was responsible for other works, in particular the *Secret History*, which are critical of Justinian, scholars have been uncertain what to make of the wholly laudatory tone of *On Buildings*, and of the extent to which it is a tongue-in-cheek literary exercise (Procopius himself draws attention at the start of the work, with reference to Xenophon and the Persian king Cyrus [*On Buildings* 1.1.13–14], to the ability of writers to enhance the status of rulers about whom they write). But whatever its status and sincerity, *On Buildings* well illustrates the ways in which objects, and particularly buildings, make power tangible.

Not that Procopius is doing anything new; we have already seen that the issue of a new wall overshadowing the reputation of the builders of an older wall is raised in the *Iliad*. It came to be commonplace to see power manifested in their buildings. The most famous case is that of sixth-century Samos: Herodotus gives a long account of Samian history, including the story of the tyrant Polycrates' power and demise, and then says that he has done so because the Samians had accomplished three remarkable engineering feats in the construction of the massive temples of the Samian Heraion, a 4,000-foot-long tunnel under a mountain, and a massive harbor mole (Herodotus 3.60). Such achievements, Herodotus seems to think, demand an adequate historical context to explain the power that they manifest.

Nor is the possible mismatch between the impression given by buildings and the actual power of the city a novelty either. Not only did Thucydides remark on this problem in relation to Sparta, but two hundred or so years later, a writer named Heraclides, who described a journey through Greece, noted that in the case of Athens, too, first impressions were disappointing:

> The city itself is all dry and does not have a good water supply; the streets are narrow and winding, as they were built long ago. Most of the houses are cheaply built and only few reach a higher standard; a stranger would find it hard to believe at first sight that this was the famous city of Athens, though he might soon come to believe it. There you will see the most beautiful sights on earth: a large and impressive theatre, a magnificent temple of Athena, something out of this world and worth seeing, the so-called Parthenon, which lies about the theatre; it makes a great impression on sightseers. (Heraclides Creticus 1.1, trans. Austin)

In late antiquity we find this trope reversed: Ammianus reports that when Constantius II came to Rome he complained "of the weakness or malice of common report, which tends to exaggerate everything, but is feeble in its description of the wonders of Rome" (16.10.17, trans. Hamilton).

What an object had to be to make an impression changed over time—if we believe Plutarch, some Athenians in the fifth century had thought that the Parthenon was inappropriately gaudy. To continue to give the impression of power, buildings needed to be upgraded. So it was that Augustus was reputed to have found Rome brick and left it marble. Expensive materials were certainly something that contributed to the production of wonder, but as Heraclides hints, they were not the only thing. Planning also mattered. Although the grid-plan city was not an invention of the fifth-century BCE, for all that it is often credited to the town planner Hippodamos of Miletos who is supposed to have laid out both his own city when it was rebuilt after destruction by Persia and Athens' port, the Peiraieus, on a regular grid. But if not invented in the classical period, regular plans and large public spaces were certainly a feature of cities founded in and after the fifth century, and the expansion of Greek city life following Alexander's conquest of the Persian Empire massively spread this urban style and colored the expectations of Heraclides and his contemporaries.

Where Hippodamos was important was in the realization that there was a link between the physical layout and fabric of the city and the political and social structure. As described by Aristotle (*Politics* 2.8, 1267b22–1269a12), Hippodamos comes across as excessively schematic: he divides the territory of the city into three parts (public, private, and sacred), the citizen body into three parts (craftsmen, farmers, and soldiers), magistrates according to three areas of competence (public, orphans, and aliens), and even law into three categories (assault, damage, and homicide). It is unsurprising to find that this is a man who proposed that inventors should be honored by the city: he treats the city community as an object that can be shaped by the material and institutional environment. Where people live and what the spaces and contexts are in which people meet determine how power is distributed.

Cities whose planning was a conscious act of social engineering never left the page of the philosophers (Plato has his own attempt with the city of Magnesia in *Laws*), but the more general lesson that if political power was to be grounded it needed to be manifested in the material reality of the city was not lost. Augustus did not merely improve the fabric of Rome; he transformed one whole area of the city, the Campus Martius, into a display of Augustan power, situating there his Mausoleum (built more than thirty-five years before his death), the Altar of Peace, and several Egyptian obelisks, one of which served as a sundial. In addition to this Augustan theme park, the first emperor also constructed a new forum close to the Republican forum, in which he surrounded a temple of "Mars the Avenger," commemorating his defeat of Julius Caesar's assassins, with a parade of the great men of Roman history in a story that led inexorably to Augustus himself, shown on a horse in front of the temple. The ordering of the city and of the objects in it played a very significant part in Augustus' success; the principate was, by the time of his death, firmly inscribed into the fabric of the city (Zanker 1988; Favro 1998). Subsequent emperors could only repeat his formulas. Trajan was reckoned, at least by Ammianus, to have outdone the Forum of Augustus with his own Forum, which "has no like under the cope of heaven and which even the gods themselves must agree to admire," and Constantius, faced with this, decided all he could do was erect, in the Circus Maximus, another obelisk (Ammianus Marcellinus 16.10.15–17; 17.4).

The vast majority of the inhabitants of the Roman Empire, however, like the vast majority of the population throughout antiquity, were much less conscious of the projection of power through monuments than they were of the projection of power through the objects of war. Something of the importance of arms and armor comes across from the decision of an Argive in the eighth century BCE to be buried with his cuirass and helmet, almost certainly the first such armor to be seen in that city. Equally, the great prominence of armed soldiers and naval vessels on Athenian geometric pottery, and the importance of military iconography on Athenian gravestones in both the archaic and the classical periods, emphasize the importance of military accoutrements for manifesting power and status. Republican and early imperial Rome was keen to keep actual troops out of the city, but with Trajan's and then Marcus Aurelius' columns, the fighting army was brought into the heart of Rome. But the very power of arms and armor made the wearing of them, in life or in representations, a sensitive matter. The classical Greek portrait type of the general seems to have depicted the general in helmet alone, rather than full armor; most Greek politicians were portrayed in civilian costume, and Hellenistic kings appeared naked in commemorative statues rather than in armor. Augustus chose to appear bare-headed and bare-footed when portrayed in his cuirass (in the so-called Prima Porta type), and in any case that type of commemoration was outnumbered by representations of him as a priest, wearing the toga and carrying just the patera from which the libation was poured.

As with the city, so with soldiers, the projection of power came not only from the particular objects—the outstanding buildings or gleaming arms—but from the ways in which the objects were ordered. The uniformity of the Roman military camp was an important way in which Roman power was expressed. Polybius, who devotes rather more space in book 6 to describing the Roman army than to his famous description of the Roman constitution, provides a long description of the way in which the Roman camp is laid out, protesting that this is something "noble and great" and "genuinely worth observation and knowledge" (Polybius Histories 6.26.12; the whole description runs from 6.26 to 6.31).

Polybius' description of the strength of the Roman army stresses discipline, skill, and courage, but technology also played a part. This was particularly the case with artillery used to attack city walls. But although the presence of artillery changed the nature of siege warfare and so literally changed the shape of towns, there is little sign of any systematic development of military machinery, and successful warfare never ceased to be a matter of skillful generalship and brave soldiers. The appearance of power created by armies was less a matter of what their armaments could do and more a product of the impression given by a large body of coordinated and uniform soldiers ready for battle.

OBJECTS AND VALUE

When the *Odyssey* has Telemachos visit Sparta to find out about his father Odysseus, Menelaos urges him to stay longer and promises him a gift on departure. In declining to prolong his stay Telemachos urges that the gift be "something that can be stored up," politely declining to take horses as a gift on the grounds that there are no meadows in Ithaka. Menelaos settles upon giving a silver mixing bowl with a gold rim that he claims is the work of the god Hephaistos and was given him by the king of the Sidonians (*Odyssey* 4.600–19). The value of this object lies partly in its precious material, partly in its creator and the technical skill that has gone into it, and partly in its illustrious former owners.

Works like that Sidonian bowl retained value throughout antiquity. The great wealth of late Roman silverware that we possess—far greater in quantity than silverware from any other period of antiquity—we owe to the unsettled conditions of the end of the Roman Empire, which caused objects that would otherwise have been gifted or melted down to be hidden for safety. The so-called Mildenhall Treasure, discovered in Suffolk in 1942, is a good example of this. Both the technical skills deployed and the adoption of classical imagery of Pan, satyrs, maenads, and other Dionysiac motifs mark the major pieces found at Mildenhall as laying claim to a long past ancestry, while the graffito "Of Eutherios" may indicate a recent distinguished owner. These were items for display, certainly, but also, and perhaps more importantly, they were stores of wealth.

Ever since the invention and development of coinage in the late seventh and sixth centuries BCE, coinage of silver and gold had offered a more convenient means of storing wealth than precious metalwork. Where other objects, like the Mildenhall Great Platter, scored over coinage was that they had other values than the strictly economic, and when displayed they might give an impression not merely of wealth, but of refinement. This is nicely illustrated in the story Thucydides tells of the experience of the Athenian envoys sent to the Sicilian city of Segesta to discover whether or not that city could really offer significant financial support for an Athenian expedition against Syracuse. The gold and silver vessels that the envoys enjoyed at every banquet turned out to be a single set that had been in part borrowed from neighboring cities and was circulated from household to household in advance of the Athenians' visits (Thucydides

6.46.3–4; cf. 6.8.2). But the impression that these vessels had given was a product not so much of a calculation of the wealth involved, but of the association of such vessels with the lifestyle of the superrich; if the Segestans all dined like *that*, the implication was, they must all belong to the wealthiest class.

The role of objects as bearers of value was very much context-dependent. What was admired as a sign of prosperity and sophistication in one context might be derided and condemned as luxury or affectation in another. A nice example of this is actually provided by Aristotle's introductory remark on Hippodamos:

> he was led into some eccentricity by a desire to attract attention; and this made a number of people feel that he lived in too studied and artificial a manner. He wore his hair long and expensively adorned: he had flowing robes, expensively decorated, made from a cheap but warm material, which he wore in summer time as well as in winter. (Aristotle *Politics* 2.8 1267b23–8)

Reactions to clothing and adornment varied across time and place, but also according to context. In some sanctuary contexts there were specific prohibitions on wearing gold or certain colors or types of garments (see Chapter 7). Theophrastus, writing in the late fourth century BCE, identifies wearing shoes too large for his feet as a mark of a country bumpkin (*Characters* 4), carrying a spherical oil flask a mark of a man out to impress (*Characters* 5), and equipping a pet jackdaw with a ladder and bronze shield the mark of a man of petty ambition (*Characters* 21). In the Roman world the differentiation of role and status by clothing became more and more regular, but the effect of that was to move the emphasis to how an item of dress was worn. Ammianus notes it as a sign of the decline of the senators in Rome that whereas those responsible for the expansion of Rome were "indistinguishable from common soldiers," those of his day "contrive, by frequent movements, especially of the left hand, to show off their long fringes and display the garments beneath, which are embroidered with various animal figures" (14.6.9–10, trans. Hamilton).

Just as the same objects lent themselves variously to admiration and to scorn, so they lent themselves to being privileged sites for the conspicuous rejection of normal values. The Cynic philosopher Diogenes is said to have thrown away his bowl when he saw a child drinking out of his hands, so as not to have been outdone in plainness of living (Diogenes Laertios *Lives of the Philosophers* 6.37). It was similarly the objects that go with wealth that Christianity signaled as impediments to spiritual wealth, as in Christ's instruction to the rich young man to sell everything that he has and give to the poor, or in the parable ridiculing the knocking down of barns and the building of new ones. But the rejection of objects was a problem for Christianity: How could the immaterial God be made visible in the world except through objects?

OBJECTS AND THE IMMATERIAL

The possibility of actually handling an object made by a god was not restricted to the fictional experiences described in the Homeric epics; in his travels around Greece in the second century CE, the Greek writer Pausanias came across a number of objects said to have been made by gods. Such objects invariably were powerful and potentially dangerous. Because gods intervene in the world, the sites of their intervention become potentially special, whether that is a matter of a holy spot where some epiphany was seen or some person or object in some way affected by the divine.[9] People needed both warning about the divine power peculiarly present at those sites and some facilities for accessing that power.

The standard Greek word for a sacred space was *temenos*, meaning literally something cut off, and the minimum needed to signal a sacred space was means of demarcation, for which a set of boundary stones would suffice, as was the case with the space of the Athenian Agora. Such boundary stones turned a piece of landscape into an object, changing its status. Most commonly such markers were accompanied by further objects—substantial walls, like the wall around the Altis at Olympia, or an altar, or a temple housing a representation of a particular god, or a building where people could be visited by the god (for purposes of healing or enlightenment), or offerings, or all of these.

Within the Greek world, no two sanctuaries looked alike. In different places and at different times, different sanctuaries attracted different sorts of offerings, different shapes of temple, and different activities. There was a tendency for the statues that represented the gods to stay relatively unchanged for long periods— the gods acquired a more or less definitive appearance, or a small number of alternative appearances, during the fifth century BCE, and those appearances were then much repeated. But what was given to the gods rarely stayed the same for long periods of time, or the same from one sanctuary to another. The gods had characters—as the Homeric epics had made clear—and people reacted to those different characters as they would to different characters in the human population by choosing to gift them with different objects.

Within the Roman world, the Capitoline triad—Iuppiter the Best and Greatest, Juno, and Minerva—became a very standardized part of Roman towns and military camps, but beyond these three the variety of gods was undiminished, and new gods continued to be added to the pantheon. This was partly a matter of imperial expansion leading to the assimilation of all sorts of previously non-Roman gods and partly a matter of the addition of Roman emperors to the realm of the gods, a process no less effective for being satirized by Seneca in the *Apocolocyntosis*.

Just what the effect was of the variety of ways in which the gods were materialized is made clear by Pausanias, whose *Description of Greece* is very largely made up of descriptions of one sanctuary after another. Pausanias is exceptionally valuable both because he was prepared to read the inscriptions on dedications and tell us about them, and because he inquired into the stories surrounding particular sanctuaries or particular peculiarities of sanctuaries. Whereas the various inventories of dedications inscribed on stone and put up in sanctuaries simply list objects, at most giving a short description, the name of the dedicator, and an abbreviated reference to the occasion of dedication, Pausanias, along with an exceptional inventory dating to 99 BCE derived from literary sources, which has become known as the *Lindian Chronicle*, gives a good impression of the way in which the objects offered themselves not simply as sights "worth seeing" to the gaze, but as stories worth hearing to the pilgrim and visitor (Vout 2018: 38–9).

One exceptional sanctuary, the sanctuary of Asklepios at Epidauros, put up inscribed texts telling its own stories of the episodes of healing that had taken place there (RO 102). These texts not only told their readers about past events in the sanctuary that had left no material trace there, but also prepared them for the significance of some of the objects they would see in the sanctuary. So we are told about Ambrosia from Athens who did not believe the stories she was told, and in consequence was made healthy on condition that she dedicated a silver pig to Asklepios as a memorial of her ignorance. But if the sanctuary of Asklepios was exceptional in recording such stories, visitors to sanctuaries knew that the objects that they saw there all had similar stories to tell. They were the physical manifestations of past divine interventions in human lives.

Just as Christianity challenged the values given to material objects, so too it inverted how sacred places worked. This was partly about replacing animal sacrifice outside a temple with a symbolic sacrifice inside a church (see Chapter 7) and partly about gathering inside a building rather than outside it, but it was even more notably about replacing narratives about people signaled by objects with a focus on narratives about God read from a book. Rather than being encouraged to model one's behavior on the behavior of others who had previously expressed their grateful relationship to a divinity in a particular way, the Christian worshipper was encouraged to follow the example and obey the instructions of one particular model, Christ.

This radical inversion changed everything and nothing. The precious metals that had figured large in temple dedications, showing off the success of the dedicant, reappeared to adorn churches and to represent God's various interventions in the world as manifested in the stories of scripture and the accounts of the saints. And the critical discourse that found displays of wealth to be inappropriate when they appeared on people's bodies and in their houses would in due course find them equally inappropriate in the houses of a God who loved the poor. The grand buildings that displayed the power of the Church enforced social hierarchies no less effectively than the grand buildings that displayed the power of Roman emperors. What had been the material evidence for secular history became the material evidence for salvation history. The Christian church, with its central conviction that human-made objects, the bread and wine of the Eucharist, could, by immaterial actions, be transformed into the divine body and blood of Christ, nevertheless thereby added a further and distinct dimension to the cultural history of objects, and ensured, in Hodder's phrase, that the world of late antiquity was even more entangled in things.

CHAPTER ONE

Objecthood

ROBIN OSBORNE

INTRODUCTION

Scholars have much debated whether the material world of late antiquity was significantly different from the material world of early Iron Age Greece. It was long maintained that the ancient world was essentially static, and that technological advance was trivial, blocked, it was held, by the prevalence of slavery that not only made labor cheap, but that made opposing labor-saving devices something in which those in power had a vested interest.[1] Archaeological discoveries, and more careful consideration of what ancient texts both say and imply, have led to a radical revision of this view. The very collapse of the ancient world, and the striking material impoverishment that ensued, bear witness to how dependent the economic life of the later Roman world was upon complex networks of production and exchange that embraced the whole vast empire (Ward-Perkins 2005). Thinking about the changing nature of objecthood in antiquity allows us to understand both the changes and their importance more fully. Fundamental to what separated the world of late antiquity from the world of Homeric epic was a changing knowledge both of the objects that made up the world and of how to deal with human relations with them.

OBJECTS AS BEARERS OF MEANING
IN ARCHAIC GREECE

The world of early Iron Age Greece—the world of Homeric epic—was a world capable of relatively sophisticated metalworking, whether for practical purposes (as with the development of iron technology itself, first to make more effective swords and subsequently to make scythes and more effective plows) or for decorative purposes (the use of techniques such as granulation and filigree in jewelry).[2] The *Odyssey* gives a memorably graphic description of the tempering of iron as part of a simile describing what happened when the stake was plunged into the Cyclops' eye to blind him:

> As when a man who works as a blacksmith plunges a screaming
> great ax blade or plane into cold water, treating it
> for temper, since this is the way steel is made strong, even
> so Cyclops' eye sizzled about the beam of the olive. (*Odyssey* 9.391–4, trans.
>   Lattimore)

What metalworking techniques enabled, however, was value. When Achilles holds games at the funeral of Patroclus, he offers a variety of prizes. These include "a lump of pig iron, which had once been the throwing-weight of Eëtion in his great strength; but now swift-footed brilliant Achilleus had slain him ad taken the weight away." Achilles announces that "although the rich demesnes of him who wins it lie far off indeed, yet for the succession of five years he will have it to use; for his shepherd for want of iron will not have to go in to the city for it, nor his ploughman either. This will supply them" (*Iliad* 23.826–35, trans. Lattimore).

But alongside these agricultural uses, metalworking techniques produced items that fascinated by their technology—and by the history they carried with them (see above p. 15):

> At once the son of Peleus set out prizes for the foot-race: a mixing bowl of silver, a work of art, which held only six measures, but for its loveliness it surpassed all others on earth by far, since skilled Sidonian craftsmen had wrought it well, and Phoenicians carried it over the misty face of the water and set it in the harbor, and gave it for a present to Thoas. Euneos, son of Jason, gave it to the hero Patroklos to buy Lykaon, Priam's son, out of slavery, and now Achilleus made it a prize in memory of his companion. (*Iliad* 23.740–8, trans. Lattimore)

In this world, objects provided the measures by which to understand history and status, assessing what could not be seen against what was known. That was not only true in terms of time, but also in terms of how writers conveyed sense of cosmic space. So Hesiod gages the scale of the world by imagining the heaviest object he knew falling through space:

> For it is just as far from the earth to murky Tartarus: for a bronze anvil, falling down from the sky for nine nights and days, on the tenth day would arrive at the earth; and again, a bronze anvil, falling down from the earth for nine nights and days, on the tenth would arrive at Tartarus. (*Theogony* 721–5, trans. Most; see Bassi 2016: 31–3)

But for all that these passages composed in the late eighth or early seventh century BCE show an acute awareness of how objects are used and how objects behave, they show little understanding of why the technologies that had been developed worked, or of what the nature of the world was.

PUTTING OBJECTS IN THEIR PLACE

Discovering what the nature of the world was like was no simple matter. It involved, as I have explored in the Introduction to this volume, a complex dialogue between theory and observation. And it was theory that was necessarily prior: only in the context where observations can confirm or disconfirm prior conjecture can particular observations be made to urge general conclusions.

Human history offered a poor basis for understanding the origin of the world. The epic poems of Homer and Hesiod attempt, in as far as they attempt to understand the nature of the physical world at all, to do so in terms of the creative acts with which they were familiar—procreation on the one hand and political power on the other. Hesiod has Empty Space coming to be first, and then Earth and then Love (Eros), who provides the motive force for further acts of generation (*Theogony* 116–20). The *Iliad* has Poseidon tell how he, Zeus, and Hades had divided up the world between them by drawing lots, with Zeus getting the sky, Hades the underworld, Poseidon the sea, and the earth remaining common to all three.

Understanding the world depended upon understanding that objects might have a history apart from human action. Arguably, the crucial perception was that one thing could turn into another: If the same thing could be solid as ice, liquid as water, and gaseous as steam, just how various was the world? Was everything just another form of water (famously the view of the man held to be the first Greek philosopher, Thales)? Or of air (the view of Anaximenes)? Or was everything a variously transformed form of energy, of fire (so Heraclitus)? Or did there need to be a small number of different substances—earth, air, fire, and water—in order to account for the world's endless variety (so Empedocles, for whom the active forces bringing combination or separation were love and strife)? Or was it all made up of tiny indivisible parts—atoms—that themselves had no qualities, but that joined to create the world as experienced (so Democritus)? Combining a small number of observations with intelligent theorizing, Greeks of the sixth and fifth centuries BCE quickly explored a full range of possible ways in which the world might be constituted.[3]

The crucial importance of these theories was that they removed the object world from the human world by introducing processes that were not the processes of biological reproduction or of human political life, and they suggested that, behind the infinite variety of particular objects, the underlying matter was much more limited in range and much more manageable. What is more, the transformation of the physical world took place independently of any intervention of a supernatural power. That did not mean that there were no supernatural powers, but their intervention was not necessary to the physical world as humans experienced it. This contention remained a sphere of controversy, and its denial was one of the marks of what was labeled by its opponents to be "magic."[4]

Hand in hand with the thought experiments of the philosophers went the practical understanding of how to do things with the physical world. Although the earliest surviving writings on mechanics—the *Mechanical Problems* attributed to Aristotle and the writings of Ctesibius, Archimedes, and Philo of Byzantium—date only to the third century BCE, use of simple machines, such as levers, winches, and (compound) pulleys, can be traced back to the sixth century BCE—levers to the beginning of that century, compound pulleys, and probably winches, to its end.[5] It is clear from the case of the pulley—the workings of which the Aristotelian *Mechanical Problems* does not fully understand—that practical use preceded theoretical understanding here. But that practical use itself transformed the relationship between humans and objects by changing what an individual could accomplish in relation to the physical world, and by making clear that such transformations could be achieved without altering the nature of the object in question.

The conceptual importance of these simple machines should not be underestimated, since they made it no longer appropriate to use man as a measure. What a man could do in relation to the physical world of objects now depended on what mechanical assistance he could be given. When Protagoras in the late fifth century BCE came to enunciate the principle that man *was* the measure, it was the *existence* of things—not their qualities—that his human beings measured. In certain crucial ways, at least, human beings now had no consistent relationship with objects; their relationships were mediated through other objects.

In their different ways, both the theories of the philosophers and the practical devices developed by builders encouraged classifying the object world. The singular properties of an object that impart value to it in the world of epic poetry become irrelevant when that object becomes simply another large object to be moved. Classification of objects as all posing the same problem was logically prior to finding a means of solving the problem. But just as explanation of how machines worked long followed the development of machines, so the great exercises in classification and cataloging of objects, which both mapped the world's resources and showed what those resources did or what might be done with them, came long after such classification had been put to practical use.

THE CULTURE-FREE OBJECTS OF PHILOSOPHY

The developing theoretical understanding of the physical world and the developing ability practically to handle that world together created an extraordinary philosophical ferment in the fifth and fourth centuries BCE. If the world was really made up of earth, air, fire, and water, or if it was really made up of atoms, then was there any possibility of having knowledge of the world beyond knowledge of that fact? Whatever an individual perceived was simply their perception of qualities possessed by a certain combination of elements or a certain combination of atoms. At one extreme lay the arguments of the fifth-century BCE philosopher Parmenides, who maintained that the only reality that could be known was singular and unchanging—that was the "way of being," all else was part of a "way of seeming." Few found Parmenides' answer to the question of what the world consisted of satisfactory, but his work was instrumental in moving the question from what existed to what could be known.[6]

The question of what can be known famously dominates Plato's dialogues. The early dialogues stage discussions of the nature of particular virtues or other qualities, asking "What is x?" where x is variously piety, beauty, courage, justice, etc., a list that includes knowledge itself. Plato variously insists that knowing what something is requires being able to give an account of why that is the case, and that it involves differentiating x from other objects. Given that any individual act that is in one circumstance pious or courageous will potentially in other circumstances be impious or cowardly, and that any object that is beautiful in one company may appear plain, if not ugly, in different company, he concludes that the only stable entities will be those that are *purely x*—that is, what are known as the Platonic "forms" or "ideas." So in the classic discussion in *Republic* 5, Plato holds that

> those who contemplate many beautiful things, but neither see beauty itself
> nor are able to follow another who would guide them to it, and who recognize
> many instances of justice but not justice itself, and likewise with everything,
> we shall declare that their views are entirely matters of belief, and that they
> have no knowledge of the objects of their beliefs. (*Republic* 479e1–5, trans.
> Halliwell)

The "forms" are for Plato the ultimate reality:

> the many conventional notions of the mass of mankind about what is
> beautiful and so on roll around between pure reality and pure unreality.
> (*Republic* 479d2–5)

To maintain this is effectively to maintain the equivalent for virtues, etc., of insisting that in the case of the material world only atoms or only the elements can be known (and indeed in *Theaetetus*, Plato rejects an account of knowledge that would make it impossible for elements to be known).[7]

The burden of philosophical discussion down to and including Plato was to separate the objects of knowledge from objects in the world of the senses. Knowledge was limited to the underlying structure of the world; of the world of things in which we pass our life, there could be no knowledge. Such a claim was at the least counterintuitive, if not paradoxical. It put all the weight on theory, and had scant concern for how one might come to know better the objects that constitute our culture. Indeed, it precisely denied that it was possible to *know* objects that had a cultural history. Bringing the sensible world back into philosophical discussion was the achievement of Aristotle.

Aristotle insists that to be an object of knowledge something must have a certain universality. We can know that triangles have interior angles equal to two right angles because this is always true. Some things that are always true are always true by definition, others because there is an explanatory connection— when an animal is sacrificed we know that it dies, because sacrifice involves killing the animal (*Posterior Analytics* 73b10–16). But Aristotle is prepared to relax this demand for universality into a demand that a thing comes about not by chance but "for the most part," explaining that

> Some things come about universally (they either are or come about in this way always and in every case), others not always but for the most part—for example, not every man has hair on his chin, but they do for the most part. (*Posterior Analytics* 96a8–10, trans. Lorenz; cf. 87b19–27)

To understand something, we do not need to know that it is universally true, but only that it is true for the most part. When we know that something happens for the most part, we will not be persuaded otherwise about it (cf. *Posterior Analytics* 72b3–4).

Unlike in the world of mathematical objects (triangles, etc.), in the natural world few things are true by definition or because of an explanatory connection. But there is, as Aristotle himself insisted, a stable and orderly arrangement in nature:

> all things are ordered together somehow, but not all alike,—both fishes and fowls and plants; and the world is not such that one thing has nothing to do with another, but they are connected. For all are ordered together to one end ... (*Metaphysics* 1075a16–19, trans. Ross)

Given this stable and orderly arrangement, the natural world becomes knowable.[8]

This redefinition of what can be known constitutes a marked change of direction in Greek philosophy, but it did not come out of nowhere. The medical investigations preserved for us in a corpus of writings ascribed to the legendary Hippocrates of Cos include systematic attempts to map what was true "always or for the most part" through such means as detailed case histories, describing the changing health of patients over the course of an illness. It is no accident that the classifications of medicine were both developed early and were markedly wide ranging: classification here had much more than an academic end, since correctly classifying symptoms is a prerequisite for treating them appropriately. The second-century CE doctor Galen would include within his voluminous writings a treatise describing numerous kinds of pulse.

The works of Aristotle and his school (Aristotle's own *Enquiry into Animals* and his pupil Theophrastus' *Enquiry into Plants* and *On Stones*) nevertheless marked a watershed in the description of the world. Earlier writers had offered more or less extensive descriptions of the customs and culture of selected parts of the non-Greek world, as Herodotus describes the customs and culture of the various parts of the Persian Empire as the necessary background to understanding the nature of the wars between Greeks and Persians. But those descriptions had focused on the habits of men, and were closely linked into the past histories of the people in question. What Aristotle and his pupils did was to turn attention away from the world of human cultures to the natural world. Indeed, what they tried to write might be described as a culture-free history of objects, or at least a history of objects that focused on those aspects that were least affected by culture.

OBJECTIVITY

The philosophers' concern with what it was possible to have knowledge of was a concern about objectivity. If what an object was like varied according to who perceived it or the context in which it was perceived, then that object was not one thing but many, and could not be known. This was not simply a problem about assessing whether something was just or beautiful or whether it was blue or purple, it was a general problem about assessing any thing that happened; nor was it simply a problem about the present, it was a problem that affected what had happened as much as what was happening. Just as growing awareness of the relativity of perceptions of the world spurred on philosophical discussion, so also the need to understand the context of past actions if their significance was to be understood (cf. Polybius 2.56.13–16) spurred on the writing of history.

Although the works of the man who stands at the head of the writing of both geography and history, Hecataeus of Miletus, who flourished *c.* 500 BCE, are lost, the opening of his *Histories* is quoted by later writers:

> Hecataeus of Miletus gives this account: I write these things as they seem to me to be true; for the stories of the Greeks are many and hilarious, as it appears to me.

More obliquely, but to similar effect, Herodotus, the earliest historian whose work survives complete, prefaces the *Histories* that he wrote in the second half of the fifth century BCE:

This is the publication of the enquiry of Herodotus of Halicarnassus, so that neither what has been done by men should become faint through time, nor the great and remarkable deeds shown forth, some by Greeks others by non-Greeks, lose their fame. (*Preface*)

It becomes clear that what threatens to wipe out the past and destroy its fame, as far as Herodotus is concerned, are the distortions that result from people telling the story about the past that suits them. The particular hallmark of Herodotus' *History* is his constant reference to the different versions of the past told by different people—versions that he flags up to indicate why one might be skeptical; as he writes later in his work, "I have a duty to say what is said, but I do not have any duty at all to believe it" (7.152.3) (see especially Fowler 1996).

How to establish what actually happened in the past remained a central problem for Greek and Roman historians alike. Thucydides notes that people believe things about the past without critically examining what they are told, simply adopting whatever version comes readily to hand, and that both poets and writers of prose adorn their accounts with more regard to charming their hearers and readers than to truth (1.20–1). He explicitly sets out the way in which he went about establishing what had happened in the Peloponnesian War by finding those who had been present at events and comparing their differing accounts, distorted as they were by partiality or simply forgetfulness (1.22.2–3). Most notoriously, he records that he had reconstructed what individuals had said, attributing to them the sentiments they ought to have uttered while keeping as close as possible to the overall sense of what they had said (1.22.1). Whether Thucydides was right or not to do so, his method involves trying to establish not the subjective impression given by speakers, but what their objective contribution was.

Thucydides' attempt to establish the objective truth is linked to his concern that his history should be a "possession for ever" (1.22.4). Just as Aristotle would assert that there was pattern in nature, so Thucydides held that "according to the rules governing what it is to be human," one would be able to predict on the basis of an accurate account of the past what would happen in the future.

Although some historians would continue to claim that their work would be useful to those involved in comparable affairs in the future (cf. Polybius *Histories* 3.31), the singularities of history rendered implausible claims that what happened in the world was "always or for the most part" like some past event. For history, there was no way out of the dilemma that the subjective perception of and reaction to events might prove more important than the objective action. Historians were a notoriously critical community, always ready to attack each other for ignorance or lapse of method. The best historians could do was to claim that their account was at least not biased by particular personal prejudices of their own—as Tacitus does when he notes at the start of *Annals* that he can write about the period in question "without anger or enthusiasm" (1.1)—and that the events of the past provided a guide to appropriate behavior for the present (see Livy *Preface* 10).

In parallel with the rise and fall of objectivity in history runs objectivity in geography. Within the ancient world, history and geography were closely linked—Hecataeus wrote descriptions of the world as well as history, and history and geography were closely interwoven in Herodotus. But there were various attempts to turn geography into an objective science. One tradition made the proper subject of geography the description of the regularities of the world—a world that there were successive attempts to divide into broadly matching zones. These attempts brought attacks from one geographer on another as critical as the attacks of one historian on another, as is well attested by the opening of book 2 (2.1–2) of the *Geography* written by Strabo during the reign of Augustus. Scholars who worked in this tradition made some remarkably accurate measurements of the world, but their work had little scope for acknowledging the place of man in the world or the place of political geography.

The *Geography* of Strabo is the greatest surviving ancient work of geography. Written in seventeen books, it engages extensively with past descriptions of the world, from Homer onward. Strabo's work is, on the one hand, a history of geography, in as far as it traces how earlier writers had described the world, and, on the other hand, a geography of history, in as far as it maps human history across the world. But all this is done from a viewpoint, or rather from many viewpoints. Some of these viewpoints are based on personal experience and strictly local—as when he describes the view from Acrocorinth, which he explicitly declares himself to have ascended, at the end of 8.6.21. Other viewpoints are intellectual—at various places in, and only in, Asia Minor (Mytilene, Pergamum, Antioch on the Maeander, Miletus, Nysa, Rhodes, Cnidus, Halicarnassus, Cos, Mylasa, Seleuceia on the Calycadnus, Tarsus), Strabo situates himself in an intellectual world by listing contemporaries who were writers and orators. But there is also a political viewpoint—from Rome. This provides both a spatial and a temporal focus, as is nowhere clearer than at the very conclusion of the work, where Strabo first offers an account of the countries of the world that the Romans have acquired, and then an account of the division of those countries into provinces, explicitly laying out the two consular and ten praetorian provinces established by Augustus, before noting that "Caesar rules the rest of the provinces," and concluding his work with the sentence "Even kings and dynasts and decarchies both are and always belonged to Caesar's portion" (17.3.25) (Clarke 1999: chs. 4–6).

The most striking evidence for the way in which Rome transformed the world as an object of knowledge, and rendered attempts at objectivity impossible, comes from the most extraordinary catalog of all to survive from antiquity, the *Natural History* of the Elder Pliny. Pliny claims to have read around 2,000 volumes by 100 authors to compile thirty-six books containing 20,000 facts (Preface 17), but he tells the emperor Titus, to whom he dedicates the work, that he does not need to read it (Preface 33): Pliny has such respect for the emperor's time that he provides, as book 1, a table of contents so that the emperor will not have to read the books. For Pliny, Greek and Roman knowledge has conquered the world, and as a result he knows the place for everything: his feat of classification is astonishing, but it is also bizarre—with much in common with the Borgesian fantasy of classification that so inspired Foucault (Foucault (1970) 2002: xvi–ix).

Pliny begins his work predictably enough:

> Book 3 contains: (i–iii) whether the world is finite and whether it is one; on the form of it; on the motion of it; why it is called *mundus*; (iv) on the elements; (v) on god; (vi) on the nature of the planets; (vii) on eclipses of moon and sun; on night; (viii–x) on the magnitude of the stars and what people have discovered through observing the sky ...

But after books 3–6 have taken us on a tour of the countries of the world, in which he claims at the end of book 6 to have treated, among other things, 1,195 towns, 576 races, and 115 famous rivers, he turns in book 7 to discuss humankind:

> Book 7 contains: (ii–iii) peoples with remarkable bodies; births that constitute prodigies; (iv–xi) how humans are born; lengths of pregnancy from 7 months to 13 months, through famous examples; signs relating to sex in pregnant women before birth; monstrous births by surgical delivery; meaning of *vopiscus*; human conception; how humans grow; cases of likeness; examples of multiple births; (xii) age limit to procreation; (xiii) remarkable lengths of pregnancy; (xiv) theory of generation; (xv) investigation into teeth; investigation into young children; (xvi–xvii) examples of great size; premature births; (xviii–xxiii) outstanding bodies; exceptional strengths; extreme speed; exceptional sight; remarkable hearing; bodily endurance; (xiv–xvi) memory; mental vigour; mercy; magnanimity ...

Here we move from an account focused on the way human biology works, through a section of a record book of human achievements, to issues to do with character of an essentially moral sort. This slippage, from a description of the physical reality to contextualizing the object in question in moral terms, occurs not simply when the objects described are human. Take the description of the contents of the opening of book 37:

> Book 37 contains: (i–x) origin of gems; on the gem of the tyrant Polycrates; on the gem of Pyrrhus; who are the best engravers and specimens of engraving; the first collection of rings at Rome; gems carried in the triumph

of Pompey the Great; when murrine vases were first imported; luxury connected with; their nature; the nature of rock-crystal; drug from it; luxury in rock crystal …

Objects in Pliny come attached to stories. They are embedded in history—they do not offer themselves simply for contemplation, they are active agents in the world, but in a world shaped by political power.

LEGAL OBJECTS

Perhaps the most pervasive way in which Roman political power changed the world of objects was through the medium of law. The question of what constitutes an object in law is fundamental to the relationship between people and the world they inhabit. Take intellectual property. We can trace back the legal protection of items and techniques of manufacture to the fourteenth-century "letters patent" in England and the Florentine and Venetian patents of the fifteenth century (Hulme 1896: 141–54; MacLeod 2002: 11). But the notion that the expression of ideas can be owned is one that does not precede the printing press. Indeed, the first copyright law was the British statute of 1710, entitled "An Act for the Encouragement of Learning, by vesting the Copies of Printed Books in the Authors or purchasers of such Copies, during the Times therein mentioned." The progressive extension of the idea of copyright and intellectual property maps the changing place—and the changing value—of ideas within Western society.

The notion that the state might step in to protect innovations was not entirely alien within the Greek world. Whether or not the Hellenistic historian Phylarchus was correct in alleging that the people of Sybaris had a law that a cook who invented an exceptional dish has exclusive rights to make that dish for a year to encourage others to invent similarly (Phylarchus *FGrH* 81F45; Athenaeus *Deipnosophistai* 521c–d), the story itself shows that protection of commercially valuable innovative objects was conceivable—even if only to mock this city of gourmands.

Greek cities seem to have had rather weakly developed categories of legal object. Although Athenian litigants distinguished between inherited and self-acquired wealth, implying that it was much worse to dispose of the former than the latter, for instance, there is no trace of such a distinction in law. Similarly, a distinction between "visible" and "invisible" property is regularly made by speakers in the Athenian courts, but exactly what the two categories are taken to refer to seems to vary from speaker to speaker (Harrison 1968: 228–35; Todd 1993: 241–3). The disputes that frequently arise in Greek cities when exiles, whose property has been confiscated and sold, return to a city after political change show clearly how no formal register distinguished land from other property, although various means of publicizing sales might be legally required (Todd 1993: 238–9, 247; for issues arising from exile see OR 132; RO 101).

This strongly contrasts with the situation in Roman law. The *Institutes* of Gaius, a Roman jurist, written in the late second century CE, lay out at the start of book 2 the law related to things by making a series of distinctions: between things under divine law (sacred, religious, and sanctified things) and those under human law (which may be either public things, belonging to no individual, or private things); between corporeal and incorporeal things; and between things capable of mancipation or not. This last distinction seems to be the earliest of all in Roman law, going back to the XII Tables of the mid-fifth century BCE, and singled out things used in agricultural production for transfer by a special ritual (mancipation). As this last example shows, these categories of thing are a result of a combination of logical division and historical accretion (the emperor Justinian would eventually abolish the ritual of mancipation).

As soon as we look into the detail of Gaius' description we discover that this classification of things is far less clean-cut than these divisions suggest. What counts within one of the categories depends upon a complex of factors, including where it is, how it has come to be in its current state, and the way in which it has been acquired. Sacred things are defined as those consecrated to the gods above. But land can only be consecrated by authority of the Roman people, either by statute or by resolution of the senate. Religious things are those left to the gods below. Land can be made religious simply by the burial in it of a body—provided that those burying have a responsibility to see that the body is buried. But land in the provinces, though it is treated as religious, cannot legally be made religious since it is owned by the Roman people or the emperor.

Particularly complex are incorporeal things, since they turn out to be in practice far from incorporeal. They consist of legal rights—inheritance, usufruct, and obligations that have been contracted. The fact that the inheritance or the contracted obligation consists of corporeal things does not matter. Incorporeal things are in general not capable of mancipation, whereas land, slaves, or beasts of burden are. The status of land or slaves that are part of an inheritance is thus quite different from the status of land and slaves acquired in other circumstances. Gaius himself observes that whereas among non-Romans someone either does or does not own something, among Romans it is possible for someone to be the owner while another has it in his estate: "for if I have neither mancipated a thing capable of mancipation nor assigned it to you in court but have merely delivered it, the thing certainly becomes part of your estate; on the other hand it will remain mine by quiritary right, until you usucapt it by possessing it" (*Institutes* 2.41, trans. Gordon and Robinson). Equally, what the legal status of a person enables depends upon the nature of the object in question:

neither a woman nor a ward can alienate a thing capable of mancipation without a guardian's authorization; but with things not so capable, a woman can alienate but a ward cannot. (*Institutes* 2.80, trans. Gordon and Robinson)[9]

The point here is not to explore the niceties of Roman law, but to reveal something of the way in which the structures of Roman law changed the nature of objecthood by distinguishing not simply between different objects, to give them different legal status, but distinguishing between objects of the same type, according to their location or the particular history of their relationship to humans. The extraordinary Roman attempt to face up to the complicated ways in which humans relate to things formalized that entanglement.

OBJECTS OF EXCHANGE[10]

When in the Homeric epics there is a need to evaluate what an object is worth, that valuation is regularly given in terms of oxen. The question of whether Glaucus was wise to exchange his gold armor for Diomedes' bronze armor is evaluated in terms of the gold armor being worth 100 oxen, the bronze 9 (*Iliad* 6.234–6). When Achilles offers prizes for a wrestling competition at the funeral games of Patroclus, we are not only given the value of the great tripod offered to the winner and the "woman, skilled in the work of her hands" in terms of oxen, but explicitly told that "the Achaeans among themselves valued the tripod at twelve oxen ... and they rated her at four oxen" (*Iliad* 23.702–5). The choice of oxen is both a choice of a common item of significant value, whose value is established by the work it can accomplish, and the choice of an item where the very perishability of the animal prevents any possible misconception that it is a particular ox that is at issue. But oxen are useful only as a measure of value; their perishability prevents their being a possible way of storing wealth, and their size prevents them being a means of exchange.

The Homeric poems have little interest in what means of exchange is employed. We are simply told that Eëtion of Imbros pays a great price to redeem a son of Priam who has been captured and sold by Achilles (*Iliad* 21.42), that Eumaeus' mother "promises to buy" an intricate gold necklace being hawked by Phoenician traders (*Odyssey* 15.462–3), and that Laertes purchases Eumaeus himself "with his own possessions" (*Odyssey* 15.483). What is required of the means of exchange is that it is widely desirable. This is a world in which the very fact that it is convertible—that it can be vaunted as a sign of power and wealth, given as a gift, and also exchanged for something or someone—makes an object desirable. That is, one reason for acquiring nonperishable objects is that they can be used as a means of exchange. The easier it is to assess the value of the object, the safer and more useful it is as a means of exchange, and there is therefore a premium on relatively standardized objects with a long shelf life.

We might wonder whether the ubiquity of some small objects in early Iron Age Greece—things like Corinthian perfume jars or clay loom weights—does not relate to their use as "small change."

Already in the Homeric poems we have seen a lump of pig iron used by Achilles as a prize in Patroclus' funeral games. In the case of the chariot race, for which he offers five prizes, the fourth prize is two talents weight of gold (*Iliad* 23.269). The pig iron is explicitly something that can be used to make other things, and the gold offered similar possibilities. But the gold also had the advantage of being worth its weight in gold (gold is the only thing in the Homeric poems that is assessed by its weight in talents). Any substance that was in relatively short supply and relatively high demand lent itself to being valued by weight alone. In the Roman world, bronze bullion would be used in this way down to the third century BCE, as attested by some huge bullion hoards that have survived (Kroll 2008). But significant advantages accrued if bullion was made available as a means of exchange, in units standardized as to weight.[11] This was particularly an advantage for those who were not themselves constantly involved with the acquisition and disposal of goods, and so were less fully informed about the relative value of everyday objects. But who was going to guarantee the purity of the substance and the accuracy of the weight?

At some point near the end of the seventh century BCE, the Lydians begin to produce stamped lumps of electrum—a naturally occurring alloy of gold and silver—of fixed weight, the first coinage of which we know (Konuk 2012: 48–9 for the date, 43–7 for the coins; see further below p. 72 on coins). Electrum, also known as "white gold," had the advantage of high intrinsic value, and the disadvantage that it was an alloy with varying proportions of gold and silver, making its value hard to assess. There are some signs that the attempt to "fix" the value of electrum by stamping standardized weights did not work—Lydia moves in the sixth century BCE to a bimetallic system, with gold and silver rather than electrum. But the idea of stamping caught on, if slowly at first. By the end of the sixth century BCE, Greek cities on both sides of the Aegean and on both sides of the Ionian Sea were producing distinct coinages.

Although early Greek coinages were worth their weight in silver, the earliest Lydian electrum coins seem to have been deliberately "diluted" from their natural alloy, and this is likely to have meant that they were overvalued. Coinage established the possibility that the value of the thing exchanged was not intrinsic to the thing itself, but conventionally established by some authority. From this point of view, coins were legal objects, their value being determined externally. But in the classical Greek world, coins never became simply token objects, and any discrepancy between the value of the coin and the value of the bullion contained by the coin could be reckoned to equate to the value of the greater convenience that coinage gave. This enabled coins to travel beyond the region in which the political power that authorized them prevailed.

The importance of the invention of coinage for the economy is not easy to assess. It is often suggested that there was nothing that coinage enabled that could not be achieved by barter (Kroll 2012: 40). But this is implausible. The Phoenicians who kidnap Eumaeus in *Odyssey* 15 have "countless pretty things stored in their ship." Those who depend on exchanging goods for goods inevitably acquire a whole host of different things, whose common quality is that they are widely desired and found attractive. Since they cannot know in detail what they will acquire, they cannot decide in advance where it will be best to dispose of it, and so they tramp from place to place. But already in the late archaic Greek world, and throughout the Roman world, traders did not behave like this. They specialized in particular items and supplied them to markets that they knew in advance (Osborne 1996; Tchernia 2016: 69–70). They could do so since they already knew for what they were going to exchange these goods. A whole pattern of trading was facilitated, if not enabled, by coinage.

Coinage was perhaps even more important at the level of day-to-day interactions than it was for exchange across the Mediterranean or for major local investment. One of the striking developments in the study of ancient coinage has been the discovery that, contrary to the express claims of earlier scholars, from the beginning Greek silver coinages frequently included fractional coinages.[12] The cumbersome nature of exchange when bullion has to be assayed (at least visually) and weighed, or when the value of a particular item has to be haggled over, is such as to be worth engaging in only when the goods being acquired are substantial. When it came to small items, although neighborly reciprocity had its problems and its limits, as Hesiod already indicates (*Works and Days* 349–59), it was simply much more efficient than any formal exchange. Coinage changed that. Small change gave a way of paying for day-to-day items in a way that cleared the bill, leaving no reciprocal obligations. Counting out coins was rapid and, short of the coins themselves being counterfeit, left no room for dispute over value. The value of coinage did not depend upon the needs of the person to whom it was offered, for it could be converted into anything. Imperishable, it could be stored as easily as exchanged, and would retain its value.

At the level of daily life, coinage enabled dramatic economic and social change. Specialist sale of small-value items became a viable occupation, and commercial relations could be extended outside the circle of those with whom one had social ties. Whether or not the various occupational names that we find in classical inscriptions indicate the professions that dominated the lives of the individuals identified as performing those occupations, rather than simply the aspects of their activity that distinguished them from others, the proliferation of specialisms is arguably something effectively unthinkable before the advent of coinage (Harris 2002, with the evidence listed at 88–97). Although the structures of lending and borrowing continued in the classical city, coinage enabled economic relations to be pursued outside the circles of social relations.[13] If there was a tension caused by the invention of coinage, as some scholars have believed, it was situated here, in the way that coinage devalued, or even rendered obsolete, the relations of power and patronage that vitally oiled relationships when goods were directly traded for goods. As Simmel long ago noted:

> The indifferent objectivity of money transactions is in insurmountable conflict with the personal character of the relationship ... The desirable party for financial transactions is the person who is completely indifferent to us, engaged neither for us nor against us.[14]

The invention of coinage added to the Greek world an object like no other— an object both fundamentally independent of human actors and totally reliant on human political structures for its existence and meaning; an object that had and could acquire no individual identity but always and only existed within a set; an object that could become anything and yet, in a sense, was itself nothing, merely the bearer of an abstract idea (for these and the ideas that follow, see Seaford 2004). It also encouraged Greeks to think differently about the world—to think, for instance, that the plurality of things observed might all be converted into a single thing, invariant in space and time, self-sufficient, and limited (the qualities that are attributed to being by the fifth-century BCE Greek thinker Parmenides), or to think that all things can be assessed by a single measure, as Protagoras asserted in claiming that man was the measure of all things. Perhaps more importantly still, the ways in which coins depend upon an initial act of authorization, of group agreement, yet operate independently, offered a template against which to measure both the need for the state and the freedom of the individual and its limits.

Those modes of thought did not need coinage to sustain them. But the economic effects of coinage were dependent on the maintenance of the monetary system. The fiduciary aspect of coinage, there from the start but of relatively minor importance, since it was always possible to exit the monetary system and yet retain most of the value of one's silver coins by turning them into bullion (which was indeed how Greek coins were used in various regions outside Greece), became more and more important over time as coins increasingly became tokens. Absent the authorizing power, coins became close to worthless. This is to be seen with the collapse of Roman power—most dramatically in the case of Roman Britain, where a prosperous fourth century CE is followed by fifth and sixth centuries from which coins disappear, and with them wheel-made pottery. Elsewhere in the Roman Empire coinage continued, but in the Western Empire outside Vandal Africa and Ostrogothic Italy it was only high-value coinage that was still minted. Without a full monetary system, the economy of the Western Empire as it had been since Augustus collapsed (Ward-Perkins 2005: 110–17).

MATERIAL GO(O)DS

Over the course of the principate, Roman emperors had got bigger. Octavian had turned himself into the first emperor, Augustus, through sheer military might. His spectacular victory over Antony and Cleopatra at Actium in September of 31 BCE left no rival for control over Rome itself and its provinces. By the time of his death forty-five years later, Augustus had consolidated the empire (through extensive military campaigns that tidied up its borders, extending Roman rule from the Atlantic to the Euphrates and from the Rhine to the Sahara), its army (reorganized to swear allegiance to the emperor alone), and its government (ending elections for public office and having provinces governed by men largely chosen by the emperor himself). No one had a claim to power that could rival Augustus, or even those who could point to descent from him. Augustus himself appeared all over the empire, in thousands of busts and statues, but, with rare exceptions (e.g. a group in which he appeared with the goddess Roma at Lepcis Magna), he and his successors from Tiberius to Claudius kept themselves within, or at least close to, human bounds. It was part of the excess of the emperor Nero, however, that he had himself depicted as a 30-meter-high colossus at the entrance of his great new palace in the center of Rome, the Golden House (Suetonius *Nero* 31; Pliny *NH* 34.45).

After the end of the Julio-Claudian line with Nero's death, emperors had to claim the right to rule on their own merits, assisted at best by real or adoptive descent from a meritorious predecessor. In consequence, they grew larger. For all that Nero's Flavian successors mocked his outsize images, Vespasian, Titus, and probably Domitian all received statues in excess of 4 meters in height in Rome (Ruck 2007). Trajan, whose lack of genetic link to the Flavians left him keen to establish himself as the new Augustus by military campaigns and building programs, created an outsize forum adorned with a large number of colossal statues. His second-century CE successors all had themselves depicted on a massive scale, not only in Rome, but elsewhere. A colossal Antoninus Pius has long been known from Béziers, and recent excavations at Sagalassos have uncovered colossal statues of Hadrian, Marcus Aurelius, and Faustina, wife of Antoninus Pius (Vout 2012: 457–8). In Rome itself, Hadrian, scholars suspect, was the emperor originally depicted by the marble colossus that was later turned first into the emperor Maxentius and finally into Constantine. And it was with Constantine, who needed to lay claim to massive superiority to justify his taking back sole control of an empire that had in the late third century CE been divided between four rulers, and with Constantine's sons that the colossal emperor returned. A colossal bronze Constantine (perhaps originally a Nero) survives from Rome, as well as the colossal marble image (for recutting of status, see Prusac 2011; Prusac-Lindhagen 2017).

The problem for emperors was to find ways of differentiating themselves from other men in ways that enhanced, rather than undermined, their authority. We have a wonderful description from the historian Ammianus Marcellinus of Constantine's son, Constantius II, arriving in Rome:

> When he was hailed as Augustus with favourable cries, [Constantius] did not shudder at the din that thundered from hills and shores, but showed himself unmoved, as he appeared in his provinces. For, when passing through high gates, he stooped his short body, and, keeping his gaze straight, as though his neck were fixed, he turned his head neither right nor left, as though an image of a man, and he was never seen to nod when the wheel shook, or to spit or wipe or rub his face or nose, or to move his hand. Although this behaviour was an affectation, it, and other aspects of his more private life, were however indications of extraordinary endurance, granted to him alone, as it was given to be supposed. (Ammianus 16.10.9–11, trans. Flower 2015)

The emperor has turned himself into a statue, laying claim to godlike power by appearing like the image of a god.

The Olympian gods offered the basic model for the powerful man who was not a man. The problem with gods had always been how to make a cosmic power who is not human, understandable to and commensurate with, but much greater than, humans. The solution had been to produce an image in human form but of outstanding appearance—outstanding because not fully human, as in the images of Hermes and of Hecate, outstanding because made of precious materials, such as gold and ivory, or outstanding because outsize like the archaic Apollo at Amyclae (Sparta, Pausanias 3.19.1) or Pheidias' statues of Athena for the Parthenon or Zeus at Olympia (though these were also of gold and ivory). Immaterial power had to be figured in material form, and both the shape and the substance mattered (Osborne 2011: ch. 7).

Nothing reveals better the range of ways in which the material world acquired meaning in antiquity than how gods were materialized. Herodotus famously remarks of Homer and Hesiod that "they taught the Greeks of the descent of the gods, and gave to all their several names, and honours, and arts, and declared their outward forms" (2.53, trans. Godley), but if it was the great poetic texts that first inspired the visual arts, it was artists' images that came to dominate the Greek and Roman imagination. Those images played not only with size but with the dazzling effects of gold or bronze, with the possibilities that marble gave to evoke the soft surface of a fleshy body and encourage physical embrace (as in the exciting stories of young men at Knidos embracing Aphrodite's naked statue in love), with the recapturing of the awe occasioned by age through the evocation of the artistic styles of the past (so that Apollo and Athena get frozen in the appearances they had at the end of the archaic period), and with the sheer enchantment offered by artistic skill.

But materializing the gods did not simply involve representing them in human form; it also meant framing those representations. Greek and Roman temples similarly run the gamut of approaches to the presentation of divine power through materials. We have the power of sheer size, as in the great archaic temples of Ionia. We have the dazzling effects of working in marble, as in the temples of the Athenian acropolis, which exploit, in the Erechtheum and the temple of Athena Nike, the possibilities of great intricacy and detail that marble offers, as well as exploiting in the Parthenon, whose choice of an eight-column rather than a six-column facade has something of the "33 percent extra free" effect, the combined force of mass and reflective power. We have imposing height, as in the podiums of Roman temples. We have in-your-face power advertisements, as in the form of external pedimental and other sculpture, from the Gorgon of the archaic temple of Artemis on Corcyra to the mustached gorgon variation in the temple of Sulis Minerva at Bath. And we have imposing surroundings—whether city acropoleis, hanging terraces like that of Delphi, or the sort of remote mountain isolation that makes the temple of Apollo at Bassai so haunting.

Christianity, dancing precariously around Jewish iconoclastic as well as Greco-Roman philo-iconic theological sensitivities, further enlarged the repertoire of ways in which divine power was materialized (see further above p. 17). Christ's insistence that his body was bread and wine made those everyday objects the focus of material elaboration through the authoritative bread stamp, the intricately carved ivory pyx, or the flagon or chalice with relief scenes or openwork decoration (the classic exhibition of this material is Weitzman 1979). But the transformation of the act of worship from the real feast provided by the eventual consumption of sacrificial meat, often taken home, to the token but immediate consumption of bread and wine also changed the requirements for the manifestation of divine power from the need for a perpetual showcase, potentially accessible at any time, to the need for a space in which god could manifest himself to his people at a particular moment. Greek and Roman temples had been houses only for the god and for the objects given to the god; Christian churches needed to host all worshippers simultaneously for the rituals in which god made himself present. This transformed the size of building needed and the nature of the space provided. It also transformed the role of the material surroundings, from offering a static display case to providing the materials for a dynamic process. The static incense burner was replaced by the swung censer, and whereas in Greek and Roman sacrifice the priest had been an optional extra, in Christian liturgy the human actors in the ritual became crucial parts of the manifestation of divine power.

VIRTUALITY AND THE IMMATERIAL

There was, in one sense, nothing special about the relationship between material objects and the gods. It was fundamental to the object world that it bodied forth some living being—typically both its maker and its user. As we have seen throughout this chapter, objects carried ideas. Saddle querns and chariots structured the way in which the world was conceived, and the way in which humans interacted with the world, quite differently from animal-powered rotary mills and Roman roads. A domestic scale of production, in which milling grain took place in each individual household and required the assignment of significant domestic labor, had been replaced by a world of bakeries (on milling see below p. 47); a world in which only individuals, and what they could carry with them, might move across the landscape had been replaced by a world in which large loads could be hauled very long distances. The world of interaction had expanded, both locally and regionally, and thanks in no small part to the advent of coinage it had expanded independently of personal ties.

It was not only the gods who needed to be materially manifested if they were to be believed to interact with the world. Even the most abstract political or moral ideas became effective only when given material substance. Democracy required its Pnyx Hill, its space for mass meetings where the people as a whole could be seen to be taking charge; the Roman Republican senate needed its senate house (for the same reason that those protesting about senatorial government needed to burn it down); jury verdicts were facilitated by specially made ballots; differential judicial penalties required the hemlock cup, or the board or cross variously used in different forms of crucifixion; benefaction required storage and distribution mechanisms for grain, costumes and prizes for dramatic festivals, or buildings for public functions—and it also demanded statues and tripod monuments by which cities could say thank you.[15]

If ideas needed objects if they were to be realized, so the realization of ideas changed the objects, and even the idea of objecthood. At the most obvious level, objects acquired a symbolic life. Statues symbolized the gratitude of a city, and this was made more, not less, plain if the statues used in one city looked like the statues used in another. This encouraged a standardization, which itself had further material and immaterial effects (Trimble 2011). The portrait statues that had once explored the distinctiveness of different individuals and of those performing different roles became the vehicles whereby all benefactors, and most particularly all female benefactors, came to be indistinguishable versions of one another. Within the Greek city, the *andron*—the room specially designed to accommodate a symposion, with its particular arrangement of benches— seems to have become the essential feature of any self-respecting citizen's house or well-equipped sanctuary. But once a house of sanctuary had an *andron*, the symposion became the necessary—and the only practical—form of domestic entertainment. This had consequences for patterns of alcohol consumption and for gender relations alike. What began as a pattern of emulation in both cases turned into a social straitjacket (Nevett 2010: 43–62; Murray 2018). Within the Roman household a similar story can be traced with the spoon, where the earliest (round) spoons seem to have been developed for particular uses, particularly the consumption of eggs and shellfish, but the spoon was then adapted in terms of bowl shape, capacity, and angle of handle to enable, first, all-purpose consumption from bowls with curving walls, and then use in particular for liquids. There looks to be feedback here between possibilities opened up by the very existence of spoons and the culinary practices that required their use (Swift 2017: 18–22).

The reverse was also true: the agency of the material changed the ideas that they conveyed. A simple example here is the use of bone for dice. The manufacturing process for bone dice, although aimed at producing a square section, actually produced a rectangular section, and the habitual way of numbering dice, with six and one on surfaces parallel to the grain of the bone, meant that the flatness was on the one to six axis. In consequence, less wealthy dice players, using dice made of bone, experienced their games of chance rather differently from wealthier gamblers, whose dice of different materials, such as rock crystal and amber, were more truly proportioned (Swift 2017: 124–46, 206–11). An intriguing example of a different sort concerns Roman uses of jet. Jet had been used in Britain during the Neolithic and Bronze Ages but then went out of fashion. Pliny ascribes to it various remarkable properties—curing toothache, driving off snakes, and detecting attempts to simulate a state of virginity (*Natural History* 36.142). Pliny does not mention its use in amulets, however, yet the jet artifacts known from the Roman Empire are largely amulets and found only in Britain and the northwest provinces. In particular, jet is carved with the face of Medusa—that is, a purely classical motif is brought in to convey the power of this peculiar material, despite the absence of any tradition of such use in more central parts of the Roman Empire (Eckardt 2014: 109–16).

***

The greater the sophistication of the object world, the less flexible the behavior possible—and indeed the patterns of thought—that that object world allowed. Roman law with its complex classification of legal objects allowed far less room for maneuver than had been possible under Athenian law, where few distinctions between types of object acquired legal status. The investment in the communication structure of Roman roads divided the world between places—and hence people—that were connected and places and people that were not connected. The investment in water mills, or other technology dependent upon access to heavy demand, required networks of economic relations that only the bureaucracy of empire could sustain. Between the world of Homeric epic and the world of late antiquity, human knowledge of the material world massively expanded, and human relations with objects significantly changed as that material world was increasingly brought under control. But the constraining of the material world also constituted a constraining of human relations, and when those human relations broke the constraints, the world of things as antiquity knew it rapidly disappeared.

CHAPTER TWO

Technology

COURTNEY ANN ROBY

TECHNOLOGIES: OBJECTS AND SUBJECTS

What does it mean for an object to qualify as technology? We might think the predicate either way, wondering either what makes an object *technology* or what makes an *object* technology. Perhaps an assemblage of material components properly becomes "technology" when we focus on its design, structure, or function: when it affords the ability to achieve some material intervention in the world. Then "technological" artifacts might be roughly defined by the ways in which we enlist them (or try) to accomplish tasks in the world, whether mechanical, exploratory, scientific, or pleasurable. As subjects, our engagements with technology objects may be adversarial or desirous, smoothly imperceptible, or fraught with complication.

Contemporary philosophy of technology, focused on the subject–object relationships formed by technologies and their users, is deeply influenced by Heidegger's attribution of *Zuhandenheit* ("readiness-to-hand") to interactions like that between a craftsman and his hammer (Heidegger 1953: 69, 1996: 64–5). Don Ihde, against the backdrop of Heidegger's work as well as Lewis Mumford's highly critical analysis of the complex of artifacts and humans he dubbed "technics," proposed a "phenomenology of technics" in which human–technology engagements exist on a spectrum from "embodiment relations" to "alterity relations" (Ihde 1990: 72–108; Mumford 1934, 1952, 1967). "Embodiment relations" are those in which the technology becomes, almost invisibly, an extension of the user's embodied sensory experience. This view makes using technology a matter of extending our own sensory and motor abilities outward into the artifact so that we *cease* to focus on its design, structure, or function.

Of course, a hammer may be an extension of a craftsman's own will and force only until it breaks. At that point we are in the realm of what Ihde calls "alterity relations," in which our relationship *with* or *to* a technology (which may be malfunctioning or merely difficult to use) comes to the fore, perhaps provoking us to beseech or threaten it in the hope that it will once again bend itself to our will. Michael Wheeler likewise draws on Heidegger to propose that skillful manipulation or "smooth coping" with technology is characterized by the tool's "transparency," which when disturbed by malfunction makes the subject–object relationship conspicuous (Wheeler 2005: 129–38).

In antiquity, "embodiment relations" make particularly vivid appearances in accounts of using instruments to construct new artifacts, where the focus is more on the product than on the tool that enables it. So, for example, Ptolemy describes the cartographer's work of transforming a data table of latitudes and longitudes into a map (one kind of information technology into another) as work done by a "hand" that functions almost autonomously thanks to the thoughtful organization of the table (Ptolemy *Geography* 2.1.4.1–13). He likewise characterizes the integration of instruments into the astronomer's panoply as a kind of bodily extension whereby one eye is applied to the sighting instrument as the hand reaches out to adjust it until the star under observation appears "glued" to it (Ptolemy *Almagest* 1,1.353.11–354.2).

Most importantly from Ptolemy's perspective, carefully constructed instruments can not only cooperate with the body's own capacities but even supplement its shortcomings. The sensory input that feeds reason is essential for Ptolemy's project of discovering the mathematical structures that form the world, which sight and hearing reveal to the astronomer or harmonicist—provided he is equipped with technology to maximize the precision of that sensory input. A circle constructed freehand may fool the viewer into thinking it is perfect, until it is compared to a circle constructed with the help of reason (Ptolemy *Harmonics* I.1.15–28). He later clarifies that producing this more perfect circle requires "a rational criterion [working] via its proper instruments": a compass for the circle, a ruler for the straight line (I.1.52–6). And so it is for the ear as well; its natural tendency to be tricked by approximate intervals of sound can be addressed with appropriate technology: the harmonic *kanōn*, to which Ptolemy attributes the ability to "straighten (*kanonizein*)" objects of sensory perception that on their own cannot tell the mathematical truth of the world (I.2.2–4). Ptolemy includes elaborate guidance on the design and construction of the *kanōn* in his *Harmonics*, from the basic monochord to multi-stringed models that enable the harmonicist to reproduce more complex arrays of harmonic intervals.

Embodiment relations with technology can apply as well between "tool" and "technician" as they do between "instrument" and "scientist." The texts of the *Corpus Agrimensorum Romanorum*, a compilation of Roman works on land surveying, offer a glimpse into what it was like for these ancient technicians to work with the tools of their trade. Frontinus (probably to be identified with the author of the *De aquae ductu urbis Romae*), writes in his *De arte mensoria* about the use of a surveying instrument called the *ferramentum*. The *ferramentum* was simple to construct yet powerful for making observations, at least if the environment cooperated. Like the similar *groma* or *asteriskos*, it consisted of a staff with a crossbar mounted on top, to which two rods were affixed in an X shape perpendicular to the staff (Dilke 1971: 66–81; Chouquer and Favory 2001: 65–71; Lewis 2001: 120–33). Material remains of the *ferramentum* and similar tools include an example from the "Workshop of the Surveyor Verus" at Pompeii (now at the Museo Nazionale, Naples), as well as funerary monuments like that of Lucius Aebutius Faustus (Figure **2.1**; Zimmer 1982: 197). Cords hung from the ends of the X, weighted down so

FIGURE 2.1 Ferramentum on the stele of L. Aebutius Faustus. Ivrea, Museo Civico. Image courtesy of Deutsches Archäologisches Institut Rom, negative D-DAI-ROM-4869.

that they would hang perpendicular to the ground. The surveyor would then sight across two opposite cords, lining them up with a distant sighting pole (held by an assistant) to produce accurate straight lines; lines at right angles were also easy to produce by sighting across both pairs of opposite cords. Frontinus advises the surveyor to balance the instrument on the terrain before aiming, to make sure the strings are taut and aligned, and then to apply the eye to project his sight across the strings (Frontinus, *De arte mensoria* 32.18–20 Lachmann; Roby 2016: 223–8). The system of *ferramentum* and sighting poles thus acts to extend the surveyor's own eye and hand, transforming his local view across the cords into the far-running grid of rectilinear lines that overlaid the Roman landscape.

But if the weather was not calm, the instrument ceased to be an extension of the surveyor's will and became an adversary. Hero of Alexandria, probably writing in the first century CE, criticizes the performance of the *asteriskos* (an instrument similar to the *ferramentum*) when the wind blows the cords around, as well as the solutions contrived by surveyors in the field (Hero, *Dioptra* 33.5–15).[1] He blames them for trying to use the instrument for tasks to which it is poorly suited, given the tendency of the cords to keep swaying for a long time when moved by the wind. Some surveyors, he says, try to fix the problem by enclosing the weights in hollow tubes, but this only makes things worse, since the friction of the weights against the interior of the tubes means the cords cannot be relied on to remain vertical (Hero in fact proceeds to a geometrical proof of this claim).[2] An *asteriskos* subjected to this kind of external interference can no longer serve as a virtual extension of the surveyor. The technology shifts from a convenience to a problem in its own right, to be solved (clumsily) by enclosing the instrument along with the surveyor in a small tent or by encumbering the simple instrument with tubes meant to shield the cords from the wind, which just cause further problems.

We may proceed with a working definition of "technological" objects as a class distinguished among other artifacts not by any criterion intrinsic to the object, but rather on the basis of individual subject–object interactions aimed at using the artifact to achieve an effect. If the effect is achieved readily, the technology becomes a kind of transparent prosthetic for our human effective capacities; if it is achieved only with difficulty or not at all, the technology's troublesome opacity comes to the fore, and it must be fixed, improved, or abandoned.

STRUCTURING TECHNOLOGIES

Technologies, of course, become culturally active only when set in a broader context, against the backdrop of social structures that created expectations for technologies, theaters in which they were used and evaluated, and environments of learning and practice that fostered their creation and development. To see our technologies against this complicated backdrop, it helps to simplify the technologies themselves into rough, "zoomed-out" taxonomies, acknowledging the serious loss of resolution along the way as a necessary evil. Indeed, we will never get to anything like a complete catalog, but at least in this failing we are in illustrious company. Vitruvius warns his reader that his account of machines will be far from complete, as he plans to focus on unfamiliar devices rather than the everyday tools with which everyone is acquainted, like "mills, smiths' bellows, wagons, carriages, lathes, and the rest" (Vitruvius, *De architectura* 10.1.6; on these objects, see Chapter 4). Vitruvius' decision to focus on "high technologies," reflected also in other textual sources, has resulted in the unhappy irony that we know much more about comparatively exotic technologies like catapults and water organs than the commonplace tools that would have played a much larger role in Greek and Roman life.

Those everyday technologies can still speak to us through the surviving material evidence. Funerary engravings in particular can offer glimpses of the subject–object relationships between craftsmen, their tools, and their products (Cuomo 2007: 77–102). Representations of mills on funerary monuments range from stylized depictions, like the flat portrait of a man flogging a mule around the central mill on a relief from Ostia (Figure **2.2**), to

FIGURE 2.2 Mule-powered mill on a gravestone from Ostia. Museo Ostiense.

the magnificently detailed image of two mills being powered by horses on a marble sarcophagus (Zimmer 1982: 112–13).

Craftsmen's tools are often carefully represented even on modest monuments, hinting at their status as what Cuomo calls "a metonymic pointer to the life of the technician" (Cuomo 2007: 97), as well as providing practical clues about the details of these well-used artifacts that often do not survive well. A stele engraved with a carpenter's tools groups a ruler with length markings, a compass, and a spoked wheel, suggesting the precise measurements that characterized the craftsman's work (Figure **2.3**; Zimmer 1982: 150). The ruler, which spans the width of the relief, hovers over the smaller images of wheel and compass in an arrangement that recalls a mosaic table from Pompeii depicting a carpenter's square from which depends a skull, itself almost—but not quite—touching a wheel below, separated by a butterfly.[3] The carefully balanced arrangement of measuring tools and finished product on the carpenter's stele, simple as it is, monumentalizes the deceased as a methodical craftsman. Contrast this with the riot of carpenters' tools scattered over the face of a votive altar to Minerva established by members of the *collegium* of woodworkers at Rome, just as they might be heaped up in a carpenter's workshop (Figure **2.4**; Zimmer 1982: 162–3). The varied iconographies of even relatively basic technologies like these hint at the rich background of practitioners' experiences, which are so difficult to reconstruct from textual evidence.

FIGURE 2.3 Stele depicting carpentry tools. Aquileia, Museo Nazionale, inv. 1231.

FIGURE 2.4 Votive altar to Minerva with carpenters' tools. Rome, Musei Capitolini, Galleria inv. 1909. Archivio Fotografico dei Musei Capitolini. Photograph: © Roma, Sovrintendenza Capitolina ai Beni Culturali.

Technological artifacts emerge from a complexly interconnected nexus of diverse craft techniques, contexts of use, and cultural associations. Taxonomic schemes were employed in antiquity as strategies to make technologies comprehensible as a class. The best-known ancient taxonomy of machines comes from Vitruvius, and the degree of difficulty of his task is apparent from the fact that no single set of categories seems to have sufficed for him. He begins in his tenth book by differentiating machines into three categories: the "climbing" type (*genus scansorium*, a gloss for the Greek *akrobatikon*), the "pneumatic" type (*spirabile*, Greek *pneumatikon*), and the "hauling" type (*tractorium*, Greek *baroulkon*) (Vitr. 10.1.1–2; Fleury 1993: 37–45). The first type involves arrangements of timbers that allow one to climb up safely to spy on enemy military apparatus; the second comprises instruments that pressurize air and squeeze it out "instrumentally" (*organikōs*) to produce sound and other effects; the third is a matter of lifting up great weights using machinery.

Each has in turn a particular virtue through which it secures its cultural relevance and value. The "climbing" type is less a matter of painstaking craft and more about the "boldness" (*non arte sed audacia gloriatur*) of interweaving connected members into a towering structure. By contrast, the "pneumatic" type is about craft first and foremost, as the pneumatic devices "achieve elegant effects through the subtleties of craft" (*elegantes artis subtilitatibus consequetur effectus*). Finally, the "hauling" type is the muscle by which its (Roman) users efficiently enact their virtues (*agendo cum prudentia summas virtutes*) in the form of magnificent constructions.

These categories depend first of all on the structure of the devices and the activities they permit—but that is not all, as those functions themselves serve to determine the cultural values and priorities the different classes of device embody. The "climbing" type becomes emblematic of the whole apparatus of siege warfare, with its arms-race upscaling of fortifications, offensive weaponry, and mobile towers for espionage and assault. The "pneumatic" type, by contrast, speaks to delicate gadgets that, even as they amuse the viewer, also provoke wonder at the human ingenuity able to exploit the subtleties of physics through craft. The "hauling" type returns us to a world populated by immense constructions, now harnessed in the service of building large and lasting structures to signal the technical power of the Roman people.

After his typology of machines in terms of their context of use, Vitruvius immediately offers another taxonomy, differentiating "machine" (*machina*) from "device" (*organon*) (Vitr. 10.1.3). *Machinae* require many operators or some other great force to move them; Vitruvius cites ballistae and oil presses as examples. *Organa*, on the other hand, "carry out their assignment by means of the skilled touch of a single operator, like the windings of hand-catapults or gear-systems" (*organa autem unius operae prudenti tactu perficiunt quod est propositum, uti scorpionis seu anisocyclorum versationes*). Here the line of differentiation traces the kinds of user experience a type of technology entails, rather than its theater of use or the cultural values it embodies. In distinguishing "machines" that demand a large input of brute force from "devices" that require a delicate, skilled touch, Vitruvius evokes not only the users who apply that impulse, but also the intentions of the designer.

Clearly Vitruvius' taxonomies tell us much more (and less) than what kinds of machines the Romans had access to. His first scheme organizes technologies by the kinds of value they might have to society: scaling ladders and other constructions of siege warfare enable acts of glorious daring, pneumatic wonders serve as elegant testaments to the possibilities of fine-grained craftsmanship, and hauling machines offer an opportunity to turn the lofty ambitions of the Roman people into concrete constructions. His second scheme hints at the shadowy world of the designers and technicians behind the machines: some technologies are relatively simple but require considerable human power to operate, while others demand less power at the cost of demanding expertise from their designers and operators alike.

Taxonomies give us the broadest possible view of technological artifacts, zooming out to find the commonalities between classes of technologies rather than focusing in on the peculiarities of their material, construction, or operation. Useful as broad overviews of such complicated territory they may be, they of course offer no clues about what it is like to engage with any particular artifact, either as a maker or a user. Few texts from antiquity explicitly describe experiences of manual technical work, not least because technological practice is always deeply informed by tacit experiential knowledge (Rihll and Tucker 2002; Baird 2004; Nightingale 2009; Collins 2010; Kogge 2012; Tybjerg 2012). Philo of Byzantium, who composed a multivolume *Syntaxis Mechanica* of which just two books survive in Greek, tells his addressee, Ariston, in the volume on catapults, "I know you are not unaware that *technē* happens to include something hard to express theoretically or track down" (*dystheōrēton ... kai atekmarton*).[4] Some components of craft knowledge are simply impossible to render into abstract theory or express verbally with precision.

At the same time, Philo urges the would-be engineer to labor over whatever attributes of the design process can be extracted and expressed theoretically. The crucial factor for rationalizing catapult designs was the discovery that the machine's payload is proportional to the size of the hole in which the spring is wound. Philo recounts the painstaking process of trial and error by which this relationship was discovered, a hard-won insight that changed the practice forever. Indeed, he compares the slow process of developing a sense for the catapult's correct proportions to the quite different craft of sculpture, adopting the tag from Polyclitus that "the good comes little by little, through many numbers" (τὸ γὰρ εὖ παρὰ μικρὸν διὰ πολλῶν ἀριθμῶν ἔφη γίνεσθαι) (Philo, *Belopoeica* 50.8; Cuomo 2007: 51–2). He likewise describes architects learning "through experiment, adding to and subtracting from the mass ... testing them out in every way" the proportions that make buildings appear symmetrical to the eye despite the optical illusions produced by the viewer's perspective (50.45–51).

Philo's recommended combination of tacit knowledge and careful refinement of plans and formulas is particularly important in a military context, where carefully designed siege engines would encounter unpredictable opposition from the enemy. The field of siege warfare was filled with devices, simple and complex, mobile and stationary, capable of pinpoint accuracy or all-out destruction, and the people on that field had to be prepared not only to face whatever tricks their opponents employed, but to outdo them in striking back. Apollodorus prefaces his *Poliorcetica* by reminding his imperial addressee that "the needs that appear by surprise in war demand versatile men and machines alike" (Apollodorus, *Poliorcetica* 138.7–12). He recalls his good fortune in having had "plenty of soldiers who either by habit or handiness were suited to high-quality craft-work" when he himself served the emperor in battle, and he wishes to keep that chain of craft knowledge intact. Apollodorus therefore proposes to send, along with his treatise, men whom he has personally trained to build his fortifications and offensive constructions, embodying his own expertise so as to be ready for the battlefield's surprises (Meißner 1999: 247). Even so, the devices he recommends in this work are in general mechanically simple, suitable for operators with limited or no specialist training. Cuomo points out that Diodorus Siculus likewise makes no reference to technicians specialized in operating Dionysius of Syracuse's novel artillery, though when he turns to Demetrius Poliorcetes' siege of Rhodes, he does mention catapult operators of some kind (Diodorus 14.95.1, 20.93.1; Cuomo 2007: 61).

Some types of siege engine are described as being operable by soldiers with no apparent special expertise in ballistic machinery. Ammianus Marcellinus describes a counterweight-driven siege engine of the type known as the "onager" (wild ass) (Ammianus Marcellinus, *Historia* 23.4.6). This heavy piece of machinery is constructed from oak, with a sling made of hemp rope or metal, and if placed on a stone wall its kick is powerful enough to destroy its supports, so Ammianus cautions that it had better be placed on a heap of turf. The onager certainly seems to fit Vitruvius' "machine" category, as it requires a team of four men to turn the windlass that winds the arm back. The onager's arm, freed from its bonds, releases its stored energy by launching itself forward; in order to prevent it from flipping over completely and flinging the stone into the ground, the device is equipped with a stopper, cushioned with a stuffed goat hide so that the arm does not snap on impact. The whole thing is bound with ropes, says Ammianus, so that it will not tear itself to pieces upon firing; that is to say, it is the very embodiment of brute force, made not for finesse but to fire a stone with the raw power to crush whatever is in its way. Even the name "onager" summons up an image of frighteningly uncontrolled force; as Ammianus notes, it is named for the wild asses that kick stones at hunters with their *back* legs—all force and no foresight, like their artificial analogs. Accordingly, the personnel who operate it are mostly there to supply manpower rather than technical expertise; the brainpower is all in the "*magister*" who recognizes when it has been fully wound up and effects the swift, targeted blow that sets the machine in action.

Contrast the arrow-firing "ballista fulminalis" described in the *De rebus bellicis*, an anonymous fourth-century work that combines imaginative schemes for economic reform with designs for military technologies that range from the practical (a javelin tipped with a many-pronged point) to the fabulous (a war chariot surrounded by whirling knives). As usual, the author does not provide a high level of mechanical detail on the "ballista fulminalis," but focuses rather on its ability to inspire wonder and fear in the enemy. The wonder associated with this device depends crucially on the fact that its mechanical complexity allows it to be operated by "only a single man, as it were at leisure ... if a crowd of men were devoted to its operation, the novelty of its craft would be diminished" (*De rebus bellicis* xviii.4). Vegetius, who likely composed his *Epitome rei militaris* a little later than the *De rebus bellicis*, likewise distinguishes heavy machinery, like the onager, from the ballista on the basis of the skill required to operate it. The ballista derives its motive power from sinew cords attached to lateral arms, which fling their payload when wound back and released. Vegetius stresses that the ballista will "pierce whatever it hits" *on condition that* it is tuned skillfully and "aimed by well-practiced men" (Vegetius, *Epitome rei militaris* 4.22.2–3). Whereas the onager's payload will crush anything in its path (Vegetius adds the detail that they can destroy horses, men, and even enemy siege engines), the ballista is more finicky, its destructive power contingent on its being prepared and operated by men with some amount of specialized expertise (Rihll 2007: 172–5).

Tracey Rihll proposes that at this time "catapult construction was returning to the same sort of pattern we saw in the early days of torsion; some catapults worked well and some didn't, and it was not entirely clear to those outside the business (and perhaps some of those in it, too) why that was so" (Rihll 2007: 248). The "practice" Vegetius' men would have been exposed to is certainly not available from the text itself: while he does list the types of drills performed by Roman soldiers with simpler arms like bows and javelins, he does not supply the kind of ergonomic detail one would need to even embark upon the exercises, let alone become expert in them. That kind of expertise requires a deep background of tacit knowledge assimilated through imitation and experience, which is put to work in an immensely more complicated framework of unpredictable variables once the battle begins.

ECOLOGIES OF PRODUCTION AND REFINEMENT

The practices and processes underlying the refinement of technologies in the ancient world have only recently begun to receive the attention they deserve. For decades, Moses Finley's assertions that the ready supply of slave labor in antiquity impeded technological innovation and that technical work was derided as "banausic" in Greek and Roman antiquity were widely accepted by scholars in many different fields (Finley 1965, 1999).[5] Finley's narrative fit neatly with a teleological impulse to ask why, given that the ancient Greeks and Romans had created some technologies, they did not manage to develop more of the same technologies we have (Loison 2016). A classic case: given that Hero of Alexandria developed the aeolipile (a pneumatically driven device to make a sphere whirl around, propelled by jets of escaping steam), what stopped him (and everyone else for centuries) from expanding it into a steam engine? On the Whiggish view that technological life has always been moving toward the present (industrialized, Western) scheme, there must have been *something* standing in the way, and Finley's hypothesis provided two easy answers: "cheap slave labor" and "elite disdain for technical work." The raft of theories Cuomo collects (and refutes) under the rubric of the "*blocage* question" cling to the idea that some invisible hand drives technological development toward an inevitable goal, ignoring the fact that technologies serve different purposes in different cultural environments (Cuomo 2007: 3–4; Berryman 2009: 39–43).

Fortunately, considerable scholarship has since emerged to correct the picture presented by Finley. Kevin Greene (2000, 2006) offers a sensitive analysis of the reasons behind the long duration of Finley's influence on a variety of disciplines. Alain Bresson provides a more realistic model for the integration of technical innovation into the ancient economy (Bresson 2016: 206–19). He notes in particular that the introduction of a technology into one sector or region does not guarantee its adoption throughout a society, not because of any hostility toward innovation, but simply because the improvements in efficiency it offers may be offset by local ecological or social advantages. As for the touchpoint of Hero's aeolipile, Paul Keyser (1992) effectively refutes the "steam engine" interpretation. Bresson has reconsidered the economic practicality of using Hero's "steam engine" as a source of power based on calculations of the economic cost and energy efficiency of combustible substances in antiquity (Bresson 2005). Meanwhile, Claude Domergue and Jean-Louis Bordes have found new archaeological evidence for mining innovations in the Roman world, while John Oleson has analyzed the material evidence for innovations in Roman well pumps, and so on (Domergue and Bordes 2005; Oleson 2005).

If we reject Finley's gloomy portrait of the artificial limitations that hampered technological innovation in antiquity, we are confronted with new uncertainties. There is only limited textual evidence for the social, political, and economic structures that fostered technological innovation in the ancient world, or for how engineers were trained, or their relationships with other types of craftsmen or with "scientific" practitioners. The "top-down" view favored by ancient historians does suggest that political structures seem to have played an important role in shaping cultures of technological development. Philo tells us, for example, that the dedicated support of Alexandrian kings who loved both glory and craft (*philodoxoi kai philotechnoi*) enabled their military engineers to realize first that the hole for the spring cord was the crucial factor in catapult sizing (*Belopoeica* 50.32–40). Philo's "many numbers" indeed offer a neat counterpoint to Finley's claim that the systematic development of technologies was unknown in antiquity.

Naturally we would like to follow up by learning about the systems of education or apprenticeship by which such developments were sustained and propagated, but unhappily we know very little about the education of technicians in antiquity.[6] Cuomo draws together epigraphic evidence that ephebes were trained as catapult operators in some Greek cities since at least the third century BCE, but this of course does not tell us anything directly about how *makers* of catapults learned their craft (Cuomo 2007: 63–5). In the Roman world, it seems likely that posts like the *apparitores*, which were often occupied by freedmen and involved a wide range of technical roles, might have been a path to technical expertise; Vitruvius himself may have been an *apparitor* at one point (Purcell 1983). The military would have provided additional options; certainly Apollodorus and others refer to military technicians, but again the specific role the military might have played in training designers of technology is unclear.

Textual accounts of the contexts in which technologies were learned and developed usually take a top-down perspective rather than revealing the experiences of ordinary workmen, but they can still tell us something about how those developments fit into the broader culture. Markus Asper has argued that technical disciplines were, with the exception of medicine, not shaped by civic institutions of competition familiar from other arenas of public intellectual life, including rhetoric, law, and drama, which might have enforced disciplinary norms (Asper 2007: 48–51). In the absence of institutionalized competition, however, informal competition could still be a powerful spur to efficiency and novelty. Diodorus Siculus reports that when Dionysius of Syracuse discovered that he needed to fortify Epipolae in a very short time, he brought in a labor force of 60,000 laymen and assigned groups of them one-stade building spaces, each presided over by a master-builder (*architektōn*) and six builders (*oikodomoi*) (Diodorus 14.18.3–8). This hierarchical combination of skilled and unskilled labor produced results so quickly that onlookers experienced astonishment (*kataplēxis*), and Dionysius accelerated them even further by instituting a competitive system of awards for completing tasks the fastest, keyed to the workers' different skill levels. Moreover, he even appeared on the construction site himself as a motivational presence, "making appearances everywhere and assisting those who struggled." His diligent involvement spurred on a spirit of rivalry (*eris*) and zeal (*spoudē*) that drove the workers to labor even into the night. Though we might be skeptical about just how helpful a king's meddling in a construction project might be, Diodorus' account highlights the cultural resonance and practical power of technological competition.

Indeed, Dionysius' informal building competition was evidently so successful that he replicated it during his preparations for war with Carthage (Diodorus 14.41.3–6). This time he principally required skilled workmen, acquiring them through edict (*prostagma*) or by the promise of high salary. His force assembled, he divided them into groups headed up by prominent citizens, with a promise of great prizes for those who produced the best arms. Again one might question the management decision of placing prominent laymen in charge of a technical operation like this, but Diodorus gives the further interesting detail that the technicians were provided with models (*typoi*) from which to work. Once again, a system of competitive gift awards created a spirit of ambitious rivalry (*philotimia*), so that the collaboration spread throughout the city, not just in public spaces like temples, gymnasia, and markets, but even in prominent homes. The crowning achievement of this competitive collaboration, says Diodorus, was the invention of the catapult, as well as the novel expansion of triremes into quadriremes and even quinqueremes (14.42.1–5). As always, Dionysius used high salaries, competitive gifts, and personal involvement with his technicians, who were inspired to ambitious feats of technical creativity. Diodorus provides few details about the artifacts themselves, focusing instead on Dionysius' *management* technology, a crucible of competition for glory and material gain.

Technical competition could come to the rescue of failed projects as well as accelerating successful ones. Cuomo brilliantly contextualizes the technical, political, and labor structures underlying the tale inscribed on the *cippus* of Nonius Datus, erected at Saldae (now in Algeria) in the second century CE (Cuomo 2011). Having been commissioned to oversee the construction of an aqueduct tunnel, Datus conducted a survey and then supplied the nearby procurator of Mauretania Caesarensis with a design (*forma*) for the tunnel. He describes himself in the inscription as a surveyor (*librator*) and soldier, and Cuomo supposes he received his technical training as an apprentice in the army; the actual work of building the tunnel was delegated to nonspecialist soldiers, a mixed group of sailors and mercenaries. Datus seems not to have exercised military-style discipline over the building project itself, as he left the scene for four years. He returned only when the project had gone terribly wrong, as two teams digging from opposite sides had both swerved to their right, failing to connect the tunnel as planned. Datus' plan to get the project back on track is more than a little reminiscent of what Diodorus tells us about Dionysius: he divided up the soldiers into small groups, each in charge of a small piece of the project, and set up a competition between the sailors and the mercenaries. Thanks to Datus' micromanagement and fueled by competitive zeal, the soldiers soon completed the project. However, the value of technical competition is not the primary focus of the tale told by the *cippus*, which poignantly highlights virtues for technical work on each of its three surviving sides: patience (*patientia*), courage (*virtus*), and hope (*spes*).

TECHNOLOGICAL AFFECTS

Although analyses of technological artifacts most often focus on their practical effects, the *affective* experiences they provoke are perhaps as important to their cultural value. Technologies designed and built for the glory and power of the state, like military machinery and large-scale public building projects, have long attracted the attention of lay audiences. These ostentatiously visible technologies evoked admiration and wonder when they were first implemented as well, along with emotions of pride and fear largely lost upon today's retrospective observers. The Hellenistic war machines we encountered earlier are exemplary embodiments of a glory that could transcend the differences between friend and foe, uniting all in amazement, as when Plutarch says of the war machinery of Demetrius Poliorcetes: "by its size it startled even his allies; by its beauty it delighted even his enemies" (*Demetrius* 20.6.1–2). In other circumstances that spectacular quality might appear misplaced in machinery designed for the protection and expansion of the state and the eradication of its enemies; Cuomo observes in the case of Dionysius of Syracuse that "Diodorus disapprovingly compares Dionysius' use of the spectacular element of siege engines to a theatrical display, almost as if one of the aims of the device, its very spectacularity, had been perverted" (Diodorus 14.112; Cuomo 2007: 58–9).

The state's spectacular technological accomplishments could of course shine in peacetime as well as in war. For sheer scale it is difficult to outdo the Roman system of roads, its storied history dating back at least to Appius Claudius Caecus' construction of the Appian Way to serve the army's needs. Since the roads' position beneath their users' feet might efface the technological achievement they represented, Statius opens up the smooth surface of the Via Domitiana in *Silvae* 4.3, reminding his reader of the many layers of different materials that make up the roads, the massive labor force needed to build them, and the deafening din of the construction process that inlaid them in the earth. The construction noise is the reader's first impression at the opening of the poem, as Statius asks rhetorically "what frightful racket of hard rock and heavy metal" (*quis duri silicis gravisque ferri/immanis sonus*) fills the coastal region of the Appian Way. As Carole Newlands observes, "dominating sound functions as a potent and ambivalent expression of imperial power—commanding, awe-inspiring, and terrifying" (2002: 295). Naturally, the racket of construction serves a greater purpose, offering the people of Campania (traumatized by the eruption of Vesuvius not long before) a convenient new travel option to Rome: no longer will they need to slog through boggy swampland, as a journey that once took a day is reduced to a couple of hours (36–7). Statius provides an in-depth view of the grueling labor that underlay the road's construction, peeling back its layers to reveal the trench that was first dug for the road, the drainage routes that channeled water away from it, the clay and tufa that filled the trench to make a stable surface for the pavement, and the puzzling together of flat-topped blocks for the pavement and the wedges that shore them up. He marvels, "how many hands labor together" (*o quantae pariter manus laborant*, 49), listing the tasks allocated to different groups of workers.

Statius' treatment of the road binds together the laborers who built it, the travelers who will use it, and the benevolent imperial power that made the project possible. He mockingly compares the project to Xerxes' failed attempt to bridge the Hellespont with a causeway, and to Alexander's aborted project of carving Mount Athos into a figure holding a city in one hand and a water reservoir in the other: the brainchild of the architect Dinocrates, who Vitruvius says dressed as Hercules to impress his patron (Vitruvius, *De architectura* 2.pr.1–3). Unlike those outlandish projects of vanity and war-making, Domitian's road-building project is the product of an emperor aiming to help his people—and this project *worked*. A massive effort of labor, based on technologically sophisticated planning, binding the Roman world together: a wonder perhaps greater, and certainly more lasting, than Demetrius's ranks of high-powered war machines. Yet for all the attention these massive marvels of state-sponsored technological power receive, smaller-scale technologies can evoke equally intense reactions of their own; I will focus here on a few that evoked particularly strong responses from devoted users, obsessive designers, proud patrons, or inspired admirers.

Timekeeping technologies were fixtures of the Roman world; they tracked chronological flows from the precise hours of the anaphoric clock to the Roman annual calendar of workdays and holidays known as the *fasti*, and far beyond to long-running administrative chronologies. Monumental structures, from inscriptions of the *fasti* to extraordinary elaborations like the "Tower of the Winds" at Athens, made time-reckoning a public, communal experience quite unlike the private appeals to a watch or phone we make now. Hundreds of sundials have now been catalogued and 3D-scanned by the "Ancient Sundials" group (Fritsch et al. 2013). The project makes available a digital database of images and 3D models of the surviving sundials and fragments, along with computational tools that make vividly apparent how Greeks and Romans could mark time with planar, conical, cylindrical, and spherical dials.[7] While the Tower of the Winds is unique, with its carved personifications of the winds and internal infrastructure that might correspond to an elaborate water clock, even small sundials often included decorative details like lion or griffon feet, curving vines, or dolphins (Noble and Price 1968; Gibbs 1976: 89–90). Some sundials include inscriptions that recall the network of people involved in their own creation, like the conical sundial from Heraclea ad Latmum (Turkey), which names not only its dedicatee, but also its maker (Gibbs 1976: #3049G).

In a fragment of Plautus' comedy *The Boeotian Woman*, a character complains of the frustrating constraints these public monuments to timekeeping place on natural, individualized human impulses. When he was a boy, he says, your only timepiece was your stomach, and it gave you all the chronological information you needed, namely when it was time to eat. Now, however, the town is chock-full of sundials, and no one is allowed to eat without the sun's approval, "so the greater part of the people creep around parched with hunger." Pliny describes an obelisk set up by Augustus in the Campus Martius and then converted to a sundial by adding a golden ball to its peak (so that the shadow's tip would not be "swallowed up" by the lower part at any time of day) and inscribing the ground below with the day curves and seasonal hour lines of a planar sundial (Pliny *Nat. Hist.* 36.70–3).[8] Unfortunately, that sundial had not told the correct time for around thirty years by Pliny's time of writing; whether because of some cosmic upset deranging the position of the earth or the motion of the sun, a local disturbance from earthquake or flood, or some other reason Pliny does not know. Yet the monument remained, constraining local perceptions of time to its inaccurate traces.

Other technologies inspire an extreme, even absurd, degree of devotion in their aficionados, despite—or maybe because of—the challenges they entail. Ptolemy's *Harmonics* lays out the systems of harmonic intervals that structured Greek music alongside a detailed description of the instruments used to make those systems audible. Chief among these instruments is the monochord: in its most basic form, a single stretched string with movable bridges that can be slid back and forth to create the desired notes. But the devil is in the details: in order to work as an instrument of harmonic exploration, the monochord has to be very precisely tuned. Ptolemy worries even about the tiny depth of bridge space that the string must traverse: How is the harmonicist to account for the discrepancy in string length from one side of the bridge to the other? Ptolemy's solution is to craft the bridges with a circular cross section, so that the string will theoretically impact the fixed and movable bridges along the edges of similar triangles, allowing the errors to cancel one another out (*Harmonics* III.2.108–14). A related analysis is introduced as early as *Harmonics* I.8, where Ptolemy describes the process of stretching the string across (ideally) spherical bridges to test its consistency. Easier said than done, of course; Creese discusses the difficulty of testing material constructions with the rigor Ptolemy aims for (2010: 306–12).

All this obsessive care goes into crafting an instrument that is only useful to the harmonicist. As Ptolemy ruefully notes, the monochord cannot really be used as a performance instrument; since it does not allow one to play two notes simultaneously, perform an arpeggio, allow a note to linger, or weave together notes of very different pitches, it is in fact the "feeblest" of all possible instruments for performing music (Ptolemy, *Harmonics* II.12.34). Though the monochord's field of application is narrow, its power as an instrument of scientific discovery is so wonderful as to justify the difficulty of its construction. For Ptolemy, refining the monochord into a maximally precise instrument aligns the user's sensory apparatus with his reason. It is only by combining these two that the mathematical beauty and order that undergirds the world becomes comprehensible: mathematics is not just about understanding beautiful things theoretically, but also reifying that comprehension through practice (*Harmonics* III. 3.38–48). As Creese observes, the monochord is "for Ptolemy an essential tool for demonstrating the rational beauty of the constructions of nature" (2010: 296). He works to give his reader sensory access to the perfect circles and intricate epicycles of the celestial domain in his *Almagest*, to the precisely interlocking musical intervals of the harmonic domain in his *Harmonics*, and (in the culminating passages of its third book) the structural parallels between the two, and between them and the human *psychē*. His obsessive refinement of the *kanōn* indeed seems very much like a kind of love for a technology capable of revealing divine truths to the human spectator.

Ptolemy was not alone in his devotion to the cosmic structures made apprehensible through technology. While ordinary stargazers could of course appreciate some of what the heavens had to offer, more robust visions into the structure of the *cosmos* depended in antiquity on doggedly patient observation, careful recording, and complicated mathematical calculations that were well out of the reach of laymen. Astronomers and astrologers (in antiquity, they were of course not the highly differentiated groups we know today) created their own tools to make the movements of celestial bodies easier to imagine. A passage from the *Alexander Romance* on the board Nektanebo used to take Olympias' horoscope shows another side of love for technology. The reader is treated to a beautifully detailed account of a set of jewels representing the sun, moon, and planets meant to be situated upon a board (*pinakidion*) of ivory and gold representing the heavens (*Hist. Alexandri Magni*, recensio γ [lib. 1], 4.34–56). The author dwells on the beauty of the board, which is indeed inexplicable (ὅπερ λόγος ἑρμηνεῦσαι οὐ δύναται), and the many-colored stones that could be laid out on it to show the horoscope: a crystal sun, sapphire Venus, emerald Mercury, and hematite Mars. The different recensions of the surviving text yield another kind of variegation (*poikilia*): sometimes the board incorporates ebony and silver along with the ivory and gold, while the sun might be a carbuncle or ruby, the moon a crystal, Venus a pearl, and Mercury a moonstone.

Fantastical as the description is, a few likely parallels to the board and gems survive: one of the Greek magical papyri describes the use of a board with markers similar to those in the *Romance*: a gold sun, silver moon, lapis lazuli Venus, and turquoise Mercury (Betz 1986: 312 [*PGM* CX.1–12]). The papyrus suggests that "a voice comes … in conversation" to the astrologer, at which point he should begin to lay out the planets on the board in their "natural order." James Evans points out that the stones representing the planets likely connect the stones' own magical attributes to the planets (Evans 1999: 288). This in turn perhaps inspires the layman to trust the homology between the shining stones on the board and their celestial analogs. Evans suggests that some of the gemstone markers probably survive among the collections of magical gems (Evans 2004: 14–20). He observes in particular the preponderance of lapis lazuli gems carved with images of Aphrodite; given the rarity of lapis lazuli (sourced from Afghanistan) in the ancient Mediterranean, the correlation between these gems and the lapis lazuli marker for Venus on the papyrus and in some recensions of the *Alexander Romance* is unlikely to be a coincidence.

Some analogs for the astrologer's board survive as well. Some seem to have been relatively simple and could be drawn on low-cost materials, like that depicted on P. Oxy. 235. But there are closer matches to the "indescribable" ivory board of the *Alexander Romance*, suggesting that these beautifully intricate windows into the cosmos were not merely the product of the author's imagination. Two ivory astrologer's boards dating to the second century CE survive from the French village of Grand, where a temple to Apollo (Grannus) once stood (Figure 2.5). The tablets were discovered shattered into fragments in a well (Béal 1993), and Jean-Paul Berteaux argues that they were deliberately destroyed (1993: 44). Now reassembled, each is a diptych with an intricate

FIGURE 2.5 Ivory astrologer's board from Grand. Saint-Germain-en-Laye, Musée des Antiquités nationales inv. 83675. Photograph: © Musée d'Archéologie nationale.

arrangement of concentric circles, showing Helios and Selene at the center, the zodiac figures around them, and in the outermost circle figures representing the three decans that make up each zodiac sign (Abry 1993). The images were originally colored and decorated with gold leaf (Evans 2004: 5)—labors of devotion indeed, at least until the portrait of the cosmos they afforded became instead a target of violent destruction.

Wonder provoked by the motions of celestial bodies through the heavens also inspired moving mechanical models of the cosmos. The most celebrated of these in ancient texts was the model attributed to Archimedes that was looted from Syracuse and brought to Rome; today the Antikythera Mechanism (on which more below) is the sole surviving example.[9] Cicero describes these devices several times in various texts, not so much in terms of their structure or function as their effect on the viewer (Jaeger 2008: 48–72). In the *De re publica*, Philus describes to his partners in dialogue how the *sphaera* of Archimedes was looted from Syracuse when it was sacked by Marcellus' troops and kept at the family home, where it was available for visitors to view. Philus recounts that he heard about the device from C. Sulpicius Gallus, who had spent enough time viewing it at the house that he was able to describe the experience to Gallus, who regales his companions with the details (*De re publica* 1.21–22). Unfortunately, any technical information Cicero may have included here is lost to us in the troubled transmission of the *De re publica*, which breaks off just as he has mentioned how the *sphaera*'s moving parts imitate the proportional motions of the celestial bodies they represent.

However, Cicero's other treatments of the device might suggest that what is missing is more an account of a wondrous viewing experience than a highly technical description of the mechanism. In the *Tusculan Disputations*, Cicero values the *sphaera* not because it allows one to make detailed astronomical calculations, but because viewing it conveys the wonderfully synoptic precision of Archimedes' model of a well-ordered cosmos, and more importantly it allows one to recognize the exacting creative effort of the demiurgic power that runs the real thing (*Tusculan Disputations* I.63). In the *De natura deorum*, Cicero's Stoic, Balbus, echoes the sentiment that as the orderly operation of human technologies communicates the control the craftsman exerted over them, so does the order of the cosmos put Nature's governance on display. After briefly mentioning sundials and water clocks, he particularly praises a *sphaera* made by Posidonius (raising the specter of Archimedes as well later in the passage) for communicating the order of the cosmos so clearly that even the barbarians of Scythia and Britain would appreciate the craftsman's representational achievement (*De natura deorum* II.87–9). Both of these accounts are short on astronomical detail: they mention the moon, sun, and planets revolving around the terrestrial center, but provide no material or mathematical specifics. The *sphaera*'s cultural importance stems not so much from the particular astronomical relationships it displays at any time, but from the wonder sparked by seeing the complexities of the cosmos played out in miniature, before one's very eyes.

The wonder of the *sphaera* never really ceased. In the fourth century CE, the poet Claudian imagines the *sphaera*'s transcending the gap between human and divine from the other side, as Jupiter himself marvels at the little machine. The human-built device provokes surprised laughter from the god, as he sees how "an old man from Syracuse" imitates the complexities of his own creation "in a fragile sphere," and wonders at the "spirit enclosed there" that makes the whole thing run. Just as the *sphaera* gave Cicero's human spectators an inkling of divine order, it shows Jupiter how "this bold diligence, revolving its own world, / rejoices, and rules the stars with human mind" (Claudian, *Minora* 51). A century or so later, a letter written by Cassiodorus on behalf of Theoderic (king of the Ostrogoths) requests that the mathematician and harmonicist Boethius construct a sundial and a water clock, to be sent to Gundobad (king of the Burgundians) (Cassiodorus, *Variae* 1.45.2–5). From the nature of the request one presumes that Boethius would understand a technical description of the *sphaera*, introduced as a "second zodiac circle, made by human ingenuity." Instead, he describes it as "a tiny machine pregnant with the cosmos, a portable heaven, a compendium of the universe, a mirror of nature for the face of the ether," revolving "with mysterious mobility." Once again, the *sphaera* evokes wonder as a miniature device whose movements reveal the immense workings of the heavens to the viewer.

The Antikythera Mechanism was discovered in 1900 among the remains of a shipwreck that occurred in the first century BCE, and it began to attract serious attention in 1902 once Spyridon Stais observed the presence of gearing mechanisms within the corroded "slab" and fragments (Jones 2017: 1–46). Like the *sphaera*, it seems to have included representations of the sun, moon, and planets, which moved through their celestial paths in the correct proportions to one another. It also included other features never mentioned in connection with a *sphaera*, like an eclipse calculator and an Olympiad dial. It was not until the 1970s that Derek de Solla Price, adding radiographic scans to the arsenal of photographic and other techniques previously deployed to study the Mechanism, published the first coherent reconstruction of the device's gearing system (Price 1974).

Michael Wright later applied linear tomographic imaging to the Mechanism, enhancing the visualization of individual planes of gears within the "slab" (Wright 2001, 2003, 2005, 2007; Wright et al. 1995). Tony Freeth and his collaborators later applied new computed tomography scanning techniques to produce a more complete image of the interior and a revised reconstruction of the gear system, in certain respects incompatible with Wright's model (Freeth et al. 2006, 2008). The Mechanism continues to attract our gaze, mediated by ever-changing imaging technologies that reveal new details about its mechanical structure and the inscriptions that describe both the mechanism itself and the cosmos it models (Freeth and Jones 2012). And indeed, in its own way it continues to provoke wonder about an intelligence beyond our own: the first question in the online FAQ for the Antikythera Mechanism project is, "Was it left by aliens?"[10]

Awe, love, frustration, wonder: technological artifacts evoked profound emotions from their ancient designers, makers, users, and dependents. Of course, a given technology may elicit quite different emotions depending on one's relationship to it. A catapult, for example, could instill in Dionysius of Syracuse a sense of pride, both in his spectacularly magnified military power and in his ability to manage his engineers effectively to produce innovative equipment. It might fill a soldier on the field with trepidation, whether he was winching back the self-destructive onager or anticipating the darts of the ballista that Ammianus describes as sparking through the sky so quickly that the pain of the fatal wound is felt before the missile can be seen (Ammianus 23.4; Cuomo 2007: 54; Roby 2016: 145). For a designer like Philo, on the other hand, the missile's swift arc is the satisfying reward of a laborious process of design and calculation, the catapult an embodiment of proportional harmony.

Though technologies are often reduced to merely a means of getting tasks done, even that apparently simple relationship turns out to be fraught with complexities of its own, as we wrestle with faulty devices or pause to reflect on the transformative experience of having a technology become part of ourselves (however briefly) as we work with it. Focusing on technologies as means to practical ends places them in a crucible of competitive development, where the goal is to isolate the features most important to the task at hand and somehow "improve" them—making them more efficient, faster, cheaper, or whatever "better" means in the immediate context of production and consumption. Even through that ruthless lens, the inextricable links between technology and human culture are clearly visible: the social structures in which technological experts are trained and consumers indoctrinated, the hierarchies and incentives that shape the workforce, and the cultural narratives we construct of technological kinds and their respective values for society. Though our knowledge of the day-to-day processes through which technologies were crafted and refined in antiquity may be scant, they still resonate through poetry, history, philosophy, and material monuments both personal and public.

CHAPTER THREE

Economic Objects

JENNIFER GATES-FOSTER

INTRODUCTION

In recent decades, the concept of "economy," as a distinct category of human behavior and its study, has expanded to encompass almost every aspect of social relations. This is due in part to the increasing awareness of the embeddedness of economic behaviors within society and the recognition that economic choices are adaptive and are keyed to wants and desires as defined by cultural expectations. Because the goals and constraints of economic choice are linked to the concerns of human social organization, it is necessary to frame economic trends not only in terms of profit or growth, but also as they relate to changing sociocultural factors. The tension between these two approaches—the rational pursuit of growth and profit and the reliance on cultural norms to define those concepts—has marked the debate around the nature, scale, and complexity of the economy of the Classical world and is encapsulated by the substantivist–formalist debates that drove much of the scholarship in this area until the last decade (Plattner 1989: 10–17). In recent years, economic historians and archaeologists have largely rejected this polarized approach, instead exploring new ways to assess growth in economic activity in the Classical past while also acknowledging the social factors that determined and constrained these trends. This shift toward a more integrated economic history has resulted in a new role for objects in discussions of the Classical past among economic historians and archaeologists and two distinct threads of scholarly analysis.

Earlier generations rejected the potential contribution of objects and object patterning in the study of the ancient economy. For Finley, object patterning could tell us nothing because quantification was always undermined by ignorance of how representative the sample was. For others, the problem was the discursive and mutable interpretive framework offered by post-processual archaeologists and their tendency to see objects as symbolic capital with no fixed meaning in the past (Gates-Foster 2016). More recently, economic history has taken a decidedly more material turn, with major initiatives focused on quantifying evidence for various economic activities in the Classical past, with an emphatic focus on assessing growth and the role of institutions designed to facilitate and support economic intensification, particularly in the Roman era.[1] This object orientation works largely at the level of broad assessments of material production and consumption and a more disciplined attention to the actual evidence (usually commodities née objects) substantiating networks of transport and exchange.

Alongside this turn toward calculation and quantification, others are working with dynamic new conceptualizations of objecthood, guided by the foundational work of Arjun Appadurai and Alfred Gell, who explore the role of objects themselves, both in their entanglement with human agents and as actors independent of human action (Appadurai 1986; Gell 1998). The agency of the thing, as further elaborated by Thomas, Miller, and Hodder, and explored by many others, doubles down on the discursiveness that so confounded earlier scholars by insisting on the centrality of the object in the telling of human (and nonhuman) stories, economic or otherwise (Miller 1987, 2005; Thomas 1991; Hodder 2012). For these scholars, because economic actions are embedded in systems of social performance and identity, the material object is a central player not only in articulating a web of social and economic transactions, but in actually defining the qualities that give significance to those actions. Notions of value and the performance of identity through consumption, production, and the act of exchange occupy a principal place, and the material contours of these transactions are of critical importance. The scope of these economic studies is not necessarily smaller, but the focus on economic and personal relations, and close attention to the material world, makes their dominant concerns fundamentally different.

Despite the bifurcation of scholarly work on the role of objects in our understanding of the economy, all agree that *economic objects*, as such, existed in the Classical past. The pervasiveness of an economic point of view and vocabulary in the description of objects and object-ness in this volume neatly encapsulates the way that economic approaches dominate our way of thinking about and with objects more generally. Value, commodification, exchange— each of these concepts, loose, flexible, and situational as they are, are deployed by scholars seeking to assess the meaning and significance of objects in the context of human social relations, and indeed the autonomy of objects as they interact with and through one another in various overlapping vectors—architecture, the body, the everyday, and so on. The economic sphere encircles them all, as the deployment of objects in human relations or in object–object relations reveals the critical common focus on the *exchange transaction* that lies at the heart of the economic discipline.

An "economic" object in Classical antiquity cannot, however, be simply defined as anything that has been or could be exchanged (see above p. 33 on such objects). This brings to the fore the difficulty of drawing a line around a coherent notion of what constitutes an "economic" role for a tangible thing. Is an economic object something that simply has value? But value in what sense? The determination of value and the appropriateness of an object as a participant in an exchange transaction are obviously related, just as the production context is related to the process of valuation. Consumption—both the desire to consume and the act itself—is culturally constrained and also bound to valuation, which is itself interwoven with socially defined notions of status and identity. The difficulty of straightforward classification is obvious, and this contributes to the tendency (again, apparent in this volume) to borrow economic vocabulary to describe a huge range of transformative human choices and agentive objects.

In the face of such slippage, it is surprising that even a cursory survey of recent works on the economy of the Classical world reveals unexpected cohesiveness in the types of objects that are framed as economic *indicia*. In most cases, these are objects that were mobile, often moving long distances (Hahn and Weiss 2013). Coins and related objects such as tokens (Figure 3.1) are a perennial favorite, while pottery—above all amphorae (Figure 3.2) and some classes of fine wares—also appears with regularity either as an independent economic indicator in its own right (see *terra sigillata*) or as an avatar for its former contents (amphorae vis-à-vis *garum*, wine, oil).

Less often, agricultural goods, especially grain, and spices are the focus of an object-oriented economic history. These categories of object are usually recoverable only through their related infrastructure such as granaries or texts that detail their production, storage, or transfer. Only rarely are we able to describe the movement of plants, fibers, and other organic commodities through direct observation despite their centrality in the agrarian world of the Mediterranean farmer. Metal ores and desirable stones, however, routinely persist in altered forms as building materials, gems, metal objects, etc., and can, when attributed to a definite source, provide an economic dimension for an object that might otherwise be viewed through the lens of its qualities as a crafted object. The trade in prestigious building stones in the Roman imperial era, for example, demonstrates how what might otherwise be the study of programmatic aesthetics also engages with questions of resource exploitation,

FIGURE 3.1 Bronze coin die from Thonis-Heraclion, Egypt. Image courtesy of Franck Goddio/Hilti Foundation and Andrew Meadows.

FIGURE 3.2 View of amphorae and ancient shelving in a wine shop attached to the House of Neptune and Amphitrite, Cardo IV Herculaneum. Photograph: Werner Forman/Getty Images.

FIGURE 3.3 Panoramic view of the interior of the Pantheon with marble pavement and revetment imported from across the Roman Empire in the second century CE. Creative Commons license.

trade, and consumption, and the entanglement of these acts with the Roman imperial command economy (Figure **3.3** and see Chapter 6).

Beyond these first-degree points of reference, there is also a parallel, booming scholarly industry focused on the material evidence of the exchange infrastructure. They include most especially ships, ports, weights and measures, and systems of marking and ownership that facilitated communication across multiple economic zones. Increasingly, these constitute their own portfolio of object-driven narratives about economic activity in the ancient Mediterranean that adds a new dimension of materiality to our models of the ancient economy. The production, movement, and consumption of things birthed yet more things that are enfolded into our narratives about the material world of ancient economic performance.

No single essay could encompass such a varied assemblage or begin to describe the diverse ways that scholars have tied these object classes to economy or economic behaviors; accordingly, this chapter aims for a more modest goal. It considers the scholarly history of some objects entangled in what might uncontroversially be described as economic relationships in Classical antiquity. It begins, rather inauspiciously, with a golden pisspot as way to consider the nature of materiality, knowledge, and value in antiquity. Then turning to money and coinage (related but separate categories of things), we examine the development and deployment of coins as an alternative to other modes of exchange that existed and persisted in the ancient world. Finally, we turn to the production and distribution of a special category of pottery, *terra sigillata*, as means to reflect on the nature of value in the face of mass production, as well as the implications of abundance and similarity for consumption and identity. Each of these interlocking categories of behavior mutated over time in service to broader social and cultural goals, and the objects integrated into these acts offer a way to assess the role that materiality played in determining economic aspects of human behavior in the Classical past.

OBJECT PRODUCTION: MAKING, VALUING, MISUNDERSTANDING

Economists have traditionally interested themselves in a narrow class of items and concepts, all of which contribute to the formation of the market: goods, commodities, money, value, price, and exchange.[2] Economists refer to these as *objects* only in relation to the theoretical framework of economics and not necessarily to the existence of the economic object as a tangible artifact in the world. Thinking of the physical artifact as a participant in an economic system relies upon an epistemological scaffolding that connects that item to a set of beliefs about the suitability of things to function within that system. To put it oversimply, economic objects are a combination of "beliefs and physical things" (Zuniga 1999: 300). There is, in other words, nothing self-evident about the suitability of an object, whether physical or otherwise, to serve as a locus for economic action. Its suitability is determined by an epistemology that determines its value in service to an economic goal. Thus, the social dimension of objects and their suitability as a location for economic agency depend upon the point of view of individuals in the past.

This process of creating an economic object—its "enactment"—could take many forms.[3] In this ontology, economic objects are social products that can be stabilized and redefined multiple times and in multiple ways by both human agents and other actors. This is best conceived of as a chain of transformations punctuated by moments where an object's value was stabilized and made singular by comparison with other goods. Production can therefore be either the crafting of a physical object—production in its traditional sense—or the solidification of an object's particular role as a commodity, defined as an example of a wider class of objects (Kopytoff 1986). For example, the potter's act of forming a ceramic bowl is a locus of craft production in which the physical object is brought into being, while its situation as one of many bowls of a type that are understood to be in economic play transforms it from a singular thing into a commodity that is eligible and appropriate for exchange, transfer, or consumption.

In this sense, economic objects can be produced many times over through *envaluation*, the process of attributing value, and commoditization, the designating of an object as appropriate for exchange by situating it among a cohort of like things. Production is an act of creative transformation, a moment when meaning and form are fixed, but not immutably; other acts are also agentive and transformative, especially exchange, which is a moment of precise valuation. Consumption frames the object's value in terms of a specific act and takes the object out of the sphere of exchange.[4] Each of these successive moments in an object's enactment are socially constructed, as are the interlinked concepts of value and worth that make an object more or less appropriate to a given task.[5] The enormous variability of human constructions of these ideas—value, commodity—in the past and present makes any universalizing claims untenable, to say the least. Value and the resulting enactment of an economic object are culturally contextual and rarely single-stranded.

In the ancient Mediterranean, objecthood was similarly multivalent, multi-stranded, and mutable. In *Histories* 2.172.3–5, Herodotus narrates an episode in which an object—in this case, a golden pisspot—is used to make a point about the nature of value and its relationship to objects, in terms of both their deceptive, changeable appearance and their material composition. Amasis, having recently become king of Egypt, struggles to impress his new subjects with his legitimacy as pharaoh because he comes from a historically undistinguished lineage. He orders that a golden pisspot, one of many luxurious items that he owns, be melted down and recast into a statue of a deity that is then put up in a public space where it is admired and worshiped. Eventually, he tells the Egyptian populace that the object of their veneration had formerly been used as a receptacle for vomit and piss, saying that he was himself like the pisspot and should be treated with respect despite his humble origins (Lateiner 1989, 1990; Dewald 2006; Hollmann 2011).

In this case, the pisspot communicates through its form an essential message about the nature of value in the Herodotean construct, and the differential relationship between form and material as aspects of value. The pisspot's resonance resides both in the material from which it is made—gold, which is fungible and easily transformed without any intrinsic loss of the material—and its social function. The fact that the object is made of gold is appropriate to its royal owner, and the misalignment between the luxurious material and the object's original function as a receptacle for vomit, among other things, serves to emphasize the extreme wealth and privilege that attended Egyptian royalty, and the inversion of ordinary practice that such a status required. In the anecdote, the object is transformed into a sacred image—the inverse of the profane pisspot—aligning its material and its function more closely, and making it an object of reverence. For Amasis, however, the statue retains a consequential association with its earlier purpose, and this retention gives the object significance that requires his interpretation. It is a tricky object, where function, material, appearance, and value are variably misaligned, creating confusion about its meaning (Dewald 1993: 59).

Herodotus uses the pisspot and other objects to construct and consider human relationships in his *Histories*. The pisspot offers a chance to say something about Amasis' qualities as a leader and to draw a connection between his humble origins and newly elevated status as pharaoh. Often, the qualities that make these objects work in this capacity is their appearance and the ways that their physical qualities—their objecthood—can be misleading or confusing for people tasked with understanding them. Sometimes, this confusion happens because the object's history is unknown or obscured by a new shape. The end results of that confusion vary considerably; sometimes, the result is a new, relatively benign perspective (as with the pisspot), while in other instances, the confusion has dire consequences for those who cannot accurately assess an object's meaning or history.[6]

While golden pisspots were hardly a common household item in the Classical Mediterranean, Herodotus' use of this and other objects as narrative devices reminds us that meaning was assigned to objects in both overlapping economic and cultural spheres that were mutually determinative. The physical form that an object took—its shape, iconography, etc.—along with its material constituents were in critical interplay as determinants of meaning, as was an object's history. The pisspot's enactment—its stabilization as an object with a particular meaning—is multiple in this episode. It is manufactured to serve a purpose and then transformed, in this case literally, into something new while still retaining memory traces of its former purpose. In both instances, its meaning is dependent upon notions of value linked to function and materiality. While the pisspot's life is perhaps more complex than most objects in the past, its many lives and its ability to instruct are important points as we consider the wide range of objects that took part in economic transactions in Classical antiquity. Mutability of meaning is the rule.

MONEY, EXCHANGE, AND THE USES OF COINAGE

The object class that most often generates direct discussion of the relationship between materiality and economy in the Classical past are coins and related artifacts, such as ingots, tokens, and dies (Figure 3.1). Widely distributed across the ancient Mediterranean, and fetishized early in the study of Greco-Roman antiquity, coins remain a primary but somewhat underutilized avenue into discussion of economy and objecthood in the Classical past.[7] Coins are often invoked as a way of fleshing out historical narratives derived from other sources or as a rich catalog of imagery for rulers, buildings, and monuments throughout the Classical world. Less often, they are discussed as evidence for the social systems that produced them (Kemmers and Myrberg 2011: 90–1).

As Kemmers and Myrberg point out, coins exist at a nexus between historical source and artifact. They bear text and are simultaneously objects, with their own physical qualities including shape, material, color, texture, etc. They see these two realms—the material and the historical—as interlinked through the iconography that coins traditionally carry, which is usually linked to the issuing authority and refracts meaning through its visual and aesthetic qualities (Kemmers and Myrberg 2011: 92–3). The social context of coins is linked to both of these aspects. Coins function as monetary objects conveying value through their metal content, text, and markings, but they also carry heavy symbolic and communicative loads.

Some of this object complexity is evident in the vocabulary used to denote money and coins in the Classical world. The Roman word for money, *pecunia*, is related to *pecus*, meaning cattle/oxen, and reflects the connection between money's function to represent value through reference to an older form of wealth that was widely used in pre-coinage exchange (see below; Papadopoulos 2012: 272ff). The ancient Greek word for coin, *nomisma*, is related to the word *nomos*, meaning law or a practice sanctioned by custom, and points to the authority implied by coin production. More ambiguous, perhaps, is the Greek word *timê*, which can also mean honor or price or, more obliquely, value. The Latin equivalent for this term was *pretium*, which could also mean worth or reward. Money, as a medium of exchange, and coinage in particular relies on the existence of a regularized and widely held system of normative value, and the range of terms used in our ancient sources to describe these objects reflects the difficulty of achieving (and describing) such a uniform system in actual practice.[8]

The variability and complexity of ancient coinage and its attendant terms is perhaps not surprising when viewed against the backdrop of pre-coinage exchange systems in the ancient Mediterranean. In the Homeric epics, goods were exchanged in kind as part of a barter system. Equivalencies were made between commodity loads—wine for oil, grain for cattle, armor for armor— without reference to a standard of value except for a generalized measure of worth expressed by a number of oxen. In the *Iliad*, we are told, for example, that Glaucus' golden armor is worth 100 oxen, while Diomedes' bronze armor is worth only 9 (6.232–6; see above p. 33).

The use of oxen as a unit of comparison reflects both the resource value of oxen in Iron Age Greek society and also the need for some way to express comparative worth at a time when valuation was largely informal. In addition to oxen, grain, salt, animal hides, and slaves were commonly used throughout antiquity as stores of value and exchanged as a form of payment even in times of intense monetization. For example, taxes were often paid in grain under the Roman imperial system, a useful reminder that major sectors of the ancient economy functioned outside the monetary system throughout antiquity.

Bronze or iron utensils, especially spits or cauldrons, were also used as a unit of equivalence in Iron Age Greek contexts. These were sometimes expressed in terms of weight, but most often the value units employed were in numbers of objects (Kroll 2012: 33–6). In the Near East and Egypt, weighed silver and gold bullion served as a medium of exchange and continued to do so well after the widespread introduction of coinage in the Mediterranean basin (Papadopoulos 2012: 265–6). These could take the form of lump metals, rings, ingots, or other goods. Outside the Greek cities of the Italian peninsula, pre-coinage took the form of rough, shapeless pieces of bronze or rectangular cast bronze bars known from the third century BCE, likely produced in Rome. These resemble

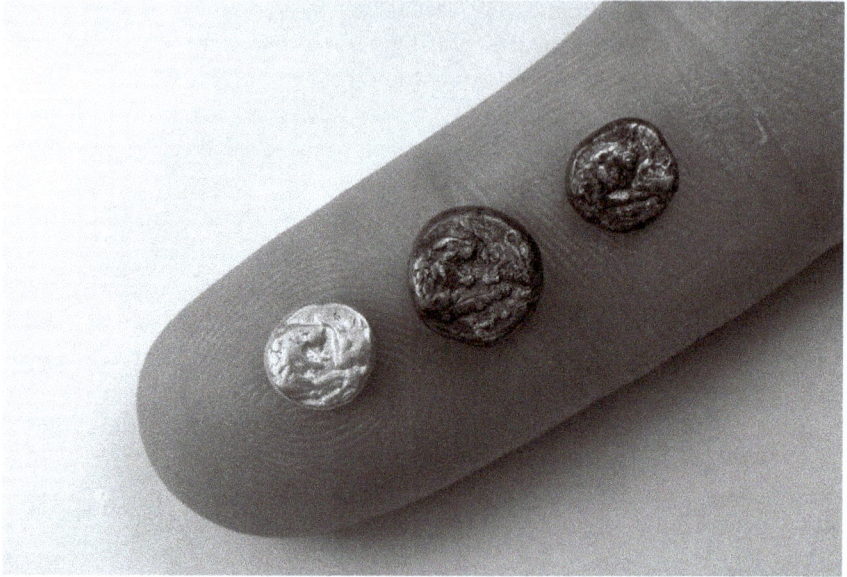

FIGURE 3.4 Gold and silver croesid 12th staters and silver croesid 24th stater from Sardis. Photograph: © Archaeological Exploration of Sardis/President and Fellows of Harvard College.

but are not identical to similar objects known from the Etruscan sphere and dating to the sixth century BCE.[9]

Coinage as such first appears in Lydia in Asia Minor near the end of the seventh century BCE. These early coins were made of a naturally occurring metal known as electrum, a mix of gold and silver, and because of their small size and limited distribution they are thought to be closer to bullion in actual function, meaning that their value was held in their metal weight.[10] Coins bearing the legend of an issuing authority and thereby deriving their value from association with that entity, and attendant implied guarantees of standard weight and content, appear in large numbers in the sixth century BCE (Figure 3.4), including in Lydia, where they gradually replace the earlier electrum issues.

In the succeeding centuries, gold and silver coinage was widely minted across the *poleis* of the Greek world and eventually in the Greek cities of Sicily and southern Italy. As coinage spread, the use of bullion as a means of exchange declined rapidly in the same spheres, but was maintained in parts of the Near East and Egypt for much longer. As discussed above, alternative means of exchange, especially barter and payment in kind, coexisted with coinage systems throughout antiquity, and were to be found even at moments of relatively high economic integration.

The early spread of coinage was profoundly linked to Greek institutions and culture and reveals something essential about the development of communities in this period. Von Reden puts it succinctly:

> The spread of coinage in the Aegean during the late archaic period is at least partly explained by the role of coinage in the process of establishing identity in Greek political communities. The production and reproduction of local imagery on a daily means of exchange created social cohesion and a focus on a collective political centre through meaningful symbols. (2010: 24)

The stamped legends of early (and later) coinage facilitated the efficacy of coins both as a way to facilitate exchange by the guarantee of metal weight and content and as a vehicle of discourse in their associated communities. Often, discussions of coinage emphasize the top-down aspect of this power by focusing on the dissemination of imagery from a political center out to passive recipients. Coins are more than a means of payment, however, and should be approached as active potential agents in their own right, capable of a broad range of transactions, economic and otherwise (Kemmers and Myrberg 2011: 99; see also Kemmers 2018). In the case of early polis formation, coinage is argued to have been a catalyst for institutional changes that shifted authority from the realm of the divine to state institutions (Von Reden 1995; Papadopoulos 2002), while others see coinage as inspiring a whole way of thought in Greek philosophy (Seaford 2004, 2012) that emphasized the individual in isolation and privileged the abstract over the concrete (see also above p. 33).

To appreciate this, we must go beyond assessments of the role of coinage in the economy that imagine its meaning to be fixed at the moment of its minting. The striking of the die enacts a coin's participation in a regime of value linked to a monetized economy. Its form and qualities—material, iconography, weight, etc.—all denote a particular role for the object as a medium for the exchange of equivalently valued objects. In execution, however, the object has a wider range of possible venues for its agency and the enactment of its value, much more so than is usually acknowledged by scholars interested in these objects.

For example, the coins of the early Principate are based primarily on the *denarius* system, which carried the basic structures of the monetized economy of the Republic into the new millennium. Weights and compositions were tied to a currency structure that fluctuated in response to the needs of consumers participating in the market, such as the issuing of smaller denominations because of the demand for small change in day-to-day transactions (Wolters 2012: 335–40). These coins bear images of the emperor or a member of his house on the obverse, including the name and titles of the ruler. Reverse types are highly variable and might feature a huge range of subjects; gods, honors, current events, monuments, or textual compositions are all common. Despite these variations, the coinage lends itself to a catalog of related, programmatic issues that appear to form a normative, broadly repetitive corpus of object type created in service to a relatively centralized economic system serving a diverse but predictable range of economic needs.

However, consideration of the actual life of a Roman coin belies such a neat picture. The turn to a culturally contextual assessment of coinage has yielded a range of studies that demonstrate the wildly varied ways that coinage was deployed in the ancient world, many of which cannot be explained in terms of rational economic choice or exchange. For example, the massing of coins in votive contexts, foundation deposits, and graves (among others) demonstrates a profound shift in their meaning and value in relation to a newly defined purpose.[11] In each instance, there are qualities possessed by the coin that make it suitable to this new arena and facilitate its redefinition. This might be the aesthetic appeal of the metal itself, the image carried by the object, or some combination of its physical properties.

For example, the use of coins in jewelry was an established practice in the Roman imperial period and widely documented in imagery and discussed in ancient sources (Bruhn 1993). As jewelry, coins and medallions functioned as amulets, protecting the wearer by activating the power of the images they carried and their decoration, much as a figured gemstone might (Figure 3.5). While the coins presumably retained their bullion value (i.e. the intrinsic value of the metal), their apotropaic potential was more potent and required a new mode of engagement and display. These reenacted economic objects demonstrate the fluidity of their function and are direct reminders that the context of a coin's deployment might involve a profound transformation in meaning that does not require a reformation—à la Amasis' pisspot—of the object itself.

CONSUMPTION AND THE EXPERIENCE OF PLENTY

The wearing of coins as jewelry is an example of the way that an object's meaning can be shifted by an individual through an act of consumption and its displacement from its previous context. As discussed above, consumption is a moment of enactment when the object's meaning and/or value is situated according to a set of culturally constrained choices. In antiquity, opportunities for consumption were abundant and at certain times marked by an experience of material sameness unparalleled in earlier periods of history. The experience of plenty—a material world characterized by abundant and duplicative objects that often moved long distances—was a distinctive economic aspect of the Hellenistic and Roman periods of Classical antiquity. The spread, in particular, of ceramic vessels, including fine black and red-gloss tablewares and amphorae, which function as transport containers, intensified and accelerated over the

FIGURE 3.5 Portrait of a woman wearing a coin-set necklace, from Antinoopolis, Egypt, *c*. 130–200 CE. Photograph: © The Walters Art Museum, Baltimore.

course of the second half of the first millennium BCE and the first half of the first millennium CE. These new types of pottery were consumed and imitated almost everywhere Roman power reached and sometimes even beyond the limits of Roman political influence (Wells 2013). Archaeological excavations across the empire, and beyond its notional borders, reveal a corpus of commonly present vessel forms that were appropriate for the full range of household functions— cooking, serving, storage, and transportation. This assemblage of forms is by no means identical from place to place, but the commonalities are clear, and they show how pervasive were the trade networks that connected spheres as distant as Britain, North Africa, Germany, and Syria.

At the top of the pyramid of Roman-era pottery across the empire are the so-called *sigillatas* (Hayes 1972, 1980, 1985, 1997, 2008; Greene 1992; Van Oyen 2016). These glossy, fine red wares imitated a type of pottery first produced in Italy in the Tuscan region, known as Arretine ware, in the second half of the first century BCE. Arretine ware was itself an Italian imitation of older Greek fine ware types imported into the Italian mainland in the preceding centuries, and imitated yet again in local types further south around Naples between 200 and 50 BCE and known as Campana A ware. Its purplish–black surfaces evoke metal vessels, as well as the dark black gloss of imported Greek pottery of the preceding centuries.

Versions of these Arretine products were manufactured throughout Italy and later in Gaul and other parts of the Western Empire in the first and second centuries CE, most famously in the Gallic region where they are known as Samian Ware (Figure 3.6). These Roman-era red wares, of which there are many regional and temporal variations, share a hard, shiny surface ranging in color from soft pink to dark red or orange and are characterized by a slip over a finely levigated body. Many forms were embellished with stamped or rouletted designs or with applied molded decoration, and the forms imitate and elaborate upon a shape corpus first established by Arretine potters.

Italian *sigillatas* were particularly popular from the first century BCE onwards, and when the Roman principate was founded at the end of that century, a taste for vessels with similar characteristics became a consistent and prominent characteristic of Roman settlements on a broad scale. Once seen as a way of indexing the embrace of a Roman elite identity (Millett 1990; Woolf 1998), these vessels are now recognized as participants in the material

FIGURE 3.6 First-century-CE Roman potter's workshop reconstruction with Gallo-Roman *sigillata* from Graufesenque. France, Musée de Millau.

negotiation between local practices and Roman influence rather than evidence of any straightforward assimilation of Roman values and ideas (Webster 2001; Mattingly 2004). Even so, the social meaning of their presence on sites is rarely discussed (Witcher 2006); instead, their importance as chronological markers and indicators of economic links is usually emphasized over any engagement with their meaning as objects or in terms of object agency.[12]

However, their widespread distribution and the duration of their consumption on sites across the Mediterranean presents an opportunity to interrogate their abundance and broad uniformity as a component of their social meaning as economic objects. The visual experience of large quantities of pottery of this type both in households and in the environment, where discarded fragments of *sigillatas* formed a small but significant component of household debris, undoubtedly shaped ideas about the desirability of particular styles and shapes, as well as the values and meanings attached to these objects.

Accordingly, it is critical to establish what abundance and homogeneity means in relation to this type of Roman-style fine ware. We can approach this along two vectors: first, temporal and spatial distribution of *sigillatas* across the empire; and second, the proportion of *sigillata* vessels in archaeological deposits and their physical characteristics. The distribution of the Gallic products demonstrates their ubiquity throughout the western half of the empire and indeed across the Mediterranean, where they are found in coastal contexts in large quantities (Fulford 2013). The market dominance of the Samian wares was eventually undercut by the pottery industries of North Africa, which began to produce red wares imitating many of the Italian and Gallic forms from as early as the second century CE; these African red slip (ARS) workshops and their products eventually came to dominate the pottery market in the Mediterranean from the third to seventh centuries CE, and their distribution is even more widespread, particularly in the eastern half of the empire (Bonifay 2004, 2007; Humphrey 2009).

From the perspective of archaeology with the benefit of its broad comparative view, these materials are unquestionably ubiquitous in the Roman Empire, and even beyond its borders, with a striking geographic range of distribution. From the temporal perspective, from the late first century BCE to the seventh century CE, the most readily available fine wares and certainly those most widely consumed would have belonged to this category, producing a remarkable aesthetic experience of similarity through a period of some 800 years. These vessels belonged to an easily recognizable, clearly desirable, and common type of ceramic with consistent and essential physical qualities that endured over time, even as modes of decoration, shapes, and production quality changed.

The ubiquity of *terra sigillata* across time and space is clear, but how abundantly present were these types of vessels—either in whole form or as fragments—in the lived environment at any given time? Part of the interest that these vessels have held for scholars is the notion that they were special, expensive, and unusual and therefore held a special pride of place for self-fashioning elite consumers who were looking to distinguish themselves by participating in a discourse of consumption practices. If they were actually the obverse—common, not particularly expensive, and broadly analogous in appearance—how does our understanding of their possible meanings shift? What are the implications for our assessment of them as economic objects?

There are some sites where *sigillatas* were superabundant and present in the landscape in a way that was clearly unusual. These special deposits are particularly sizeable and are associated with manufacturing sites and dumps at harbors. The Gallo-Roman production site at La Graufesenque (Bémont and Jacob 1986) is a well-known and particularly evocative case of the first kind. Hundreds of thousands of waster vessels as well as dumps of vessels broken after production have been recovered at the site, along with graffiti that give numbers associated with specific workshops (Hermet 1979). In several cases, workshops are listed as producing more than half a million vessels each, and the accepted estimates for a single firing from the La Graufesenque kilns is around 29,000 vessels. The quantities involved are staggering, especially when the multi-decade life of a site like La Graufesenque is taken into account.

Along with these special kiln deposits, dumps near harbors are also documented and represent repeated disposal episodes after a cargo had presumably been damaged and no longer had value. The morphology of these fine ware dumps is similar (even if the scale is not) to the massive middens of amphora that have been recovered in Ostia, Rome, and across the empire, the most famous of which is the Monte Testaccio in Rome, estimated to contain between 40 and 50 million discarded amphorae (Almeida 1984). Entire wharf structures built of discarded amphora have also been documented in the early Roman harbor at Myos Hormos (Figure 3.7).[13] These deposits, as well as shipwreck assemblages, demonstrate that fine ware cargos were typically dominated by large groups from a single manufacturer, with a long tail of smaller groups from other manufacturers included. The dumping of certain types of similar pottery created an unusually large concentration of fine ware fragments, much larger than was likely to accrue through any regular activities.

A recent study of Samian or Gallo-Roman—the closest local source for *sigillata*—red wares in Britain has yielded some useful numbers for assessing abundance in more typical deposit contexts (Willis 2013). Across a broad sample of both rural and urban British sites during the first and second centuries CE, Samian ware consistently represent about 5 percent of the estimated total number of vessels in an assemblage (usually less on rural sites), while fine wares overall represent about 10 percent of the assemblage. Alongside imported *sigillatas*, local imitations of the same forms often appear, although in a distinct, usually

FIGURE 3.7 The early Roman quay at Myos Hormos, Egypt, constructed of discarded transport amphorae. Image courtesy of L. Blue and D.P.S. Peacock, University of Southampton.

differently colored fabric (Lamm 2012). These percentages of imported fine wares are similar in later contexts where ARS vessels dominate, with ARS fine wares forming a significant percentage of pottery overall on a given site, sometimes as much as 10 percent, and fully half of the tableware (Fentress and Perkins 1988; Zanini 1996). These numbers suggest what most Roman pottery specialists instinctively observe—that whatever *sigillata* was the dominant product of the monument is likely to appear in quantity and in associated "sets" in households and dump deposits across the empire. In antiquity, the tendency was to acquire tablewares in groups, for reasons that are hard to reconstruct, but the end result was that anyone who was able to dominate the supply into a particular area or market was likely to move their products in quite large quantities to meet a very high demand for pottery groups, rather than individual vessels.

Sigillatas are more common in urban contexts and coastal centers, and appear less commonly at rural sites or inland centers, with some major exceptions. The presence of the Roman army in the Western Empire, for example, correlates with higher percentages of *sigillatas* as part of domestic assemblages. The number of fragments of fine wares of any kind are everywhere dwarfed by the huge quantities of amphora fragments, but nevertheless these wares represent a significant component of the tableware in any given context and are relatively abundant and highly visible in the archaeological record.

Another important feature of the *sigillata* industries is the remarkably homogeneous character of production over time and space. As already mentioned, variations in quality, shape, and decoration can be associated with different regional traditions or even certain workshops, but these variations are remarkably subtle. Michel Bonifay (2004, 2007) has argued that the most common vessels produced in the ARS workshops in Tunisia changed very little between the fourth and seventh centuries CE, making it difficult to distinguish between early and late examples of common forms.

In Italy and the Western Empire, applied molded decoration was favored in early sequences (in imitation of metal), while vessels from the second century CE onward tend to be rouletted or stamped, with motifs repeated across centuries (Arthur 2007). ARS deployed both of these decorative types. These high levels of standardization are remarkable since most production seems to have taken place in small workshops that were aggregated into collective manufacturing centers or in unrelated *ateliers*. This suggests that the demand for uniformity was a response to consumer demand and also, perhaps, a result of the technological means of producing these vessels; the use of molds to produce many *sigillata* vessel types is known from a range of production sites (Hayes 1972), and the stamps and tools used to decorate ARS could be used many times. Standard measurements for certain vessel types, such as plates and cups, can also be observed in the Italian and Gaulish products of the first two centuries CE. Mimesis was clearly the goal of these manufacturers, and duplicative objects the expectation of the contemporary consumer. It may indeed have been the point of these objects.

This is a ceramics industry with remarkable physical continuities on a massive temporal and spatial scale. Masses of red slipped wares would have been present in the physical environment of many urban centers, both as intact vessels owned by households and perhaps more commonly as discarded, fragmentary sherds distributed in middens and as sheet refuse in common spaces. The tactile and visual linkages between these fragmentary pieces and the active, usable vessels would have been clear, as would the association of these types of vessels with a long and stable tradition of consumption.

The massing of quantities of these vessels was part of the meaningful performance of social status, and the relative uniformity of the objects themselves an expression of continuity with previous acts of consumption. The fact of their abundance in the environment was critical to making that connection and to establishing these objects as commodities of mass meaning, which at certain moments might have included prestige (as something different from status), but these concepts were locally determined. Interlinked notions of abundance and consumption were certainly distinguishing characteristics of social hierarchy in Roman society. Outside of Italy, to have more, and more *terra sigillata* in particular, might have been a demonstration of wealth and status (although not necessarily of Roman-ness). In both cases, the consumption of sameness was a way of tying oneself to a genealogy of material performance across time and space in which the physical qualities of the objects involved were of critical importance.

The materiality of *terra sigillata*, then, was critical to its efficacy as an economic object, just as the physical qualities of coinage were key to its value and transformative potential. Glossy red, shiny, visible even in discard and reuse, and mimetic in shape, decoration, and assemblage—the physical qualities it possessed facilitated exchange and consumption in wildly diverse contexts in the Roman Mediterranean. The reason it appealed to the consumer and how it was ultimately deployed or enacted undoubtedly varied across time and space, but its essential homogeneity was a thread highlighting a sprawling network of economic connectivity.

CONCLUSIONS

At the beginning of this chapter, I spent considerable time deconstructing the idea of an "economic object" with a fixed meaning or value while at the same time acknowledging that antiquity was full of objects that facilitated and shaped networks of exchange, underpinned acts of (sometimes rather extraordinary) consumption, and mediated discourse on the nature of knowledge through their material form. Each of the categories of object under consideration here—coinage, *terra sigillata* and Herodotus' extraordinary pisspot-cum-statue—highlights the complex way that enactment of an economic object depended on its materiality and physical characteristics, as well as the social scaffolding that assigned meaning or value to those aspects.

The emphasis on movement and the transference of these objects from hand to hand and place to place is also notable. Whether it is the marble of the Pantheon floor or the amphorae that constituted the quay at Myos Hormos, the "from elsewhere-ness" of the objects has moved them into the category of being an economic object. This displacement is the result of the chain of exchange transactions and transformations that resulted in their arrival at their spot of residence, where they have gone on being meaningfully transformed. In the case of the Pantheon's marbles, they were integrated into a rededicated sacred context in the change of the pagan temple into a church, now a tourist attraction. In Myos Hormos, the amphorae were recovered by archaeologists *in situ*, but redefined as archaeological evidence and moved into an entirely new category of significance. *Terra sigillata*'s itinerary is almost always obscure, but we can appreciate the chain of enactment and redefinition that has resulted in its deposit in a midden somewhere in the Western Roman Empire, the result of a consumptive act that assigned it a new meaning—rubbish.

This brings us back to Herodotus' golden vessel. Transformed and transformative in its ability to affect knowledge and to change the point of view of its observers, the golden pisspot remains a kind of imagined emblematic economic object despite its less vaunted travel itinerary. It moves from the bedroom to the temple *temenos*, with a stopover in a craftsman's workshop, but its makeover does not erase its connections to its previous form and uses. What makes it useful to think with is the way that its changed form and redefinition are ongoing; it retains a trace of its former associations and is at the same time emblematic of the new social order that Amasis' kingship represents. Its mobility lies in its transformed state and its multistranded meaning. It presents us with a palimpsest of past time and actions, collapsing all of these into its objecthood—valuable, beautiful, and meaning-laden.

CHAPTER FOUR

Everyday Objects

LIN FOXHALL

INTRODUCTION

The identification of what constituted "everyday" objects for people in the Classical world is not at all self-evident from our distant perspective. We might start with the idea that "everyday objects" were those that were so deeply embedded in daily routines and activities that they became simultaneously indispensable and overlooked, like pens, dishcloths, and toothbrushes are for us, or rags, knives, and nails were in the ancient past; essentially becoming ephemeral, material manifestations of habitus. Hence, they are surprisingly hard to find in our sources. They rarely feature prominently in texts precisely because they were largely unremarkable, and the best we can usually hope for are a few offhand references. In visual and iconographic sources they sometimes helpfully appear, but often, literally, as part of the background. Although some survive as archaeological artifacts, for many reasons I will explore below, even more probably do not, and this skews our perspective on what the "everyday" looked and felt like.

This fleeting, ungraspable quality of everyday objects is made more complicated by the fact that what constituted an assemblage of everyday things was different for different people. Beyond temporal and spatial variations, what things were inextricably entwined with people's daily lives depended on a range of social factors, especially wealth and status. Hence, objects like painted fine ware pottery or silver drinking vessels in antiquity—or designer-brand clothing for us today—that might have been "everyday" for some people were not for others, and some people certainly filled their lives with many more "everyday" objects than others. Crudely, it is probable that the majority of people in the ancient world engaged with relatively few everyday objects on a day-to-day basis, while the bulk of the actual objects that we can identify as "everyday" in our evidence were associated most closely with a small, relatively elite sector of the population. However, not all objects that a person might encounter daily necessarily belonged to them or were in some sense directly under their authority. For example, personal slaves regularly handled objects such as fine textiles or silver cups that were "everyday" to their elite owners who used them regularly. But these objects played a very different role in the lives of slaves who did not use them personally but instead engaged with them on their owner's behalf.

Further, some "everyday" objects and the frequency with which they were regularly used (or consumed) varied specifically with, and were indicators of, gender, class, occupation, group identities, age, and other aspects of an individual's social persona that were entangled with, but also reaching beyond, wealth and status. In effect, this means that the assemblage of the "everyday" was different for every individual, and varied over time—over the course of a day, seasonally, and through a person's life cycle, but while also adapting to collectively changing habits and fashions. Potentially this raises interesting issues around how "everyday" a specific kind of object such as a ceramic vessel might have been for any particular person or type of person, since, though individuality and idiosyncrasy occasionally shine through in our evidence, as archaeologists and historians of the Classical world, we are better at identifying types of people than individuals. Moreover, the everyday meanings, values, and users of an object might change over the life cycle of the object (see below, p. 104).

Texts, visual representations, impressions in other materials, and occasional rare finds reveal many kinds of everyday objects that do not generally survive to be recovered as archaeological artifacts. The bulk of these were items made of perishable materials, including string, textiles, basketry, wood, or leather, or were consumed through use, such as perfume or makeup. Such items are found reasonably intact only where unusual environmental conditions enhance preservation, such as in waterlogged deposits from shipwrecks or desiccated contexts in Egypt. This is not surprising since, even in our own world of non-degrading plastic, many quotidian items remain perishable. Pottery, of course, survives in abundance, but the disappearance of most of the perishable (or other rarely recovered) items with which pots were used can easily deceive us into overestimating their "everyday" importance in relation to other kinds of objects. Moreover, "natural" items such as handy sticks, stones, stumps, or trees, appropriated to serve a specific purpose but generic in their morphology, especially when we do not know the use context, can be difficult to recognize as "everyday" objects in the archaeological record, even when we find them. Such objects might not even have a particular owner,

FIGURE 4.1 A hunter carries his prey home on a stick, Attic black-figure lip cup by Tleson from Vulci, mid-sixth century BCE. London, British Museum 1867,0508.946. Photograph: © The Trustees of the British Museum.

but simply be left available for any user, such as canes for knocking fruit or nuts off trees (Foxhall 2007: 128, fig. 5.5), a handy stick for carrying things (Figure 4.1), a rope and bucket at a well, or a rock for holding a gate shut.

VALUING EVERYDAY OBJECTS

For interpreting objects as "everyday" in archaeological contexts, especially settlements and houses, it is critical to consider how people in the past valued them. We value objects for many reasons. Sometimes their economic and/or prestige worth is the key to why we consider them precious. But "everyday" objects that are comfortable, familiar, have critical practical or sentimental value, or are in some other way so much a part of our lives that we feel we could not possibly do without them may be treasured just as much, even if they are not prestigious or costly.

The substantial number of excavated Greek houses dating to the fifth to fourth centuries BCE at the sites of Olynthos (over 100) and Halieis (about twenty-five houses in part, with five fully excavated), where assemblages of artifactual material can be associated with individual buildings, enables us to compare what we know from visual and written sources about how domestic objects were used with what we find and do not find left behind in houses. For example, Nevett (1999: 43–50) presents a useful analysis of objects depicted with people on a sample of 600 Attic red-figured vases. Items regularly depicted with women include chairs, stools, footstools, mirrors, small chests, wool baskets, small containers including alabastra and lekythoi, and various cushions, clothing, and textiles. Men appear in both gymnastic and bathing scenes with aryballoi and strigils. Symposiastic vases often show a range of dining and drinking vessels both in use and hanging on the walls, as well as furniture (couches and tables) with textiles and cushions.

Olynthos is interesting because while the data set is not perfect for a number of reasons, we do know that most inhabitants left over a fairly short period at the time of the invasion and capture of the city by Philip of Macedon in 348 BCE (Nevett 1999: 57–9; Cahill 2002: 24–5). For the Roman world, some of the less disturbed houses in Pompeii similarly provide important information about the choices people made to take things or leave them behind at the time of the eruption in 79 CE. Allison's (2006) study of the household assemblages associated with individual houses in the insula of the House of Menander provide a useful body of data that is roughly comparable to the Greek assemblages at Olynthus and Halieis. The data for five sample houses are summarized here in Table **4.1**. However, the houses of Pompeii, like many houses in Roman Italy, were occupied for much longer than the earlier Greek houses of Olynthos and Halieis, so that it can be difficult to ascertain when or for how long over the lifetime of a house an object was in use. Also, the extraordinary circumstances of Pompeii's abandonment may sometimes have distorted the choices about objects that people made. Hence, we must interpret this material with caution.

The processes of abandonment of these sites enable us to gain insight into the range of relationships that people had with different elements of portable material culture and everyday things. In these archaeological contexts, the most valued "everyday" things were generally *not* ones that people disposed of or left behind, so frequently we do not find them, or we do not find them in the numbers that we might expect they were used. This is supported by texts such as the so-called Attic Stelae, an official Athenian inventory of items confiscated from the houses of prominent Athenians prosecuted in 415 BCE and auctioned by the state. Here, too, it appears that many valuable items had already been removed or disposed of by their owners and other parties before the magistrates arrived to sell the property (Lewis 1997: 65–7). At Olynthos and Pompeii, abandoned

TABLE 4.1 Everyday objects recorded in five sample houses in Pompeii (Allison 2006).

	House I 10, 1	House I 10, 2–3	House I 10, 4	House I 10, 7	House I 10, 8	House I 10, 10–11
Knife/blade			6	10	3	1
Hook/bill hook/pruning knife	1		32	3		7
Sickle			2			
Mattock			1			
Hoe			19	3	1	
Shovel/spade				3		
Fork				1		
Rake				1		
Ax			9	3		5
Pick			3	2	1	
Chisel			1	24		
Hammer				2	1	
Saw				1		1
File				9		
Gouge (woodworking)			1	1		
Tongs				2		
Shears			1	1		
Clamp				1		
Fishhook					1	
Spindle				2 (bone)		
Loom weights	1	2	10	3	1	1
Needle			1 (bone); 1 (bronze)	11 (bronze); 3 (bone); 2 (bronze/bone)	1 (bronze)	
Scalpel				6		
Strigil	1 (bronze)		2 (bronze); 1 fragments (iron)	2 (bronze)		
Razor				3		

Continued

	House I 10, 1	House I 10, 2–3	House I 10, 4	House I 10, 7	House I 10, 8	House I 10, 10–11
Mirror				1		
Jewelry		1 pendant (bronze)	2 bracelets (gold); 1 bracelet (bronze); 1 ring (gold) by skeleton; 3 rings (gold); 3 rings (bronze); 1 stamp seal ring (bronze); 1 ring (silver) stuck to key; 2 rings (iron), with finger bones; 1 ankle bracelet (silver) by skeleton; 3 pendants (bronze); casket in chest with gold jewelry [Table **4.2**]	Necklace, pair of earrings, ring (gold) in cupboard; 1 ring (gold); 3 rings (bronze); pair earrings (gold)	3 pendants (bronze); 1 ring (iron)	
Toilet/ cosmetic/ medical instruments	1	2	1	13		2
Spoon		1 (bone)	19 (silver, stored in chest); 1 (silver, possibly associated with skeleton), 1 (bone); 1 (bronze)			

in the face of impending disaster, it is probable that the inhabitants took with them things they felt to be most essential. Once a house is abandoned, anything left falls victim to looters. So, with some important exceptions, archaeologists usually only find the things that people considered least important. The logical corollary is that what we *do not* find, especially if it was not economically valuable, is potentially a good indication of what was most meaningful and/or essential—the items that people thought of as "everyday" objects.

However, there are complications (for Olynthos, see Cahill 2002: 48–61, 67–70). Additional unwanted refuse and trash from elsewhere was often dumped on abandoned house sites. Sometimes settlements were partially reoccupied shortly after large-scale abandonment (this happened at Olynthos to some extent). Squatters may also occupy abandoned houses, or buildings that were once houses may be reused for non-domestic purposes. Objects deposited in such post-occupation phases are not always very easy to distinguish from those that were part of the use-life of a house.

Among the objects associated with the use-life of a house, it is unlikely that many obviously costly items such as metal vessels would remain, since those would have been taken or looted. We cannot always guess what perishable objects might have been left behind. We might expect some (though not necessarily all) clothing and household textiles to have been taken, since they were economically valuable and sometimes meaningful. Some items that might have been taken in their whole state may well have been left behind if broken or incomplete. The effect is that such objects appear occasionally in house assemblages, but not as often as their widespread and regular use would lead us to expect. Some items may have been left because they were either too heavy, awkward, or fragile to transport.

The objects we might expect to have been used but do not find fall into two main categories: tools and personal items. Iron and bronze tools, including knives, are rare in Greek house assemblages and less common than might be expected at Pompeii. In the five sample Pompeian household assemblages in Table **4.1**, no house has a large number of knives, a small and general tool with a wide range of uses that people would surely be inclined to take on departure (the largest number is 10 in House I 10, 7). However, two houses (I 10, 4 and I 10, 7) have substantial numbers of specialist carpentry and agricultural tools that were left behind. At Halieis, a cleaver, a shovel, a pruning knife, two spearheads, and a few knife blades and sickle blades are all that appear.

At Olynthos, a range of blades and tools appear as one-offs or in small numbers, but they are relatively rare across the site. The Attic Stelae (*IG* I³ 422.116–65; 425.4–14; Foxhall 2007: 204–11) show that agricultural and other kinds of tools, sometimes in multiples, were important components of Classical Greek household equipment, though these texts suggest that many tools were kept in storage buildings out in the fields, not in domestic houses. This might partially explain their absence in house assemblages, especially in cities. Tools have both economic and practical value, but individuals may also become fond of a particular tool, or attribute sentimental value to it.

Loom weights and spindle whorls—weaving tools used in textile manufacture largely by women—appear in numbers lower that might be expected. Virtually no Greek houses have enough loom weights to operate a warp-weighted loom. Most of the loom weights found at Olynthos, where they appear to be more or less in primary contexts, seem to have been stored rather than in use on a loom (see Cahill 2002: 171–9, though here the number of weights needed for a loom is underestimated, and many of the so-called weaving rooms are storage areas; cf. Foxhall 2011). The five fully excavated Halieis houses contained between eight and twenty-five loom weights, mostly deposited in ones and twos (Ault 1994: 244). Similarly, in the five sample Pompeian houses in Table **4.1**, loom weights and spindles appear only in tiny numbers. I have argued elsewhere (Foxhall 2011, 2012, 2018) that we rarely find the large caches of loom weights and other weaving tools we might expect because women valued them, even though they were not inherently valuable, and when they abandoned a house they took most of them away.

Personal items are rare in Greek houses but somewhat more common at Pompeii, where the scale and speed of abandonment was probably much greater (Table **4.1**). Some of these may have served medical as well as cosmetic functions, as in House I 10, 7. At Olynthos, several types of small bottles suitable for perfumed oil (guttae, small lekythoi, alabastra) regularly appear, but in contrast, only three turn up in Halieis (miniature lekythos: House 7-HP2686; squat lekythoi: House A-HP2987, House D-HP2587). Items related to personal body care, such as toilet sets, tweezers, ear spoons, and cosmetic spatulae, do not appear in any Halieis house. At Olynthos, cosmetic spatulae are found in small numbers. Sixteen were inventoried, and the eight with a known provenance all come from houses; none appear in graves (Robinson 1941: 352–4). Similarly with tweezers and ear spoons: the seven cataloged examples of tweezers (Robinson 1941: 355–6) and the eight cataloged examples of ear spoons (Robinson 1941: 354–5) were all from houses or streets, not graves.

In contrast, the pattern with strigils and razors, implements that must have been regularly used in a domestic setting on an everyday basis, is completely different. These items are rare in houses, even in Pompeii (see Table **4.1**). At Halieis, two strigils (HM1364, HM1189), one fragmentary, and a razor (HM1377) were found, all in House D. At Olynthos, no razors were recovered. Of the fifty-three inventoried strigils, only two were found in houses (no. 522 strigil fragment, House A-1; no. 544 strigil, House A vii 2, room a) (Robinson 1941: 175, 178). The rest had been deposited in graves, both male and female, and occasionally in children's graves (Robinson 1941: 172). Grave 264 is a good example of a female grave containing both a strigil and a loom weight (the latter are quite rare in graves). Strigils are most often associated with men in Athenian visual sources, particularly in the context of the gymnasium and athletics (Nevett 1999: 45), but their use was clearly not restricted to men. Razors, too, could have been used by both men and women.

Ten bronze mirrors were inventoried from Olynthos, but more may have been found. Mirrors or fragments of them appear occasionally in houses at Olynthos (though there are only two for certain; e.g. no. 512, House A iv 9, room g). More often they appear in female graves (Robinson 1941: 163, 171; Cahill 2002: 112). They are absent from Halieis (there is one fragment of a bronze disk that could, by a stretch of the imagination, be part of a mirror, but this is not certain, House A-HM1200). Only one appears in the sample Pompeian houses in Table 4.1. These certainly seem to have been personally and economically valuable enough to take away.

In the sample Pompeian house assemblages in Tables 4.1 and 4.2, it is clear that some of the jewelry found was being worn or was dropped by people attempting to escape. Only two houses have substantial amounts of jewelry, but these provide interesting examples of collections of jewelry that were left behind: a cask stored in a chest in Houses I 10, 4 contained twenty-six pieces of gold jewelry (Table 4.2), and three pieces of gold jewelry were found together stored in a cupboard in House I 10, 7. One actual stamp seal with a name on a ring was found, and several of the bronze and gold rings bore incised images that could have been used as stamp seals.

Bronze jewelry, including fibulae, earrings, pendants, bracelets, and rings, and beads in various materials, appears in small quantities in both the Halieis and Olynthos houses. Most of the jewelry found was not costly, and items like single earrings or the occasional bracelet might simply have been lost. Twenty-three single earrings or bits of them were found in and around houses in the North Hill and Villa sections of the city, while thirty-two earrings (including

TABLE 4.2 Pompeii, House I 10, 4: cask of gold jewelry in chest.

Object type	Number of objects
Ball	1
Locket	1
Bangle bracelets	2
Necklace	2
Earrings	6 (3 pairs)
Rings	11
Hair clip	1
Pins	2

thirteen pairs) were deposited in graves. Interestingly, they turn up only in children's graves positioned just above the shoulders, suggesting they were worn (the excavators assumed these were girls' graves; Robinson 1941: 93–4).

Although there is extensive textual and archaeological evidence for the widespread use of personal stamp seals (Richter 1968: 149; Boardman 2001: 236) that, in the form of bronze rings, were not necessarily particularly expensive items of jewelry, comparatively few stamp seals, or rings with stamp seals or engraved as stamps, have been found in houses. At Olynthos, only four stamps or seals were discovered, and the only one with a provenance was from House A v 9, room e (Robinson 1941: 347). Engraved finger rings made as stamp seals were more common. These were almost all bronze, with only three examples in silver. At least thirty were found in houses or streets, but at least fifty-eight rings came from graves (Robinson 1941: 132–3), though it is not clear that all of these were seal rings. Presumably because these were associated with personal, or even formal, identities (as suggested by their regular deposition in graves), they are not common in house assemblages because inhabitants must usually have taken them away. When found in graves they were always on the left side of the body, and in cases when they were still on the body, they were on the third finger of the left hand. In one fourth-century BCE grave, the seal ring dates to the before the 430s, suggesting that it was an heirloom (Riverside cemetery, grave 4, no. 468: Robinson 1941: 146, 1942: 2).

At Halieis, although many other oddments of bronze jewelry appear in houses, seals of any kind are rare. One bronze seal ring was found in House A (HM1360). A circular bronze stamp appears in House E (HC815) and a cylinder seal in House D (HS 517) (Ault 1994: 303).

Some categories of objects seem to be regularly left behind when houses were vacated. The first is furniture, for which there is much indirect evidence in both Greek and Roman houses; this is discussed in more detail below (p. 108). Perhaps less portable, it was often clearly considered less essential than other kinds of items when people departed under duress.

The second category consists of terracotta figurines, protomes, and decorative plaques, and the third is miniature vases. At Olynthos, two or more terracotta figurines, protomes, or plaques appear regularly in houses, and a few houses have substantial numbers (Robinson and Graham 1938: 348; e.g. Cahill 2002: 85, 95, 104–6, 111, 120, 123–4). Similarly, miniature pottery is surprisingly common; mostly it appears in ones and twos, but in a few cases miniature "sets" are found. Cahill (2002: 92, 140–1) has interpreted these objects as ritual, but if that were the case one might expect that these would be more valued as meaningful personal or household items, which would then have been removed on abandonment. Figurines and miniature vessels appear regularly in the Halieis houses as well, but in much smaller numbers, and at least one figurine was bronze.

Leaving behind portable stone altars or louteria makes more sense as these are heavy and not easily transported, but if figurines and similar decorative items were profoundly meaningful to their owners, ritually or in any other way, why were they not taken when the owners left? Perhaps this pattern suggests that their purpose was largely decorative (and that aesthetic value was less important than other considerations of value when abandoning a house), or that they had some other, non-ritual function, for examples as toys.

Indeed, portable objects that are unambiguously ritual or "magical" are largely absent from Greek household assemblages. At Olynthos, two beads in the form of grotesque heads found in the House of the Comedian have been interpreted as possible amulets, but this is not certain (Cahill 2002: 140). Magical objects such as curse tablets that turn up in houses and other buildings mostly seem to have been deposited after they have been abandoned (e.g. Young 1951: 222–3; Rotroff and Ntinou 2013: 82–3; cf. Jordon and Rotroff 1999). However, in fourth- and third-century BCE Athens, a much-discussed group of sacrificial deposits in houses and buildings, some clearly associated with the presence of craft activities, documents rituals involving animal sacrifice practiced both during periods of occupation and occasionally after abandonment. Rotroff has persuasively argued that these were associated with the protection of workers from misfortune or injury and/or purification rituals in relation to industrial accidents (Rotroff and Ntinou 2013: 75–85).

The following sections of this chapter will explore in more depth specific functional categories of objects that, in one way or another, people from all walks of life and in all periods must have encountered on a daily basis. The aim is to investigate how and by whom these objects were used, and how the objects themselves and their use might vary in different social, temporal, and regional contexts.

FIRE

Whatever their position in society, everyone encountered fire in some way on an everyday basis. However, to be useful for heat, light, and cooking, fire must be domesticated, and its use mediated through objects in culturally specific ways. Both wood and charcoal were burned in houses, though they latter was more expensive and probably more commonly used in urban settings. Although wood produces more smoke, charcoal produces carbon monoxide that could potentially have been an issue in poorly ventilated spaces. Fixed hearths are comparatively rare in Greek houses of the Classical and Hellenistic periods; there are only seven at Olynthos, one among the houses excavated in proximity to the Athenian Agora (Tsakirgis 2007: 226), and three at Halieis (Ault 2005: 55, n.151). When they appear, it is sometimes in courtyards, as at Kolophon (Holland 1944: 124; cf. Tsakirgis 2007: 226), not in rooms, suggesting their main practical function was as summertime cooking places.

For heating and cooking, small portable charcoal-burning braziers and similar cooking devices were probably much more common, and were moved around the house as needed with the changing seasons. These were low and generally seem to have been used set on the ground (the significance of this is considered below). However, they are almost never found in their original use contexts in houses. Those we know of are almost all ceramic, although it is likely that some metal braziers were used but have not survived. A rare example in bronze from Olynthos (Robinson 1941: 182) was found buried in a corner of a room before the house was abandoned, suggesting that the owner valued it and hoped to return to retrieve it. In Classical Athens, eleven of the contexts where braziers were found are wells, which were commonly used as trash dumps when they had dried up, and five are other kinds of fill deposits, mostly associated with building or renovation. The majority of ceramic braziers from Athens were recovered from wells, where they had been tipped after they had been broken and discarded and were no longer in use (Tsakirgis 2007: 228). Of the sixteen firmly contextualized deposits in which braziers and similar cooking devices were found in the area around the Athenian Agora, only one is in a house (House K: Young 1951: 244–5; Sparkes and Talcott 1970: 378, 386; Table 4.3). The fragmentary condition of the two braziers found there suggests that they are unlikely to have been in the original place where they were used (in a marble workshop). Rather, they were probably part of the fill of trash and marble chippings deposited on the floor when the building changed use in the mid-fourth century BCE.

The patterns of use, find spots, and disposal of braziers suggest that people usually removed them when a house was vacated or abandoned unless they were broken or nonfunctional. It appears that even ceramic braziers were valued, though they were not particularly costly—their owners' attachment to them

TABLE 4.3 Athenian Agora, cooking devices, and their archaeological contexts (all dates BCE) (Young 1951; Sparkes and Talcott 1970; www.agathe.gr).

Object number	Object description	Context number	Context description
2020	Tripod (P23129)	5th-century context	
2017	Cylindrical stand/ brazier, horseshoe shaped	A 18–19:1	c. 500–450; deposit in large cutting in bedrock, ostrakon fill
2039	Eschara	C 12:2	c. 375–325; well, depth 18.12 m; dumped fills of material dating to 2nd and 3rd quarter of 4th century, not deposited until 3rd century

Object number	Object description	Context number	Context description
2035	Eschara	C 12:2	c. 375–325; well, depth 18.12 m; dumped fills of material dating to 2nd and 3rd quarter of 4th century, not deposited until 3rd century
2033	Eschara, fragmentary, looks like part of fill	C 19:5 (b)	Late 5th–1st half of 4th century; house fills; b represents 2 fills from marble working area, one from period of shop, the other dumped over it, not easily distinguishable (Young 1951)
2040	Eschara, fragmentary, looks like part of fill	C 19:5 (b)	Late 5th–1st half of 4th century; house fills; b represents 2 fills from marble working area, one from period of shop, the other dumped over it, not easily distinguishable (Young 1951)
2034	Eschara	F 11:2-U	2nd half of 4th century; well, part of earlier system of wells and cisterns west of Tholos. Includes G 11:4
2037	Eschara	G 11:4	2nd half of 4th century; well, part of earlier system of wells and cisterns (F 11:2) west of Tholos
2029	Eschara	G 13:1	c. 500–475 and later; pocket, debris filling over bedrock, mostly early 5th century, Agora IV
2019	Cylindrical stand/ brazier, horseshoe shaped, typical second half of 5th century	G 18:1-M	3rd quarter of 5th century to c. 410; well, 3 dumping events of cleared household debris, of which this is the middle one
2028	Eschara	G 3:1	c. 500–470; pit, debris fill, considerable traces of burning. Agora IV; Hesperia 9 (1940): 300, center
2038	Eschara	H 7:1	c. 435–425; fill, behind retaining wall of Stoa of Zeus, debris identified as part of pottery workshop destroyed when Stoa was built
2023	Barrel cooker; comparable to Corinth example (C-27-354) from well fill of last quarter of 5th century	J 18:4-L	c. 550; storage pit, household pottery with name, Thamneus, scratched on. Hesperia 17 (1948): 159–60, pl 41.2–3

Continued

Object number	Object description	Context number	Context description
2022	Cooking bell	M 20:3-L	400–380 or later; well excavated to 9.3 m; 2 dump events separated by 2 m of mud
2018	Cylindrical stand/ brazier, horseshoe shaped	N 7:3	c. 460–440; well cleared to 10 m where walls collapsed, use filling not reached so this is probably post-occupation; deposit of tableware and household equipment
2030	Eschara	N 7:3	c. 460–440; well cleared to 10 m where walls collapsed, use filling not reached so this is probably post-occupation; deposit of tableware and household equipment
2036	Eschara	O 18:2	c. 350–320; well, excavated to depth of 6.25 m, deposit included many terracotta figurines
2027	Oven	O 19:4-U	c. 350–320; well, excavated to depth of 6.25 m, deposit included many terracotta figurines
2021	Cooking bell	Q 12:3	590–490; well beneath gutter of Stoa of Attalos opposite Pier 1, excavated to 9.7 m; identified as stock of potter's shop dumped in cleanup after Persian sack
2016	Cylindrical stand/ brazier, horseshoe shaped	Q 13:5	c. 575–540; well excavated to 5.3 m, beneath Stoa Terrace Fountain, dumped fill
2026	Oven	Q 13:5	c. 575–540; well, excavated to 5.3 m, beneath Stoa Terrace Fountain, dumped fill; same deposit included frags of at least 6 others
2031	Eschara	R 13:5	c. 420–390; well, depth 8.5 m, dumped fill, much roof tile at bottom, small amount of fine and table wares
2032	Eschara		Probably 3rd quarter of 4th century

may well have gone beyond their purely practical function. In Greek culture, the symbolic concept of the hearth (regardless of their physical absence in most houses) was embodied in the name of the goddess of the hearth, Hestia, and was a central element of domestic religious practice (Vernant 1983: 147). The rituals performed at the "hearth" were specifically associated with the life cycle of the household and its changing membership. They included the acceptance into the household of a newborn child or a new slave, and elements of wedding ritual focused on the hearths of both the bride's and the groom's houses (Tsakirgis 2007: 230). If, in practice, braziers served as "the hearth" in both practical and symbolic terms for most Classical Greek households, this could have provided an added impetus not to leave them behind. Though the ceramic brazier was among the most banal of everyday objects, it offers a good example of how the ordinary and the religious can become entwined. A house cannot function properly without warmth and cooking, thus it seems fitting that the rituals that attempted to ensure the smooth functioning of the household over time should be focused on this humble object.

In the elite houses of Roman Pompeii (like many other Roman houses), there were specialized "kitchens" with a fixed cooking platform or hearth in the form of a substantial rectangular bench. In Allison's (2004: 30, 99) study of thirty houses, forty-four kitchen areas were identified. Some of the most opulent houses had more than one hearth, suggesting that they might be used for cooking for different groups of people or at different times of the year (e.g. in the case of hearths located in porticos, as in the Casa del Fabbro, portico 10). Iron braziers also appear in houses and garden areas, which Allison (2004: 102) suggests were used for different types of cooking than the hearths. Such a plethora of kitchens with large fixed hearths and cooking devices also suggests that they might serve as a way of displaying the conspicuous consumption of fuel in wealthy households. While "kitchen" areas and hearths were occasionally situated in proximity to images or shrines of household gods (e.g. in House I 10, 18, room 9, where there is a Lararium painting on one wall of a room with a hearth; Allison 2006: 369–70), this is not always the case.

LAMPS AND LIGHTING

The regular presence of lamps (generally only one or two) in Pompeian kitchens (Allison 2006: 63, 86–7) is an interesting reminder of how difficult it was to cook at night: a good bed of hot coals gives off very little light, and handling pots of boiling liquid in the dark is lethally dangerous. It seems most likely that in Greek and Roman houses of all periods, most major activities, including cooking operations, were carried out in daylight.

Oil lamps in ceramic and metal and other lighting devices such as torches and lanterns were ubiquitous everyday objects because they were necessary for any movement or activity, however minimal, at night or in dark spaces. Although there are visual representations of torches, and we know something of how and when they were used from texts, our knowledge of the extent of their use is limited. There is much more that we know about lamps and their uses. Greek and Roman ceramic oil lamps produced remarkably little light— about the equivalent of a single candle for a normal, single-spouted lamp, or 1 lumen (Griffiths 2016: 168). By comparison, a dim modern electric lightbulb of the equivalent of 25 watts produces 200 lumens; a 40 watt-equivalent light bulb produces 400 lumens. Most modern kitchens have far more than one low-powered lightbulb. Indeed, except for dining and entertaining by elites and some religious rituals, most people did not do a great deal in the dark most of the time because artificial lighting was inadequate and, for many, too expensive.

Although lamps are regularly found in Greek and Roman houses, there are fewer than one might expect, and the find spots are significant since they suggest that generally the lamps we recover were not in use at the time of abandonment. In the Greek urban houses at Olynthos, ceramic lamps turn up in small numbers in cooking and storage areas (including in the pastas, a roofed area in the courtyard) and occasionally in a dining room (Robinson and Graham 1938: 347). Of the forty-one houses in which lamps were found, over half of them (twenty-three) had one to three lamps (Table **4.4**). Only two houses had over eight lamps, both of which seem to have served as commercial premises: A iv 9 (sixteen lamps) includes three shops (Robinson and Graham 1938: 85–8; Cahill 2002: 108–13) and A v 7 (twenty lamps) consists of irregular rooms off a large courtyard where a substantial number of coins (sixty-one) were found (Robinson and Graham 1938: 95: Cahill 2002: 268, 272). It is possible that some activities, perhaps connected with business, may have been carried out after dark or needed extra light (see below). This may also be the case with the one house with eight lamps (A v 10, with two shops; Robinson and Graham 1938: 97–8; Cahill 2002: 113–18). In rural Attica, the Vari House had two lamps with small fragments of two or three others

TABLE 4.4 Olynthos, number of lamps found in individual houses.

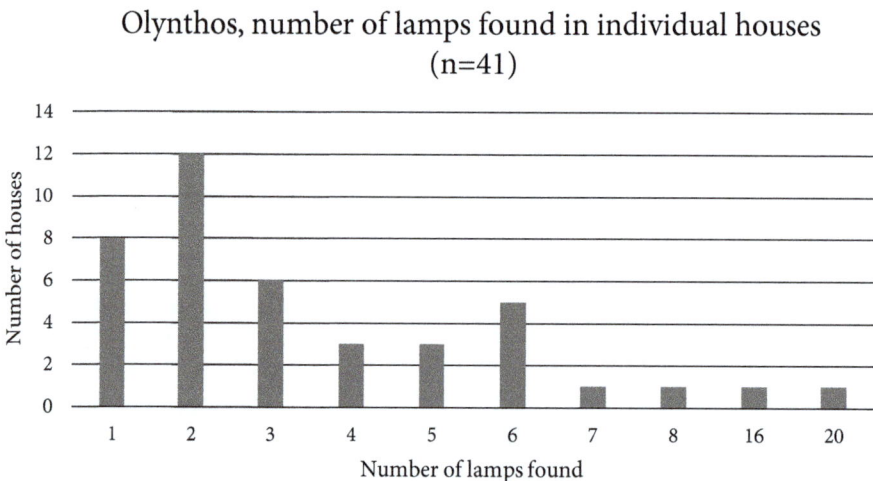

Olynthos, number of lamps found in individual houses (n=41)

(Jones et al. 1973: 381), and the more elaborate Dema House had two lamps with fragments of six others (Jones et al. 1962: 93, 100). It is likely that the lamps represented only by small fragments were not in use in the final period of occupation.

The pattern is similar with Roman houses. At Cosa, the House of Quintus Fulvius was destroyed in a destruction event around 70–60 BCE, datable from a hoard of 2004 denarii buried in a jar under the floor. The house had been adapted from previous structures on the site not long before this destruction event, and was probably inhabited by one of the most elite families in the town (Bruno and Scott 1993: 94–7; Fitch and Goldman 1994: 13). However, only nine ceramic lamps that were possibly associated with the occupation phase of this house were recovered, only one of which was nearly complete. Most are very worn and fragmentary. Three of these fragments were found in a cistern, one in a cesspit (dropped in by accident during a nighttime toilet visit?), and three in the street outside the house. While this could be the result of the destruction event, it is also possible that some of these lamps broke and went out of use earlier in the life of the house and had already been discarded as rubbish. However, it also seems possible in a house of this status that metal lamps and other lighting devices less likely to survive in the archaeological record had also been in use.

The evidence for lighting in Pompeii is complex and has been analyzed and discussed in depth by Griffiths (2016; cf. Allison 2006). The material from Casa del Chirugo, occupied in five phases from the mid-second century BCE to the eruption in 79 CE, presents an opportunity to see changes in the numbers of lamps used in different phases before the abandonment of the town with the eruption. Fifty lamps were recovered from the pre-eruption occupation phases of the house, but the numbers recovered from any one phase were small: four in the period c. 150–100 BCE; none from c. 100–25 BCE; twenty-three from c. 25 BCE–15/25 CE; thirteen from c. 15/25–62 CE; and ten from c. 62–79 CE (Griffiths 2016: 84).

At the time of the eruption, in Pompeian houses where the positioning of lamps could be fairly accurately ascertained, the pattern of finds is reminiscent of Olynthos, even across houses of different sizes, perhaps because both towns were abandoned over a short time. For example, the Casa della Ara Massima (200 m²) had a large number of lamps for its size: twenty-seven ceramic lamps and three bronze ones, but twenty of the ceramic lamps were in storage in a single room (Griffiths 2016: 107–8). House I 10.8 (265 m²) had ten lamps and a bronze lampstand, but seven of the lamps were in one storeroom (Griffiths 2016: 110). The Casa del Fabbro (I 10.7; 320 m²) had twelve ceramic and five bronze lighting devices, most of them in a dining room that may have been in use as a dining room (Griffiths 2016: 119). The Casa del Efebo (I 7.10–12; 650 m²) contained thirty-five ceramic lamps, all but one of which were in storage in two rooms (Griffiths 2016: 119–20). It is interesting that the large majority of lamps and lighting devices even in the wealthiest Pompeian houses were ceramic, and that most of them were in storage (though in some cases that could be an outcome of the abandonment process). Nonetheless, it seems likely that, as at Olynthos much earlier, not all lamps were in use at the same time. It is probable that some lamps and other lights went with the fleeing inhabitants. The bodies of ten people attempting to escape from the House of Menander were found with ceramic lamps and one or two bronze lanterns to help them find a way out (Griffiths 2016: 131).

A remarkable papyrus document of the third century BCE can provide further insight into where and how artificial lighting was used. This papyrus probably belongs with the archive of Zenon, who managed the accounts for the estate of Apollonios, an important official under King Ptolemy II (Westermann 1924). It documents the daily allowance of lamp oil allocated to particular individuals for

TABLE 4.5 Lamp oil in the estates of Apollonios (Westermann 1924).

Recipient	Kotylai	ml*	Lighting hours**
Accounting office—Athenagoras	1	270	18
Accounting office—Demetrios	1	270	18
Accounting office—Dionysodoros	0.5	135	9
Scribe's office—Iatrocles	1	270	18
Scribe's office—Artemidoros	0.5	135	9
Philinos—bakery	0.5	135	9
Bannaios—silver storeroom	0.25	67.5	4.5
Steward's storeroom	0.25	67.5	4.5
Philistios and Menodoros	0.25	67.5	4.5
Pyron, steward's records	0.125	33.75	2.25
Herophantos	0.125	33.75	2.25
Herakleides, stable attendant	0.25	67.5	4.5
Solon, stable attendant	0.25	67.5	4.5
Euboulos	0.25	67.5	4.5

* The kotyle varied in volume in different places between about 250 and 330 ml; 270 ml is an approximation.
** Based on Griffiths' (2016: 170) experiments with a ceramic lamp. Metal lamps may have been more efficient (Foxhall 2007: 93).1 kotyle = 270 ml.
1 lamp: 18–20 hours.
2 lamps: 9–10 hours.
3 lamps: 4.5–5 hours.
4 lamps: 2.25–2.5 hours.

carrying out specific duties. In Egypt, this was castor and sesame oil, not usually olive oil as in the Mediterranean. The key recipients of this allocation were the accountants and scribes, the baker, the man who polished and guarded the silver, the steward, the stable hands, a bath attendant, and various sanctuary attendants with special duties in religious festivals (including keeping the sanctuaries lit), and especially to those cooking for these festivals. One of the allocations is specified as going to "the man cooking food by night destined for the Serapeum" (Westermann 1924: 243), again suggesting that large-scale cooking after dark was out of the ordinary. A number of the recipients are indicated as working at night, and some of the others may well have been working in dark environments such as bakeries and storerooms. Nonetheless, the amount of light some of these allocations would have provided was quite limited, as is evident from Table **4.5**. A minimum allocation of one-eighth of a kotyle would have kept a single lamp lit for about two hours, so most of these allocations of lamp oil would have provided only a few hours of light at the most.

CONTAINERS AND CERAMIC ITEMS

Pottery was ubiquitous in Classical antiquity in all periods, and is probably what most people think of as "everyday" in the ancient world. Dio Chrysostom, writing in the first century CE, represents the poor farmer/hunter he encountered in a remote part of Euboea as listing his few tools and possessions one by one, but not bothering with an inventory of the pottery because "why would anyone talk about the ceramic items?" (Dio Chrysostom 7.47). Many things other than pots were made of fired and unfired clay, including tiles, architectural elements, spindle whorls, loom weights, and decorative/votive figurines and toys, and it was commonly used as a building material and for plaster.

The kinds of fine ware and decorated vases most often illustrated are not the kinds of pottery that were necessarily the most used. Most Classical Greek tablewares were plain black slipped, and most of the pottery in everyday use was unslipped and undecorated. Romans perfected the art of mass-producing beautiful decorated tablewares, as the mold-made red-slipped products of Lezoux and La Graufesenque in Gaul and the African red-slipped pottery of late antiquity testify (see above p. 78). Nonetheless, throughout Classical antiquity, utilitarian wares were more important in everyday life, and potters were adept at formulating clay recipes by choosing and refining clay from particular sources and mixing it with other ingredients such as sand, mica and other crushed rocks, ground fired pottery, or organic matter to produce clearly defined fabrics suited to specific purposes, producing a range of vessels and wares that were highly standardized in most times and places. They could make cooking pots in tough fabrics that were resistant to thermal shock and water jars that were soft and porous, allowing evaporation through the walls to keep the water a bit cooler.

Large, thick-walled storage vessels (pithoi/dolia) and smaller, more portable amphorae were used to contain a wide range of foodstuffs and were sometimes coated with resin or other substances to improve preservation. Manufacturing very large vessels such as pithoi or highly effective cooking pots is technically more challenging and in some cases demands more specialist materials than making basic fine wares for table use. It may well have been the case that many of the utilitarian vessels that have traditionally been overlooked were more valuable and valued that some of the tablewares.

It is easy to forget that pottery and ceramic items were designed to be used in conjunction with other kinds of common objects and materials that no longer survive. Tableware for the wealthy included metal items, or in some cases metal probably replaced ceramics altogether. The Greek word for the object on which large pieces of meat or other elaborate dishes were served is a *pinax*. This literally means a board, and leaves open the possibility that wooden boards or (in elite circles) metal "platters" were used that no longer survive. Although we do have examples of ceramic plates in most Greek and Roman pottery repertoires and assemblages, they are relatively rare in comparison with the number of bowls and cups. Some cooking pots and pans were bronze and many implements such as tripods, spits, graters, ladles, and knives were made of metal, although comparatively few survive (Cahill 2002: 187–90). Numerous basketry, wooden, leather/skin, and textile implements such as baskets, paddles, skin containers, sieves, sacks, nets, and mats were also commonly used with pottery (Figure **4.2**). The use of some ceramic vessels depended on elements made of other materials that we no longer have. For example, many of the less-robust ceramic mortars that survive would have broken had a stone or ceramic pestle been used with them, so it seems probable that with these wooden pestles or pounders were used. Pots were regularly hung from walls by their handles or suspended with string, while rounded everted rims were perfect for tying a cloth over the top and bottles with narrow necks suggest stoppers in organic materials (cork, wood, cloth). Lids were sometimes ceramic but could also be made of wood or metal. So, what made pottery such an important "everyday" object in the Classical world was not simply its durability and ubiquity, which are what we see in the archaeological record, but rather its versatility and utility in combination with objects made of other materials.

Fired clay is a resilient material, so broken pots and tiles were regularly and spontaneously repurposed. Amphorae were recycled to make drain pipes (Allison 2006: 353) and stands for round-bottomed cooking vessels (Allison 2004: 101). Broken pottery was reused for other purposes, including filling holes in roads and as ostraca, the ancient equivalent of Post-it notes. Both pithoi/dolia and amphorae were recycled as containers for corpses or cremated ashes in burials across a range of periods. Fragments of roof tile were sometimes shaped for other purposes such as lids or weights.

FIGURE 4.2 Domestic scene with women. *From right to left*: a woman holding a small chest for storage; a woman holding a full basket; a woman sitting next to a wool basket probably making roves of wool to wind on a distaff or perhaps spinning. Attic red-figure pyxis by a follower of Douris from Athens, late sixth to early fifth century BCE. London, British Museum 1873,0111.7. Photograph: © The Trustees of the British Museum.

The reuse of ceramic loom weights is regularly documented. A good example is provided by two sites in the Metaponto countryside. At Sant'Angelo Vecchio in the fourth century BCE, discarded loom weights from a house were reused as separators in a kiln on the same site, serving to ensure that pots were not touching each other during the firing process (Foxhall and Quercia 2016). At the Pantanello sanctuary, loom weights dedicated as votives by women in the sixth to fourth centuries BCE were recycled as kiln separators in a second- to first-century BCE kiln built on the site after the sanctuary had gone out of use (Foxhall 2018). Along the same lines, it seems likely that the small numbers of odd loom weights sometimes found in Pompeian kitchens (Allison 2006: 87) and in shipwrecks (Panvini 2001: 62, 95) were used for purposes other than weaving. These offer a particularly interesting case of where we can be fairly certain that the change of use indicates different users and new and different meanings associated with the objects themselves. Loom weights in use for weaving had strong symbolic and ideological associations with women in the Classical world (Nevett 1999: 40; Foxhall 2011, 2018). So, while men might not be keen to be seen using them for weaving (though we know that some did, especially in Roman times), secondary users in kilns and on ships seem more likely to have been men, repurposing them in completely different ways.

CUTLERY AND EATING HABITS

When it comes to eating and drinking, surviving vessels—mostly ceramic— and visual representations of dining are informative, but in addition numerous literary texts survive that reveal how people used objects in dining. Many of these textual references are preserved in the early third-century CE work by Athenaeus, the *Deipnosophistai* (*Wise Men Dining*). Written in the form of conversations among a group of intellectuals over dinner, it presents the various courses and elements of a Greco-Roman banquet through a pastiche of short quotations ("fragments") from earlier literary works, many of which are now otherwise lost to us. Although immensely valuable, it must be used with caution since we lack the original sociopolitical and textual contexts for these literary fragments, and they have been recontextualized by Athenaeus from the perspective of his own, much later, time period.

Greeks and Romans mostly ate with their hands (Athenaeus 4.134f, 4.135b–c), so forks, spoons, and table knives were not actually everyday objects. Bread, served in baskets (made of metal and other luxury materials in elite settings), was used to mop up bits, sauces, juices, and broth (e.g. Athenaeus 4.149a–b). However, the rarity of surviving spoons is particularly interesting since many Greek and Roman dishes, especially those eaten by the poor, consisted of boiled ingredients and seem to have had the consistency of soup. This is confirmed not only by textual evidence, but also by the shapes and types of surviving cooking pots that are designed for preparing foods boiled in liquid. Cooking pots were also sometimes put directly on the table as serving vessels, even in elite settings (e.g. Athenaeus 4.147a). The special mention of the gold spoons handed out to guests at the wedding of the Macedonian king Karanos (Athenaeus 4.129c) so that guests could eat from a centrally placed communal vessel, though legendary, suggests that such a practice was unusual in elite settings in historic times. It could signal the serving of a luxury version of a particular (perhaps "traditional") dish normally associated with non-elites, and the usual manner of eating it was simultaneously "gentrified" in the story by the spoons of gold.

It seems almost unimaginable that in non-elite settings boiled foods were prepared or eaten without using spoons. One possible solution to the normally invisible spoons could lie in the very large numbers of small ceramic bowls (Figure 4.3) that appear in even quite modest Classical pottery assemblages. Hypothetically, these could have been used to scoop liquid food out of a cooking or serving vessel and consume it, though this sounds messy. However, the most likely solution is that spoons were normally made of wood. A few ceramic ladles survive, but most of these must also have been made of wood.

Spoons appear more regularly in a range of contexts in Roman times. For example, a collection of nineteen silver spoons for dining carefully stored in chest was recovered in House I 10, 4 at Pompeii (Table 4.1). They are normally made of metal, often silver, so are items that would have been used by wealthier people. The ends of the long handles of these small spoons are often pointed, and this feature has led to the suggestion that their primary purpose was for removing the ends from and eating eggs (Figure 4.4). In Petronius' description of Trimalchio's extravagant dinner party, egg spoons were handed out for one of the courses (Petronius, *Satyricon* 33). However, observation of the wear patterns on spoons indicates that they may have been used for a wider range of purposes (Swift 2014).

FIGURE 4.3 Small bowl (2285-1) used for dining, fourth century BCE, one of a number of such small bowls found in the Umbro Greek rural farmhouse, Bova Marina, Calabria.

FIGURE 4.4 Roman spoon, bronze. London, British Museum 1968,0626.28. Photograph: © The Trustees of the British Museum.

HARD SURFACES AND SOFT FURNISHINGS

The remains of ancient buildings always look hard and cold because we are missing the soft elements that made them comfortable. Although we think of textiles primarily as clothing, in various forms they surrounded everyone in daily life. Even poorer homes were sparsely and simply equipped with textiles and furniture. However, the houses of the wealthy, which are for the most part the ones we know and recover, were full of cushions, spreads, throws, rugs, and mats, as well as wooden and metal furniture.

Most Classical Greek furniture, even in opulent settings, was comparatively light and portable, as for example on a pelike in Oxford attributed to the Pan Painter (Figure **4.5**) where a young man is shown carrying a couch and a table.

FIGURE 4.5 A young man carrying a couch and a table, Attic red-figure pelike by the Pan Painter from Gela, first quarter of the fifth century BCE. Oxford, Ashmolean Museum AN1890.29.

This is consistent with the tendency for many elements of Greek material culture to be easily moveable and sometimes modular—that is, easily disassembled and reassembled. This is probably related to the lack of specialization of built space: in houses and elsewhere, spaces often did not have a single fixed function and were used for a number of different activities at different times over the course of a day or seasonally. Furniture and other equipment such as looms that can be readily moved and/or dismantled make it easier to use space flexibly in this way, but also add a transitory feel to the way in which everyday space may be constructed and shaped by the changing flow of everyday things.

Common items of furniture in Greek urban houses appear to be boxes and chests, along with seats of various kinds and couches and a few low tables. This is reflected in the Attic Stelae, where a variety of tables, chests, stools, couches, and the occasional bed are listed. These are accompanied by numerous throws, spreads, curtains, cushions, and other textiles to be used with and on these items of furniture (e.g. *IG* I³ 421 col. 4.160–209).

Visual representations of furniture from all over the Greek world similarly depict couches and simple seats. The latter include small, easily stored folding stools, stools with rush seating, and wicker chairs, all light and portable. Seating and workspace could also be provided by the stone benches built along walls in Greek and Roman houses of all periods. Couches and seats are regularly shown in visual images as covered with textiles and cushions (Figure **4.6**). Furniture was never upholstered in Classical antiquity (Richter 1968: 117); textile items are always placed on the basic stone, wooden, or metal frame (see Richter 1968: fig. 179). This also made moveable items of furniture more portable. Compared to modern or even Roman furniture, most Greek seats and tables, beds, and even high-status couches for dining were low, although

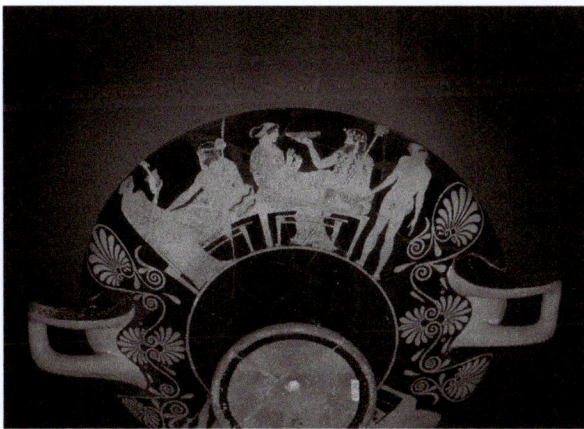

FIGURE 4.6 Couches equipped with cushions and textiles, Attic red-figure kylix by the Codrus Painter from Vulci, third quarter of the fifth century BCE. London, British Museum 1847,0909.6. Photograph: © The Trustees of the British Museum.

a few more elaborate chairs with backs are sometimes represented as higher (e.g. in depictions of seated deities or important people such as the deceased on funerary stelae).

Chests, boxes, and other items of furniture are directly documented at urban sites such as Olynthos, largely abandoned before Philip's invasion in 348 BCE, and Halieis, also abandoned in the fourth century BCE, by finds of pieces of metal sheet, bone, ivory, and metal fittings, handles, plates, feet, and nails, sometimes found in clusters that are all that remain (Cahill 2002: 102, 124; Andrianou 2009: 63–81). Many of these chests and boxes served as containers for other kinds of objects such as stored textiles (Figure **4.2**; see also Richter 1968: fig. 386). In rural Greek houses, by contrast, even rather grand ones (Jones et al. 1962: 83, 1973: 372), evidence of such purpose-built furniture is virtually never found. In more elegant dwellings such as the Dema House, the owners may have removed all of the furniture when the house was abandoned. However, in more modest rural dwellings, it seems more likely that the inhabitants never used the kind of crafted furniture that was "everyday" to wealthier urban residents.

Many items of Roman furniture were similar to those of the Greeks. However, to judge from the visual representations and the few surviving pieces, including the household assemblages from Pompeii, well-off households crammed more pieces of furniture into their homes (see Richter 1968: fig. 586), which were also often more ornate, and sometimes higher (e.g. in the case of couches). As in earlier Greek houses, many metal fittings from items of furniture that no longer survive were found in the houses of Pompeii (Allison 2006). Perhaps because Romans surrounded themselves with more things, an important Roman invention was the freestanding store cupboard (*armarium*) (Cova 2013: 385), which by late antiquity also seems to be adapted to serve as a book/scroll store and desk (Figure **4.7**).

FIGURE 4.7 Roman sarcophagus of a physician from Ostia, early fourth century CE. The deceased is depicted as a philosopher, reading a scroll and seated in front of the cupboard in which are stored the tools of his trade. New York, Metropolitan Museum of Art 46.76.1. Gift of Mrs. Joseph Brummer and Ernest Brummer, in memory of Joseph Brummer, 1948. Creative Commons license.

In all periods, furniture and furnishings in the houses of the poor, though much less well documented, are likely to have been quite different in character from those that surrounded the occupants of well-off urban households. The poor, such as slaves in urban households, probably spent much of their time squatting, kneeling, or sitting on very low seats just off the ground when they were working indoors. To some extent, a preference for low seats when working seems to have been common to all classes in Classical Greece. This is probably because the most commonly used work surface was the floor, even in better-off households, and tables were comparatively rare and not so regularly used as work surfaces. Stone benches, a feature that appears regularly against the interior walls of ancient houses, could, of course, have served as both seats and, from a seated or kneeling position on the floor, as work surfaces. Depictions on Attic pottery of individuals working at various tasks show clearly this preference for low seating, such as the armorer working on a helmet in Figure 4.8, the carpenter working on the ground in Figure 4.9, the shoemaker in Figure 4.10, and Ajax and Achilles playing a game (Figure 4.11), who sit on what appear to be chunks of columns or cut logs—the latter could be the kind of seats that might be found in poor households.

Textiles were expensive to make in time and materials, so it is unlikely that poor households enjoyed the number or quality of cushions and throws

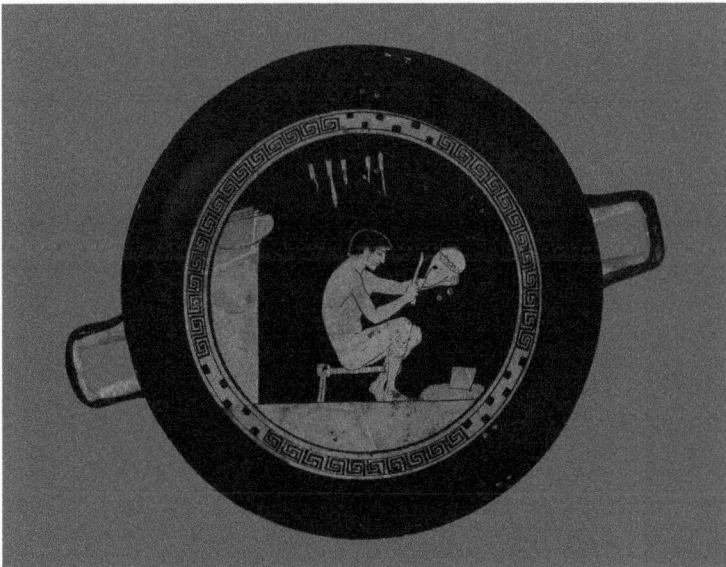

FIGURE 4.8 Armorer working on a helmet, Attic red-figure kylix by the Antiphon Painter. Oxford, Ashmolean Museum AN1896-1908.G.267. Photograph: © The Ashmolean Museum.

FIGURE 4.9 Carpenter working while kneeling on the ground, Attic red-figure kylix from Vulci, late sixth century BCE. London, British Museum 1836,0224.231. Photograph: © The Trustees of the British Museum.

FIGURE 4.10 Shoemaker at work, Attic red-figure kylix, second quarter of the fifth century BCE. London, British Museum 1865,0722.14. Photograph: © The Trustees of the British Museum.

FIGURE 4.11 Ajax and Achilles on low seats playing a game, Attic black-figure amphora by the Lysippides Painter from Chiusi, third quarter of the sixth century BCE. London, British Museum 1851,0806.15. Photograph: © The Trustees of the British Museum.

that adorned the furniture of wealthier people. In the elite households documented on the Attic Stelae, rags were kept (*IG* I³ 421 col. 4.163), and they appear to have been worth selling. Rags were important in a world with no specialist towels, bandages, diapers, and sanitary products, and, like string, had a plethora of additional possible uses. For the poor, clothing may have doubled as blanket and bedding; Greeks and Romans had no equivalent of pajamas or, as far as we know, underwear. Although the well-off who owned dining couches also sometimes used them as beds, the rarity of dedicated beds suggests that many inhabitants of even comparatively well-off households slept on bedding on the floor that could be rolled up and stored during the day when the space was needed for other purposes. It therefore seems highly unlikely that the poor regularly had access to couches or beds. Even in Roman times, the orator Dio Chrysostom (7.65) claims that when he stayed in the remote house of a Euboean farmer/hunter, the bed (*stibas*), also used for seating, was made of a pile of leaves covered in skins. The description of similar Spartan "beds" said to have been used for the festive dinner known as the "*kopis*" (Athenaeus 4.138f) suggests that Dio Chrysostom's account is not entirely imaginary. The likelihood, as suggested by the archaeological and visual evidence, is that the everyday environment of the poor, especially the rural poor, was very sparsely furnished.

CONCLUSIONS

As in all times and places, everyday things entangled in people's lives also partially shaped and defined the spaces they inhabited. By investigating a selection of sites in detail, we can show that conceptions of the everyday were very different from anything we experience, and experiences varied radically, especially along the lines of wealth and status. Nonetheless, it is still possible for us to get some sense of what it felt like to inhabit that world, although this small sample provides only a glimpse of the range of everyday experiences in the Classical past. While some everyday objects, especially for elites, were valued for their costliness or for the prestige they were felt to confer, many more everyday objects were taken for granted for their practical utility: if they worked, no one thought too much about them. However, this does not mean that some kinds of mundane objects were not valued beyond their functionality. Some plainly acquired sentimental, religious, or symbolic significance in particular contexts. However difficult it is to access "the everyday" in Classical antiquity, the objects associated with it can tell us much about who people thought they were, what they valued, and how they lived.

CHAPTER FIVE

Art

MIGUEL JOHN VERSLUYS

Let's talk about radicality. Let's talk about the kind of radical exoticism of things that Segalen discusses, the estrangement from a sense of identity that results in the creation of a form of vertigo through which all sorts of things can occur: affects, concepts, prospects, whatever, but always something insoluble, something unresolved.

(J. Baudrillard in Baudrillard and Nouvel 2002: 9–10)

INTRODUCTION

The perception that objects are active agents in their relationships with people was a familiar one in antiquity. In the Greek and Roman worlds, images of gods, for instance, were effectively treated as if alive and positioned as partners in social relationships (see above p. 37).[1] As such, they certainly had agency in the sense of that term famously employed by Alfred Gell.[2] References to and anecdotes about "the animated image" are readily found in Greek and Roman writers (see Bussels 2012). The story of the man who fell in love with Praxiteles' Aphrodite of Cnidus (Figure **5.1**) is told by several ancient authors: hiding in the temple at night, he tried to make love to her, a stain on the statue being the evidence of his lust.[3] Equally famous is the story of the artist Pygmalion, who makes a naturalistic female figure in ivory and then begins to believe it is a real woman and falls in love with the statue (Figure **5.2**) (Bussels 2012, 32–6; Grethlein 2017: ch. 6). More mundane and certainly more regular examples of such haptic engagements include the clothing, kissing, garlanding, and anointing of statues as if they were living beings in need of caretaking.

FIGURE 5.1 Version of Praxiteles' Aphrodite of Cnidus, the so-called Capitoline Venus. Rome, Musei Capitolini, Palazzo Nuovo. Photograph: Stijn Bussels.

In many instances statues are destroyed, too; such an act of *damnatio* equally testifies to the statues' agency (Stewart 2003; Varner 2004; Myrup Kristensen 2013). These examples all show the power of objects in a way that seems to be largely dependent on their mimetic, naturalistic qualities. Semi-iconic and aniconic objects could occupy similar places in social relationships between objects and people, however.[4] The introduction of the *mater deum magna Idaea*, the Magna Mater also called Cybele, is a fine illustration. Toward the end of the Second Punic War (218–201 BCE), an oracle urged the Romans

FIGURE 5.2 Pygmalion asks (a statue of) Venus to animate the statue of a female
he has made himself and fallen in love with. Late eighteenth-century painting on the
origin of sculpture by Jean-Baptiste Renault in Château de Versailles, salon des nobles.
(Wikimedia Commons: Coyau) (cf. 8.4).

to fetch a sacred stone, probably a meteorite, from Asia Minor in order to
defeat Hannibal. This meteorite *is* the Magna Mater. The main evidence for
the introduction comes from Livy (29.14.10–14) and Ovid (*Fasti*, 4.343–7),
both Roman authors writing about the events centuries after they had taken
place.[5] They recall how the Magna Mater arrived in Ostia in 204 BCE and
was welcomed in a grand ceremony by P. Scipio Nasica and the chaste Roman
matron Claudia Quinta, both by special appointment of the Senate. Crowds
lined the Tiber and welcomed the stone with gifts and prayers. Following its
arrival in Rome itself, the meteorite was delivered to the temple of Victory
at the Palatine. Pomp and circumstance surrounded this stone, especially in
the presence of Cybele's crew of eunuchs and sometimes even self-flagellating
priests and musicians, clad in colorful robes. Would the crowd along the Tiber
have whispered magical binding spells to ward off the potential evil agency of
this intrusive object arriving from the East? We do not know. The stone and
along with it the goddess from abroad were installed on the Palatine—and only
a few years later the war ended in Roman success.

Scholars of the ancient world have relatively recently become interested (again)
in objects as active agents, while still only hesitantly embracing the material turn

at large.[6] In this respect, two different approaches should be distinguished.[7] One approach, and the one perhaps most enthusiastically pursued so far, is to focus on *what people make of objects* and on documenting individual examples of human–thing entanglement, like the ones mentioned above. Such interpretations often deal with individual objects—often objects perceived as art, like the Aphrodite of Praxiteles or the Pygmalion statue—and mostly concern material engagement on the short term, within a chronologically rather limited period of time.[8] Often the human–thing entanglement is *conscious*, an encounter as exemplified in Figure 5.2.

A second approach investigates the question of agency on a more general level and asks *how objects make people and culture* or, in other words, how the history of the ancient world evolves through the particular relationship between objects and people.[9] Such interpretations mostly deal with classes of objects and groups of people, or even cultures, and concern material engagement in both the middle and longer term. The chapters of this book provide ample example of that, too.[10] Often these concern a more *subconscious* human–thing entanglement and therefore tend to go unnoticed in ancient texts—or at least they do not receive a similar explicit focus as the cases of the Aphrodite of Cnidus, Pygmalion, or the Magna Mater do. In order to trace them, we must try and document changes in the repertoire(s) of material culture available in a certain context over time and investigate how human behavior and society is molded through these alterations of the *object-scape*.[11] Identifying (classes of) objects as "game changers" and looking at their impact will thus allow us to investigate their agency.

This chapter is concerned with both approaches, as it looks at how objects were able to have an impact in particular historical encounters and situations (i.e. the particular) and how objects and categories or repertoires of objects were able to shape sociocultural possibilities in antiquity (i.e. the general). It is in better understanding of how object agency worked that the contested concept of "art" will prove to be hermeneutically most useful. I shall argue that calling an object "art"—whether this is done by the ancients or by us—is an attempt to grasp the impact (on them or on us) of the object as a special kind of (sensory) experience. Calling an object "art," I argue, thus simply serves to thematize the special kind of agency that the object is thought to possess. Potentially, therefore, all objects can be art, as Modern Art is constantly reminding us. Whether this is true or not is irrelevant in the context of this chapter; if we are interested in how the agency of objects works, what matters is whether people *consider* something as art—because that (emic) definition shows that they perceive that something special is going on in terms of the impact and agency of objects. Calling something "art" must be considered as a viewer response toward an object that is felt to evoke a singular experience. This is why we say that art moves us. But we could also speak of singular objects to characterize their experience by humans, as Baudrillard and Nouvel do, or of excessive objects, as Van Eck does (Baudrillard & Nouvel 2000; Van Eck 2015a, 2015b). The argument of this chapter is that such objects provide a privileged vantage point for studying agency.

I deliberately do *not* start by discussing ancient and modern definitions of "art" and the relations between them, as most previous contributions to the debate have done. Instead, we will first look at object agency in antiquity in a rather general way by investigating how and why certain objects were functioning as partners in social relationships with people—as *actants* in the definition of that term by Bruno Latour (1991)—and how this human–thing entanglement was perceived in antiquity. Only subsequently and from that perspective will we draw in and investigate notions of "art" and, later on, "aesthetics." This is a useful maneuver, I argue, because these notions and all the discussions on their meaning can only become really relevant for a cultural history of objects when framed in terms of the general problem: object agency.

OBJECTS AS *ACTANTS* IN ANTIQUITY

I start with four selected examples of object agency in antiquity.[12] The examples both illuminate the practical workings of object agency in the ancient world and simultaneously work towards a better understanding of *objects as art* in antiquity.

1. It is probably no coincidence that already the earliest Greek literature that has come down to us—Homer's *Iliad* and *Odyssey*—reflects on the mutual dependence between the world of humans with their ideas, emotions, beliefs, etc., and the world of things with their affordances.[13] The utmost importance of objects for these stories themselves as well as for their narrative structures and techniques has been demonstrated clearly in a long-standing and still burgeoning debate on *ekphrasis*: the description of works of art in ancient literature.[14] The description of the silver wine mixing bowl of Patroklos in *Iliad* 23, 740–9 serves well as an example—note that the text qualifies the object in question as "*tetugmenon*," which means something like "exceptionally well crafted"; a term not infrequently translated as "art":

> At once, the son of Peleus set out prizes for the foot-race:
> a mixing bowl of silver, a "*tetugmenon*," which held only
> six measures, but for its loveliness it surpassed all others
> on earth by far, since skilled Sidonian craftsmen had wrought it
> well, and Phoenicians carried it over the misty face of the water
> and set it in the harbour, and gave it for a present to Thoas.
> Euneos, son of Jason, gave it to the hero Patroklos
> to buy Lykaon, Priam's son, out of slavery, and now

Achilles made it a prize in memory of his companion,
for that man who should prove in the speed of his feet to run lightest.[15]

The bowl is characterized as a singular object first of all on the basis of its superior design (what we could also call its stylistics), the quality of its craftsmanship, the material used, and, finally, the fact that it was distinctly nonlocal—something underlined by mentioning both the Sidonian craftsmen and the Phoenician middlemen. But the other reason why this object is so very special and is presented as the ultimate prize for the footrace is its biography; it was passed on first to Thoas and Euneos, and then to Patroklos and Achilles. The object is presented as having a life of its own and being a protagonist in various human stories (Kistler 2010: 70–1; Crielaard 2015: 354). Objects like this bowl are known from the archaeological record, and it is likely that they were indeed perceived as active agents by contemporary users and viewers. The example from the *Iliad* suggests that their agency was located in what could be called the particular *design* of the object (its style and execution, the material used) and its *biography* (coming from for away and having passed through prestigious hands).

2. A glass bowl from the Iranian world, dated to around 500 BCE and found in a late-Hallstatt burial *tumulus* along the Rhine 3,500 km from its place of production, underlines this premise (Kistler 2010) (Figure 5.3). Such vessels were very special objects in the Achaemenid world, where they acted as highly symbolic gifts from the King of Kings to his court members. These courtiers used the objects to build or maintain relations with the local rulers— the *satraps*—on which the geographically very large Empire depended for its coherence and survival. In a world not yet so full of objects, where glass bowls were very rare—the industrialization of glass production by new techniques like glassblowing would only start centuries later (Degryse 2015)—this will have been a very special object by definition. Singular objects like this vessel could be said to have held the Empire together. We possess no viewer responses concerning the vessel, like the ones presented indirectly by the *Iliad*, but its agency becomes clear in more general terms through the prolongation of its life. Via trans-Eurasian networks, of which the Mediterranean trade routes formed the most western branch, the object continued its life in a Celtic burial mound. It certainly was a singular object along the Rhine: contextual analysis of such distinctly nonlocal objects shows that their attraction depended on both their particular stylistics and their biography, or, to use a more general term for the latter affordance, on their "social exoticism"; the fact that they originated from elsewhere.[16] Through these affordances, they would often have a major impact on the societies they entered, whether in the short term, as the example of the Achaemenid bowl in the Celtic tomb shows, or in the longer term, as is testified by repertoires of such intrusive objects that would soon be part of and make

FIGURE 5.3 Achaemenid bowl from a Hallstatt burial in Ihringen (Germany), around 500 BCE. Photograph: Kr. Breaigau-Hochschwarzwald BW.

up the societies they entered. Examples of such "impact repertoires" include Near Eastern-style metalwork that populated Greek sanctuaries and Greek-style pottery deposited in Celtic (burial) contexts.[17] Repertoires like these radically transformed the societies they entered.[18]

3. Let us now move ahead several centuries in time to a sculpted relief and a context we are better informed about historically. Somewhere around the middle of the first century BCE, a large stele was installed at a site now known as Nemrud Dağ, high up in the Taurus Mountains in southeast Anatolia, near the upper Euphrates. This temple–tomb was built by a Hellenistic sovereign named Antiochos I, who ruled the small kingdom of Commagene between *c.* 70 and 36 BCE. Antiochos I had constructed this monument for reasons of ideology, social order, and canon-building and he sought to achieve these goals by means of a strategy of *bricolage*; putting together (stylistic) elements from different regions and periods.[19] The large relief (2.6 m high and 1.5 m wide) shows two figures: a ceremonially dressed man in Persian-looking attire on the left and a nude, bearded man with a club in his hand on the right (Figure 5.4). The figures can be identified as a Commagenean king shaking hands with Heracles. In all respects this will have been an excessive object to contemporary viewers, given the monumental dimensions, the unprecedented iconography, the enchantment evoked by the detailed depiction of the king's costume (as is underlined by the nudity of Heracles), the context of display amidst other monumental reliefs

FIGURE 5.4 Nemrud Dağ (Commagene), West Terrace, (*left*) *dexiosis* stele, depicting Antiochos I and Artagnes-Herakles; (*right*) cast of the relief made at the end of the nineteenth century. Photograph: Forschungsstelle Asia Minor, Münster.

and even more colossal statues, the location on the top of a high mountain, and the fact that the region had never seen an object like this before. But what did this relief *do*? As no viewer responses have been preserved, and as there are no signs of a deliberate destruction of the relief nor of different life stages of the object in antiquity beyond its initial placement by Antiochos I, our evidence to answer this question is circumstantial. However, the agency of the object must partly have relied on the fact that the king was depicted. Representations of gods and kings in the Hellenistic and Roman worlds were not merely depictions but *were* the god or the king, literally re-presenting them. The relief will therefore have immediately signaled "kingship" and probably have made the contemporary viewer kneel or at least lower his or her voice. Moreover, also in this case, the object seems to have been singular through both its design and its biography, or rather *the biography of the (stylistic) elements from which it was made up*. Its design was singular in execution (dimensions, iconography, craftsmanship), rather than its standard sandstone materiality. The biography of the constitutive (stylistic) elements of the stele signaled social exoticism in several ways, although very differently and in a more complex way than the Achaemenid bowl in the Celtic tomb did. The naturalistic style we call Greek had a long and turbulent life in Eurasia after the Classical period and generally did extremely well in its entanglement with peoples and cultures: this is why large parts of the Hellenistic and Roman worlds often look distinctly Greek. In contexts like late-Hellenistic Commagene, the agency of this Greek style was particularly strong through its associations with civilization and modernity: a local ruler aiming at a place on the global stage could not but use the visual formula known as Greek. This is known as Hellenism. The Persian associations making up the stele had a very different biography. The particular style that was so easily recognized as Persian, by them and still by us now, was created to re-present Achaemenid kingship in the first place and understood as such throughout antiquity. Moreover, Persianism flourished through its many entanglements with peoples and cultures overtime, and Antiochos I, who wanted to profit from the allure of Achaemenid kingship to legitimize his own position, also used it eagerly (for Strootman & Versluys 2017 see Persianism). This is how the biography of certain semantic elements characterizing objects—the way in which these visual formulae had been used over time, bundling, as it were, the meanings of all these previous entanglements within their agency—could have a major impact on peoples and societies, even haunting them.[20] The agency of our piece of sculpted sandstone, then, comes from its design as well as from the biography of the iconographic elements making up that design—and, I would argue, especially from their novel combination and confrontation within this singular object.

4. Finally, let us move ahead several more centuries in time again to a statue of a goddess called Allat Athena, dated to the second century CE, made of Pentelic marble and found in her temple in Palmyra (Figure 5.5).[21] Archaeologists who have excavated and reconstructed the cult place for this goddess have interpreted it as distinctly "Classical" on the outside, while being "Near Eastern" on the inside. This temple was destroyed and then rebuilt as part of a Roman army camp in Palmyra at the end of the third century CE. In this new, rather different-looking phase, the more-than-life-size (3 m) marble statue in distinctly Classical style (at least a century old by then and perhaps related to a very similar example from the Antonine period that has been found on the Athenian agora) was added to the sanctuary as its main cult statue and displayed under a four-column canopy. However, the excavators found it deliberately mutilated and buried within the temple, placed with its face to the ground. The head had been smashed into several pieces and especially the nose as well as part of the left side of the body had been violently destroyed. The attack seems to have been selective—singling out the cult statue and the temple's central altar while other statues were left unharmed—and recalls contemporary human–thing entanglements in Palmyra that have shocked the world.[22] As the statue was excavated from a securely dated archaeological stratigraphy, the attack can be placed in the final decades of the fourth century CE. In this period, Christians went around pagan sites to destroy temples and statues of the pagan gods, and it seems clear that the mutilation of the Allat Athena statue should

FIGURE 5.5 Cult statue of the goddess Allat Athena as found in her temple in Palmyra with deliberate mutilation of the nose and the left side of the body. Formerly in the Palmyra Museum, present whereabouts unclear. Photograph: Troels Kristensen.

be understood against this background. Managing object agency was a central concern for the transformation of temples to churches in the most general terms (see Hahn et al. 2008 for the theme and many examples). It is important to note that, in the case of Allat Athena, the *damnatio* proved successful. The temple of Bel, a much more prominent and important sanctuary in the city, was turned into a Christian church and continued to be a place of religious worship until the Middle Age mosques that had followed the church were demolished by the French excavators of the 1930s. Allat Athena, however, would not live on in this way, but died at the end of the fourth century CE in what will have been a spectacle of destruction by means of which her agency *had* to be destroyed—until the moment she was excavated in the twentieth century. At the end of the fourth century CE, that agency was located in her origins—that is, the fact that she was a pagan statue from a pagan temple—but perhaps also in her stylistics; how otherwise can we explain the selective mutilation of the nose? During earlier phases of her life in Palmyra, she had impact through different stylistic and biographical affordances: she could have been selected as a cult statue because she was an antique object, or because she looked distinctly Classical, or because she came from Athens, or because she matched local understandings of Allat. This is impossible to tell—the only viewer response toward her agency that can be documented is the late fourth-century CE attack.

OBJECT AGENCY AND THE CONCEPT OF ART

The question of what was art in Antiquity and whether the concept as such existed in the ancient world has received a large amount of attention.[23] Let me briefly summarize the *communis opinio*. There clearly were aesthetic considerations in the production and consumption of (visual) material culture—and art history as we understand it nowadays was "invented" in antiquity (Tanner 2006; Porter 2010; Summers 2010; Squire 2015). That is to say, in the Hellenistic and Roman worlds in particular, objects were defined as art in terms of "an autonomous province of meaning" and were analyzed, discussed, traded, and displayed as precisely that (Tanner 2006: 205). A picture by Laurens Alma Tadema, tellingly entitled *Un Amateur Romain* (Figure 5.6), encapsulates this state of affairs, showing us four classically draped figures in a costly and stately Roman *atrium* silently contemplating a silver statue. The fact that the reclining man seems most interested in the gazing women and their experience of the statue in terms of sociocultural (or perhaps economic or sexual) capital only underlines that Alma Tadema imagines the object as being art. At the same time, it is clear that the reconstruction of Roman (-emic) understandings of objects as art as presented in the painting is very much determined by contemporary (-etic) notions specific to the context of the consumption of art that was the second half of the nineteenth century and, of course, specific to the artist Alma Tadema himself. The double hermeneutics at play here are as fascinating as they are difficult to disentangle, as formulations of the concept of art in the second half of the nineteenth century took their impetus from ancient texts and, moreover, modern interpretations of those texts.

In an important article from 2012, Michael Squire has argued that Classical archaeology and the study of antiquity more generally are very much in need of having the concept of art as part of their methodological toolbox.[24] Art history, he argues, is strong in analyzing "modes of seeing" in a way material culture studies are not or are less so. Calling a statue or a painting or a vase

FIGURE 5.6 Laurens Alma Tadema, *Un Amateur Romain*, 1886. Glasgow Art Gallery and Museum. Photograph: © Glasgow Art Gallery and Museum.

from antiquity "art," therefore, would bring across much better the fact that these objects have a presence of their own and are able to constitute their context. This "ongoing presence" has continued strongly to influence us up until the present day; indeed, we can speak of a life history of Classical art from antiquity to the present in which objects from the ancient world can be shown to "make up" the various historical periods they populate (Vout 2018; see also Boschung 2017). In other words, *spolia* are important elements in a story of cultural transference and never just *spolia*.[25] However, Squire argues, talking about statues or paintings or vases from antiquity as *objects* has resulted in privileging (archaeological) context above the object and its presence itself. Considering such objects as *art* would force us to rethink the dichotomy between context and form and, moreover, show that the biographies of objects are also contextualized by their own aesthetics, as, in Squire's words, "images imply contexts" (Squire 2012: 471). Although I very much agree with Squire's analysis of the *status quaestionis* within the field of Classical archaeology at the time, I think that the material turn, as exemplified by this and other volumes, now allows us to move beyond the dichotomy he sees between *context* (= archaeology and anthropology) on the one side and *object* (= art history) on the other. What is more, the material turn can bring these fields—*the* three disciplines that have objects at the very center of their cultural analysis—closer together.

To illustrate that, I have discussed the four examples from the previous section without using the word "art" at all. Although the Homeric crater, the Achaemenid glass bowl, the Commagene relief, and the statue from Palmyra could all find a place in overviews of ancient art, I hope to have shown that discussing their ongoing presence as well as their impact on the contexts they populated does not require describing them as art. Rather, it requires putting the notion of object agency central to our investigation and asking the question: *What do objects do?* Or, when shifting our attention to the object perspective within human–thing entanglement, asking even more explicitly: *What do objects want?*[26] There clearly can be a place for art within the study of objects, but we should see these categories as not mutually exclusive and use art to signal the special kind of agency some objects are thought to possess. As such, objects considered as art are a privileged vantage point for studying agency as that agency is documented by the very notion itself: art is a viewer response toward an object that is felt to evoke a singular experience.[27] It follows that potentially all objects *might* be understood in terms of art.[28] Material culture disciplines like archaeology and anthropology should therefore actively turn toward art history in developing the material turn, as art history is experienced in understanding objects as active agents in their relationships with people like probably no other discipline investigating material culture. It is telling that innovative recent interpretations of, for instance, material culture from Iron Age temperate Europe or the Scythian steppe used and needed the concept of art to arrive at their novel interpretations.[29] They deal with the same objects as previous generations of archaeologists and anthropologists, but (only) investigating these objects as art has brought out questions of agency, impact, and experience to the full. Evoking the concept of art might therefore be useful hermeneutically, despite the burden—discussed in the next section—that it brings. Be that as it may, I think that a cultural history of objects can only fruitfully use the concept of art when this is framed in terms of object agency, as this chapter does.

THE BURDEN OF ART—AND AESTHETICS

Calling an ancient object art often came with the serious and probably inescapable burden of transposing our typically normative, modern, Western views of what art is onto the ancient evidence—and tended to leave a lot of ancient viewers, objects, and contexts outside the analysis, resulting in a very incomplete picture of the ancient world. However, once we see the concept of art not as an -etic category but rather as an -emic concept, it becomes an effective tool to investigate object agency. As such, the study of objects as art has tremendous potential, and not only for the period of antiquity. Notwithstanding that conclusion, evoking the notion of art is not a necessary precondition for studying object agency in a fruitful manner in my opinion. For that reason, and because art will probably always remain a contested concept in itself, in the remainder of this chapter I will briefly explore two other concepts relevant to studying objects as active agents: aesthetics and exoticism. Although these concepts are themselves contested and come with their own burden as well, they arguably allow a closer investigation of object agency, as has already become clear from discussing the Homeric mixing bowl, the Achaemenid glass, the Antiochan relief, and the Allat statue. In analyzing these objects and their agency, the concept of design was used to describe their particular stylistics. Other scholars frequently use the concept of aesthetics to do so. Might drawing in the concept of aesthetics itself as well as the ancient and modern debates about it help us to better understand how objects' agency in antiquity worked (and may still be working)?[30]

The Greek notion of *aisthēsis* "fused such modern ideas as sensation, perception and intuition. It was the ongoing apprehension of particular things, as opposed to *noēsis*, which was reflective and analytical, general and rational. ... Modern aesthetics was ... associated from the beginning with prerational and intuitive judgment and ... is concerned with taste, with judgments of beauty and quality, but the term also quickly assumed much broader dimensions, becoming in effect the collective imagination, worldview, style or sense of form of cultures, peoples and historical periods."[31] This definition clearly shows, I think, the importance of the concept of aesthetics for the study of object agency. In the first place, aesthetics is about impact, not meaning; about phenomenology, not analysis—and hence very much about the sensory and affective aspects of material encounters we are trying to analyze.[32] Secondly, aesthetics is simultaneously about the short-term and *conscious* human–thing entanglement as well as, through its broader dimensions, about more *subconscious* human–thing encounters in the middle and longer term. Aesthetics is therefore not at all about Plato and Aristotle contemplating art, as scholars not so familiar with the debate often still seem to think. Rather, as in particular James Porter has shown, aesthetic sensibility in antiquity was very much concerned "with the sensuous surface of material objects or with felt appearances ... one even finds an exclusive interest in this aspect of aesthetic experience at the expense of, say, attention to meaning, morals or religion."[33] As such, the concept has great potential for investigating object agency in antiquity: it is about what things do to people, why they have this particular impact, it indirectly documents viewer responses toward objects, and it allows us to analyze the impact of (shifting) repertoires and culture styles.[34] There is therefore a lot to gain from actively engaging with debates on the value of aesthetic value for scholars of material culture (Porter 2012).

THE RADICAL EXOTICISM OF THINGS

Let me turn then to the affordance that was repeatedly evoked as being crucial when analyzing the agency of the four case study objects: being nonlocal in time or space, or, in other words, their exoticism. I think this notion has great potential to help us better understand how object agency worked, at least when we use it as a positive term with critical currency, as was proposed by Victor Segalen (Figure 5.7).

Segalen (1878–1919) was a French polymath (doctor, poet, writer, ethnologist, archaeologist, and traveler) who thought hard about the Other and, in relation to that, about the sensory and affective aspects of material encounters with "foreign," nonlocal objects. In his *Essai sur l'exotisme*, a collection of manuscript fragments written over the years 1904–18 that draw on his extensive travels and archaeological and ethnographical research in Asia and Oceania, he developed a theory of exoticism as, what he calls, an *aesthetics of diversity*.[35] With *aesthetics* Segalen means to say that exoticism is a phenomenological rapture, a confrontation resulting in the inability to comprehend. With *diversity* he means to say that only a confrontation with the Other, the nonlocal, can bring out the alterity of the Self. For Segalen, therefore, exoticism is not about cultural translation, or even about cultural contact in the traditional sense of the term at all. *Exoticism is about the sensorial and affective experiences evoked by the confrontation with something foreign*. Through this "anxiety of the real," this confrontation resulting in a singular experience, "all sorts of things can occur: affects, concepts, prospects, whatever, but always something insoluble, something unresolved."[36]

Segalen's ideas resonate strongly with our analysis of the object agency of the Homeric mixing bowl *made by Sidonian craftsmen*, the *royal, Achaemenid* bowl, the relief from Commagene juxtaposing *Hellenism and Persianism*, and the *distinctly classical* Allat Athena statue. In all these cases, the biography of the objects was shown to matter a lot in the sense of their *being nonlocal*. Together with the style and execution of the objects, this resulted in a design with a profound agency. Segalen's ideas help to explain why exoticism, understood

FIGURE 5.7 Victor Segalen (1878–1919). Image: bretagne-chine.org, Wikimedia Commons.

as the phenomenological experience triggered by (certain) objects, is able to impact society: *the tension that this experience creates makes all sorts of new things possible*. As we have seen, intrusive objects entering societies are indeed often radically transformative, as are "impact repertoires."[37] Segalen's theory of exoticism as an *aesthetics of diversity* explains why they have this particularly strong agency and why "objects in motion" are often innovating objects. This is not so much because they transfer (cultural) meaning or part of their biography in a direct way. What they achieve through their *aesthetics of diversity* is the creation of a *Denkraum* in which it is possible to think outside the box—and innovate.[38]

THE AESTHETICS OF DIVERSITY OF THE PRIMA PORTA AUGUSTUS

As a conclusion to this chapter, let us briefly analyze the agency of an object that has been hailed as a Classical art masterpiece from the moment it was found in 1863 and that probably is less obviously characterized by multi-temporality and multiculturalism than the Homeric mixing bowl, the Achaemenid glass, the Antiochan relief, and the Allat statue discussed above: the Prima Porta Augustus (Figure 5.8). Discovered in the ruins of an imperial *villa* north of Rome and restored by the sculptor Pietro Tenerani soon after, the statue was immediately seen and used as *the* symbol of the first Roman emperor and his Principate. It continues to be perceived as a singular object in the present day and probably was similarly regarded in the Roman period, based on the fact that approximately 150 copies and versions of the Prima Porta-type head have been preserved. How to account for the agency of this object? Much emphasis has been put on the fact that the statue was part of a keen strategy of propaganda that very actively used material culture to disseminate ideological messages in order to try and change Roman *habitus*: Augustus and his power of images (Zanker 1988). This certainly played an important role; the statue was not merely the depiction of a person, but a political metaphor embodying *corpus imperii* in all respects and in a very subtle way (Meister 2012). However, as it turns out, much more is going on.[39]

The design of the statue is exceptional. It is larger than life-size, at 2.04 m, and is carved from very-high-quality *lychnites* marble from the island of Paros. Through its counterbalanced contrapposto, the statue has an excitingly dynamic diagonal pose. Moreover, the posture of Augustus seems to be deliberately ambiguous: he is clearly standing and addressing an audience (passive), while at the same time moving and showing the way forward (active). The execution itself is equally exceptional. The body of Augustus is almost visible under the cuirass, which makes the statue look simultaneously naked and clothed. Through the color scheme, which is now no longer visible, a refined game was played with the depictions on the body and the body itself. The statue's biography was as multilayered as its stylistics. As in the case of the Antiochan relief discussed above, it does not concern the biography of the statue (type) itself (about which we know relatively little), but the biography of the (stylistic) elements of which it was made up. It has long been recognized that the sculpture refers back to *fifth-century BCE* prototypes, the high *Classical* style of the Doryphoros of Polykleitos in particular. The cuirass, however, is a *Hellenistic* type. In terms of association, the cuirass is a sign of military power, characterizing Augustus as a successful *Roman* general. This *Republican* rhetoric contrasts with the overall focus on portraying the emperor as having a strong and beautiful body and hence signaling masculine power in a *Greek* and *Hellenistic* tradition. References to the nonlocal and noncontemporary—that is, in time and space—continue in the decoration on the cuirass: the central scene depicts a distinctly *Oriental* figure facing a Roman general; *Barbarian* captives, most probably referring to conquered Celtic and Iberian tribes, are depicted around it. The scene refers to Augustus'

FIGURE 5.8 The Prima Porta statue of Augustus, around 20 BCE. Height: 2.04 m, made from Parian marble. Rome, Musei Vaticani inv. 2290. Photograph: Bettmann/Getty Images.

recovery of Roman military standards lost to the *Parthians* by the famous general Crassus at Carrhae in *53 BCE*, an important date in Roman history.

Large parts of the *oikumene* and some distinctive parts of its history thus come together in this statue. This prime example of Roman art in fact seems to be characterized by its multi-temporality and multiculturalism in the first place. In order to understand the impact of the Prima Porta Augustus, I do not think we should try to decode these different elements in an iconological way. Instead, the power of the statue, and that of the Augustan *Bildersprache* in more general terms, seems to be located in its embracement of ambiguities. The answer to the question of *why* embodying these ambiguities in a single statue and through the novel and unprecedented combination and confrontation of multi-temporal and multicultural elements was so successful that it resulted in a singular object brings us back to Segalen: it might have been the exoticism of the statue as an *aesthetics of diversity*. The tension that this experience created indeed made all sorts of new things possible, like the momentous shift in ancient history we call the Augustan cultural revolution.

CHAPTER SIX

Architecture

RABUN TAYLOR

INTRODUCTION

We humans think through material culture. By nature, objects interact with us, and we with them. If we take literally the etymology of the word *objectum*, "thing thrown against," we intuitively grasp that it is primarily sentient beings (persons, animals) against which they are hurled, for the simple reason that, as vehicles of subjective experience, we invite the disruptions they make—disruptions that, once inside our heads, can trigger a pinball game of contingent disturbances. The ways by which we respond to such perpetual bombardment constitute perhaps the most elemental mechanism of thinking, or being, in human experience (Heidegger 1971, 1996; Clark 1997; Merleau-Ponty 2005). Human cognition relies on material objects because the symbols constitutive of thinking cannot exist independently of material referents. And those referents come to us through bodily sensation (Renfrew 2004; Hodder 2012).

In everyday language, the freestanding noun *object* is rarely used of buildings, cities, landscapes, roads, or infrastructure. This usage reflects a cultural habit conditioned by a more or less arbitrary scale of mass and fixity that conforms to our embodiment as humans acting in the material world. Ironically, our proverbial term "immovable object," by virtue of its implicit impossibility, signals that all objects are movable—and not just in a potential sense, but in a genuinely phenomenological way. We expect objects in our sensory universe to be capable of displacement by the agency of people, animals, natural forces, or other objects. Yet things that are *not* comfortably defined as objects can also move or be moved. Fire and liquids move. Tides, magma chambers, and tectonic plates move. The planets move; seabeds rise into mountains over time. The simple noun *object*, then, is defined in terms of the temporal and dimensional limitations of our bodies. It is not just "thrown against" our senses; rather, we presume that our senses can, in effect, pick it up and throw it again. In consequence, a simple object must be fairly solid, cohesive, and limited to a size that makes tangible, not just visible, sense to our bodies. A speck of powdered sugar, unmagnified, is no more an object than a mountain range, though both are apprehended before our eyes. Magnified on a screen, its simulacrum becomes an object only because it has reached a scale that seems manipulable.

Yet when the object noun is coupled with a noun in the subjective genitive case, material quality and quantity lose their significance. Now *anything* (titanic, tiny, abstract, concrete, real, imagined, ephemeral, durable) can be an object *of* attention, *of* desire, *of* persuasion, *of* pilgrimage, *of* defacement, *of* a person, *of* the gods, etc., as long as some kind of agency is implied in the genitive noun. Cognitively speaking, then, almost anything—or anyone—can be an object, as long as someone or something interacts with it. Simple objects just exist; objects-of-something are bound up in the actions of subjects, which may in turn, by being thus entangled, develop reciprocal relationships, trading roles of agent and patient. It is in this more expansive sense that we should regard architecture and urban form as objects.

An object cannot be so diffuse or so insignificant that it is incapable of drawing or holding attention, but it need not have hard boundaries either. A neighborhood can be an object in the expansive sense (e.g. of pride or shame), but as such it may have no defined borders. In fact, a lack of precise boundedness characterizes a great deal of built space. If a building—say, a villa or a farmstead—has dependencies, are they part of the building? As a concept, the Forum Romanum, the center of public life in Rome, was an *object* of continuous and urgent interest in antiquity (Figure 6.1).[1] But ancient Romans could define its topography no more precisely than anyone today can define, say, Harvard Square, which is no square at all but rather a confusing tangle of winding streets and small, irregular plazas. The problem lies not so much with the center, but with the periphery. Do we include everything down to the Colosseum valley? Up the slopes of the Palatine and Capitoline Hills? Buildings up side streets from the main plaza? (Surely nearby merchants would want to take advantage of this prestigious place name, and they might test its geographic elasticity.) The Forum, in brief, had no skin. But it had flesh and a center of gravity, and as such it was an object, or potential object, of an infinity of action nouns. And it still is. Not only is it a popular tourist destination, but it continues to provoke serious study. It lives a rich and full symbolic afterlife through its attachment to famous Romans, momentous events, and resonant political ideologies. It also activates a host of abstracted concepts and derivative meanings attached to words like "forum" and "forensic."

FIGURE 6.1 The Forum as seen from the Palatine Hill, Rome. Photograph: Jean-Christophe Benoist. Wikimedia Commons CC BY 3.0. Modified. https://creativecommons.org/licenses/by/3.0/deed.en.

So where does architecture fall in the endless catalog of objects? First, like any physical thing understood from an anthropological perspective, it is partly concrete and partly abstract. There is the material object, and then there are the cultural potentialities or relationships inhering in it or adhering to it that have been variously called tendencies, affordances, indices, dependencies, fittingness, entanglements, etc.[2] In its more abstract or analytical guises, architecture's role as object can be categorized in numerous ways: for example, as *historical object* (what is its story?), as *processual object* (how was it designed, built, or used?), as *material object* (what is it made of?), as *semantic object* (what does it signify or symbolize?), as *affective object* (how does it makes us feel or act?), as *economic object* (what is its commodity value?), as *instrumental object* (e.g. how does it help us mail parcels or conduct weddings—or how does it influence our thinking?), and even as a mathematical abstraction transcending design. Many other categories of object value could easily be identified, and those I have named could just as easily be reconfigured by the application of alternative names.

From this welter of possibilities I have chosen to focus on three salient characteristics of Classical architecture. The first, commoditization and value, fits most comfortably into the category of architecture as economic object, if we understand buildings or built space to be embedded in a broad social economy that extends far beyond purely monetary considerations. The second characteristic, cognition and memory, straddles categories, but holds its larger shares equally in the categories of architecture as instrumental and as affective object; it briefly examines how a particular kind of architecture, the Greek theater, assists in creating and recording memorable experiences. The third characteristic, style—specifically, the Classical columnar style—also crosses several categorical boundaries, but in my particular treatment it most comfortably occupies the semantic and instrumental categories.

COMMODITIZATION AND VALUE

Literally and figuratively, objects move among us, and we move among them. One important way of looking at how we negotiate the world of objects is by regarding them as vehicles of value (i.e. of cost and benefit). We use objects transactionally, often as gifts, loans, or proxies for other objects or labor.

It is now commonly recognized that objects have social lives; that is, they operate as things of value within or between societies. When involved in exchange, they are called commodities. I take the term *commodity* in an expansive sense to refer to almost anything subject to exchange, be it through sale, barter, rent, or gift; all these processes are akin, sharing motives that are ultimately transactional (Bourdieu 1977: 171–83; Appadurai 1986: 6–16). Such things can be unique or mass-produced, concrete or abstract, valuable or cheap. Having physical and temporal durability, commoditized objects (or those that are candidates for commoditization) have lifespans, biographies, and (often) afterlives, even if, unlike people, their identity and individuality can be blurred over time by physical modification, repurposing, dissolution, recycling, replication, and so forth (Peña 2007a).

Not surprisingly, portable objects have dominated the anthropological literature on exchange. This may be simply because they can circulate easily through space and are thus more suited to transmission between owners. But nobody would deny that land and the structures built upon it also function freely as commodities. In complex agrarian societies, buildings have always been among the costliest of human material investments and among the most essential. We should thus expect them to loom large in any command or market economy. Indeed, from the word *economy* itself (i.e. "housekeeping"; Greek *oikonomia*) one may summon intimations of architectural materiality, even if the "house" (*oikos*) is meant as an abstract collectivity of assets; for in the ancient Greek world, as in most sedentary societies, such assets were concentrated in and around one's dwelling. A house, if used and occupied, was highly distributive, a node for the comings and goings of people and assets. Indeed, at its core, the verb root *nemo* in *oikonomia* means precisely "distribute."

Like movable property, real estate, too, circulates in markets; it is bought and sold, rented, and enjoyed by usufruct. The law of immovable property in Classical antiquity was highly developed, its sophistication reflecting the importance of land not just in the discourses of wealth and status, but in the sustenance of ordinary life (Kehoe 1997; Maffi 2005: 259–66; Temin 2013: 139–56). Owning and profiting from rental properties was normative behavior for the landed class. Motivated individuals could speculate in real estate, too, as we learn from the notorious story of the plutocrat Crassus buying burning properties in Rome from panicked owners during fires for redevelopment at a massive profit (Plutarch, *Life of Crassus* 2.4). But benefit also accrued to those who displayed their wealth materially; this is where buildings made the most of their status as objects.

A portable object can usually be tracked by its physical proximity to its owner. But with architecture, the owner may be absent, in which case those occupying, managing, or curating it—possessors, in Roman technical parlance— have no direct agency in its exchange, if by exchange we mean legal transfer of ownership. From an anthropological perspective, however, legal ownership alone—whatever that may mean in a given society—fails to characterize the complex social lives and proprietary structures of buildings. In general, the most important buildings in the Greek and Roman world, and thus the most *displayable*, belonged permanently to the public, to gods or (later) the Church, or, in the case of monarchies, to the ruler's patrimony. With the notable exceptions of war, invasion, or the absorption of pagan cult properties into the Church discussed below, they rarely exchanged hands. Did they thus fail to function as commodities?

Such buildings could be regarded as "terminal" commodities, initially subject to exchange but quickly retired from the market; a similar pattern is thought to characterize the biographies of many *sacra* such as cult objects and relics (Appadurai 1986: 23–4). But to the contrary, monumental buildings—whether sacred or secular—seemingly have always engaged in an ongoing social and political commerce. Indeed, it is hard to argue otherwise, given their durability (even through episodes of complete renewal), prominence, popularity, and utility within their urban and sanctuary landscapes. The Latin word *celebritas*, referring to a thing's popularity with an interactive public, could almost itself be translated as exchange; and it is precisely this property of celebrated buildings— the hard, gainful use, the give-and-take between architecture and its clientele— that marks it as a commodity.

Such buildings, even if they remain permanently off the real estate market, are never really "terminal" commodities; they remain involved in the real economy. In effect, their assets are perpetually available for rent—even if the rent is assessed not in monetary terms, but rather in terms of enjoyment, use, or status. The impulse to exclude them may rest on an excessively binary understanding of exchange at value, as if an object's participation in a market (and even "market" is hard to define) can be switched on and off. More recent perspectives have challenged this simplistic dualism (Thomas 1991; Hodder 2012). Here, I list but a few ways in which major public buildings could remain perpetually engaged with the social economies of their human clientele.

- *Patronage and symbolic capital.* Many prominent buildings in the Greek and Roman world were strongly associated with patrons, either individual or collective. In the Classical period, the dynastic patronage patterns of tyrants often yielded to more democratic, *polis*-centered modes of sponsorship, but they were no less ideological for that. Patronage-by-monument is aggressively transactional, and not just at the beginning of a sponsored building's lifespan. In fact, such buildings were implicitly meant to carry forward a patron's relationship to his clientele indefinitely. *Pari passu*, the clientele would implicitly continue to use and maintain the building in tribute to the patron. For centuries, every human encounter with a Greek city's treasury at Delphi or Olympia generated or reinforced a discourse that aimed to exact from the visitor a quiet tribute to that city and its erstwhile leaders (i.e. the patrons) as well as its glorious history.[3] Distant victories were evoked; mythologies were burnished. Admiring such buildings and consuming their messages constituted a psychic investment. Concomitantly, the buildings invested in their admirers, relying on a reciprocal dynamic of prestige to maintain or burnish their status, upkeep, and appearance.

- *Production.* Buildings are not produced in the same manner as portable objects, which tend to emerge complete from the workshop. Construction of buildings is public theater: the generative act is a complex, multi-act work of art in its own right, its narrative arc inspiring desire and anticipation. The public may participate in its creation as an audience participates in a new play, hanging on its narrative and navigating to its conclusion. The multisensory experience of the building's emergence—sights, sounds, smells—excites anticipation and pride. It promotes a sense of investment, a kind of co-ownership, among the community. While ownership in some sense accrues to the maker of a thing (Hodder 2012: 25–6), with buildings, and especially prominent ones in urban areas, where a building is permanently "thrown against" the senses and sensibilities of the public, that feeling is much more widely shared. But especially in premodern societies, the maker is often perceived to be the patron, not the architect or builder.

- *Consumption.* Greg Woolf has remarked on a highly visible phenomenon of Roman expansion in the provinces, which in Gaul began under Augustus—a "consumer revolution" marked by a colossal influx of goods from around the Roman world (Woolf 1998: 169–205). It betokens not just prosperity, but acculturation: the production of new tastes, values, and habits. This trend was similarly manifested in elite consumption of villas and tombs, built in Roman style, which proliferated alongside all that stuff. Here, we are dealing with commodification of material goods in the manner that chimes most insistently with modern capitalism. Much of the Romanizing architecture of the local aristocracies around the empire was the artificial object of manufactured desire.

- *Dependencies.* Buildings may look like neatly bounded essences, but they are endlessly entangled in their environments (Hodder 2012: 10–14, 51–2). Infrastructure—drainage, water supply, street frontage, delivery access, etc.—does not inhere in the building, but the building depends on it, and vice versa. Services are every bit as much commodities as objects are, and their constant bombardment of buildings—from which they exact a price for that bombardment—should make us very skeptical that living buildings are ever dead to exchange. A particularly vivid example of such a transactional nerve center was the Colosseum, with its impressive drainage system washing human and animal effluvia into the Tiber and simultaneously protecting its fragile structure from the infiltration of rainwater, while fresh water was delivered to fountains around its lower three decks (Taylor 2003: 82–4, 162–4). Those drains, and the aqueduct supplying the water from a nearby hill, were commodities in their own right, providing necessary goods or services. Indeed, aqueducts, providing a hybrid of both goods and services, might be regarded as architectural commodities *par excellence.*

- *Maintenance, renewal, and technological reciprocity.* By the very nature of their scale and complexity, monumental buildings not only lay claim to cultural supremacy within their urban, suburban, or sanctuary environments, they also place permanent demands on their users and beneficiaries. Bold, daring buildings—or simply those subject to heavy use, like baths or stadia—required high maintenance and were subject to many reconfigurations, modifications, and repairs. By aiming to maintain or improve the functionality of buildings and extend their social lives, these interventions may be taken as a perpetual form of commoditization. Whereas the generative force for a monument was credited to the patron and (at the technical level) the architect, over time that partnership of *auctoritas* (authorship) and *techne* (artful craft) became, in a sense, the property of the curating entity, which had to summon, *in loco parentis*, some of that generative creativity in order to maintain the building and fix its faults. The city of Rome preserves the histories of many buildings that were repeatedly repaired or remodeled and, after disasters, rebuilt on a new design. Agrippa's Pantheon—which retained its patron's proprietary inscription even after its redesign from the ground up in the second century CE—is only the most famous example of a building with such a biography (Figure **6.2**) (Boatwright 2013).

- *Injury, dismemberment, and death.* Many buildings suffered and died within our period of interest (roughly 500 BCE to 500 CE). Injured, sick, and dead buildings—we typically call them dilapidated or ruined—are an interesting but understudied component of towns, sanctuaries, farms, or other architectural agglomerations of Classical antiquity. Buildings that suffered in a non-catastrophic way—perhaps by pure neglect and dilapidation, or by trauma that could not be completely remedied—often played profoundly interactive roles in their landscapes. In exceptional circumstances, ruins themselves became monuments of cultural memory; for example, the Archaic temple of Athena on the Acropolis of Athens, destroyed by the Persians in 480 BCE, seems to have been preserved as a war memorial not unlike ruins enshrined in some cities today (Ferrari 2002). More commonly, dilapidated sites hosted marginal or illicit activities, attracted investment in redevelopment, or contributed recycled materials to new construction or repairs elsewhere. These latter two functions in particular qualify them as commodities: on the one hand, dissolution

FIGURE 6.2 Pantheon, Rome. Photograph: S. Borisov/Shutterstock. https://www. shutterstock.com/support/article/Standard-License-vs-Enhanced-License.

activated opportunity, as we see repeatedly in the form of aggressive
building programs in Rome after devastating fires; on the other hand,
the repurposing and exchange of used building materials contributed
vitally to the building economy (Taylor et al. 2016).

- *Afterlife.* Of course, buildings themselves, as well as their parts, could
  be recycled or repurposed in many ways, acquiring new functions and
  identities in the process. It is hard to characterize such a complex and
  varied phenomenon in any meaningful way until late antiquity, when an
  enormous demand for ecclesiastical buildings coincided with the severe
  contraction of the long-range stone trade (Kinney 2001; Hansen 2003;
  Russell 2013). Using prestige materials in monumental building became
  a zero-sum game. Columnar architecture in particular was ransacked on
  a massive scale to adorn tombs, baptisteries, sacristies, bishoprics, and
  especially the naves of churches. More to the point, public or sacred
  buildings and spaces were simply remodeled into churches or other
  Christian structures. As the old religious cults dwindled and died, their
  derelict land holdings and buildings reverted to the state, becoming
  easy targets for the burgeoning Church (Taylor 2017: 274–7). But
  negotiating the shift of identity between old purpose and new was a
  matter of great anxiety that often involved a nearly complete alteration
  of the building's form. Therein we face a problem of an object's ontic
  continuity: form, function, identity, and name all changed, but spatial
  fixity and some semblance of an architectural skeleton remained the
  same (Figure **6.3**). Ironically, however, questions about the object's
  persistence in space and time do not threaten its status as a commodity.
  Objects come apart, and their material components are reassembled
  into new objects all the time. What matters is that (1) value was
  conserved, generated, or augmented by reconstituting or reconfiguring
  parts or *properties* (bricks, floors, warm southern exposure, etc.) of a
  neglected building; and (2) value was understood broadly in terms of
  human consumption—be it spiritual, psychological, or material.

In the great majority of cases that did not involve a complete reappropriation,
the ongoing commoditization of a building can be understood as a perpetual
use history in which certain of its parts or properties were consigned,
temporarily or permanently, to independent entities. Those entities, in turn,
may have benefited the building (by giving it attention, supplying it with
water, paying for its maintenance, etc.) or contributed to its dissolution (by
dismantling and reusing its components). But more to the point, they benefited
third parties—either persons or things—that exploited the building's parts,
qualities, or features as assets of their own—in short, as commodities. The
so-called *Marmorsäle* of imperial Asia Minor are particularly salient examples

FIGURE 6.3 Narthex of the Cathedral of Syracuse, incorporating the Doric peristyle of the fifth-century BCE Temple of Athena. Photograph: Di Giovanni Dall'Orto. Fotografia autoprodotta/Wikimedia Commons.

among countless others less easy to interpret archaeologically. These lofty, theatrical halls inserted into monumental bath–gymnasium complexes could host a wide variety of ceremonial events unrelated to the building's primary functions (Burrell 2006).

The notional basis for this partitioned kind of commerce is high *use value*—the commodity's potential to be useful—supplemented in some cases by *prestige value*, as when a space is chosen for events because of its particular grandeur, embodied perhaps in rare imported columns of colored marble. Prestige has an endlessly variable parentage, but certainly *labor value* (based on the quality and quantity of work that went into it) and what Colin Renfrew calls *prime value* (assigned to highly prized materials) play important roles (Renfrew 1986: 157–60). But social and historical considerations also help to determine prestige value—as when, for example, a patron bestowed upon his hometown a building that happened to be the first and only one of its type in the city. Under those circumstances, demand may have been high on account of the building's local uniqueness, novelty, or patronage connections.

But we should not underestimate the symbolic benefits accruing to the entire building, too. This was especially true in the event that a single patron sponsored it, as often happened in the Hellenistic and Roman periods. The building was a kind of fetish for the patron, embodying his or her spirit and authority. Sumptuary laws reflected a genuine fear that if a single man built too much, his personal physical (and thus symbolic) presence would grow accordingly, almost as if he were supersizing his own body out of all proportion to others. In Rome of the late Republic, an entire class of architecture was subject to a sumptuary law: venues of spectacle. By design, the city had no permanent theater or amphitheater—purportedly because spectacles and entertainments were morally degenerate, but more truthfully because a huge convention center sponsored by and celebrating a big man threatened to inflate him further by a hundredfold; and as that building developed a history and a biography, it would merge into the big man's own.

Repeatedly, ambitious magistrates staging plays or spectacles were compelled to build their venues out of temporary materials and then, public duty discharged, dismantle them. Only in the early 50s BCE did Pompey the Great finally break the taboo, and only by resorting to a legal fiction: he would erect a grand new theater of concrete and stone (Figure **6.4**), but on the pretext that it was actually a sanctuary for a small temple of Venus perched atop the seating area (Tertullian, *On the Spectacles*: 10.5–6). Pompey's rivals could not stop him, though they recognized that a theater in his name, even if ruinously expensive, would represent an immense boost in his cultural wealth. In sheer prestige value, it would stand alone. The theater remained his property until his death, but in essence it was a semipublic place from the start. Even if he had donated it to the public it would have adhered to him—as it does still today, long after the physical annihilation of both the man and the edifice. Great urban monuments are "sticky" or culturally inalienable. As Marcel Mauss might have concluded, they are gifts and thus share the essence of the giver, who cannot shed himself of them (Mauss 1990: 14–16). Let us recall the Pantheon, which stuck to Agrippa even after a demolition and a complete redesign. In a very real sense, monuments were meant to reap rewards for the patron. By *producing* a conceptually unitary commodity of high prestige value, Pompey was also *consuming* the prestige along with all of its attendant advantages, such as expanded social networks.

FIGURE 6.4 Theater of Pompey in Rome, reconstructed view from A. Limongelli. 1937. "Parere dell'On. Prof. G. Q. Giglioli." *Capitolium* 12: 105–6.

Monuments therefore epitomize the principle of symbolic capital (Bourdieu 1977: 171–83). By the high Roman imperial period, such munificence was the norm in cities around the empire. This particular model of commoditizing public buildings reached its apogee, perhaps, among the shifting ranks of the urban elite in Asia Minor, where munificence was employed as a tool of political and social dominance (Gordon 1990: 224–31; Zuiderhoek 2009: 113–53). Public projects—bath–gymnasia, aqueducts, stadia, libraries, temples, etc.— needed only to satisfy normative expectations. But the process was reciprocal. Simultaneously, these gifts to the people were construed, by their popularity, to be the currency by which the public *gave back* to the patrons in the form of consent (Beetham 2013). By accepting and adopting architecture, they ratified it as a monument to the patron's legitimacy.

The visual character of these buildings conformed to a normative Romanness, clothed in the Classical columnar style that would have seemed familiar and comfortable to any visiting emperor and his senatorial entourage. Though certain architectural types (such as bath–gymnasia) bore a distinctly regional imprint, there was little to be seen in these buildings that might be understood as an architecture of hybridity—by which I mean a visible cultural negotiation between a dominant and a subordinate culture—let alone of resistance. Local elites in Asia assimilated readily to Roman rule, and that fact may in turn suggest that their clienteles were similarly assimilated. Other Roman provinces, however, tell different, and subtler, stories. The Agora at Athens, now in the province of Achaea, held a special place in Roman sentiment because of its outsize cultural and political legacy. But by the early Empire, most of the city's creative energies had dissipated, and its foreign overlords proceeded to cram the formerly open plaza with sacred and secular buildings reflecting Roman priorities, while moving commercial activities to a new agora nearby. All of this building or rebuilding—some of the "new" structures were old Classical temples uprooted and moved from sites well outside Athens—was calibrated to generate not just an artificial Roman nostalgia for the Greece of bygone days, but in subtler and more complex ways to grant the local Greeks an opportunity to temper their powerlessness and humiliation with a kind of memory theater that intensified local pride (Alcock 2002: 51–71). In particular, the hulking odeion of Agrippa (*c*. 15 BCE) and, east of the Agora, the library of Hadrian (*c*. 132–134 CE) not only served to enshrine cultural activities still critically important to the Athenians (oratory, music, philosophy, literature), but signaled by means of their elite patronage and monumentality (prestige value), utility (use value), and rare materials (prime value) that the city still merited its renown. The Augustan building program in particular evoked Athens' glorious military past and its tradition of Attic-style oratory, favored by the Roman elite at that time, who were often educated in Athens itself (Spawforth 2011: 59–86).

A true architecture of *resistance* to central Roman authority, though urgently sought, remains something of a chimera. What we find in abundance instead is hybrid architecture—especially in the western provinces—that reflects a careful balancing act among the elite local sponsors of urban projects. The tremendous investment of symbolic capital in the physical Romanization of cities and sanctuaries profited most when it exercised a subtle, calibrated pushback to excessive, top-down uniformity. The non-Roman customs and traditions of local populations responded best to Roman hegemony when the new architecture allowed breathing room for local rituals or customs—what Woolf calls structured differences (Woolf 1998; Revell 2009). Perhaps the best-known hybrid architecture of the western provinces, however, retains a much more powerful strand of traditional experience. Gallo-Roman temples in Britain, Gaul, and Germany were concentric structures that often featured a wraparound, shed-roofed veranda (Figure **6.5**). They bear little resemblance to the conventional elongated Roman-style temples favored by the military garrisons in these regions, yet their colonnades and masonry walls owe a debt to Roman practice.

FIGURE 6.5 Reconstructed Gallo-Roman temple, Archaeological Park of Martberg, Pommern, Germany. Photograph: D. Herdemerten (Hannibal21). Wikimedia Commons CC BY-SA 3.0. Modified. https://creativecommons.org/licenses/by-sa/3.0/ deed.en.

The core impulse animating every party in a negotiation is to maximize self-interest. In such contractual circumstances the objects of negotiation—in this case, architecture and the rituals that mold it—behave as barter or currency (Mattingly 2010: 223–6). Because native traditions are often most fiercely expressed in the religious sphere, the proliferation of Gallo-Roman temples in towns and the countryside can be perceived as a win–win outcome for both hegemon and the locals: a magnanimous concession to the natives from above and an uncontested pied-à-terre from below.

COGNITION AND MEMORY

According to Merlin Donald's influential evolutionary model of the development of human cognition and culture (Donald 1991, 2001), the third and final great developmental stage of the human mind, after mimesis (a largely prelinguistic mode) and mythic culture (which accompanies the development of language) is what he calls theoretic culture, a mode of representing knowledge and memory by means of external symbolic storage—cultural media, especially writing systems, that allowed symbolic information to be stored and transmitted in durable, independent formats. By enabling what was in effect a new mode of transcribing and recovering memory, such systems "transformed the collective architecture of cognition and changed how the larger human community thinks and remembers" (Donald 2001: 304).

Obviously, visual art is classified among these systems, especially if it tells a story; the earliest examples of symbolic representation on the walls of European caves predate writing systems by some 25,000 years. It is perhaps less immediately obvious, however, that architecture functioned in similar ways. It has recently been proposed that at the dawn of the Neolithic period in the Near East (*c.* 10,000 BCE), built space constituted the very earliest external symbolic storage system in that region (Watkins 2004). Sites such as Jerf el Ahmar and Göbekli Tepe, a site that merges dramatic, formalized stone structures with artistic representations in relief, may have functioned as theaters of memory, enculturating people to ritual life and institutions by shaping ritual space and infusing it with intelligible symbolic meaning. From the start, these sacred buildings were objects to think with.

How might architecture of more complex premodern societies, and specifically the Greek and Roman, to which this chapter is devoted, have acted as objects of deep enculturation? There are many ways in which architecture of the Classical word emulated its predecessors, especially in ritual contexts. But there may be no better embodiment of such theaters of memory than the Greek theater itself. Architecture, being powerfully attuned to the enactment of ritual and story, has always been theatrical or participatory, shaping collectivities of individuals to engage in communal behaviors. Architecture is also collaborative. A theater works with the performance. A church interacts with the liturgy. Built space gives shape to ritual, and vice versa. But it bears emphasizing how thoroughly the Greeks took this collaborative character to its logical conclusion, building works *exclusively* for performance. There was nothing obvious or inevitable about such a development, and it invites the question: "Which came first, the assembly or the assembly place?" The question may seem pointless, since both certainly coevolved; but we may nonetheless ask, if only as a thought experiment, how much of the *object of collective perception*—let us call it a play, a term that usefully aggregates a creative work in the abstract, and its performance in real time and space—was embodied in the *architectural object*, never to be replicated again. Reports or scripts of ancient performative activities such as drama, political meetings, court cases, etc., come down to us in disembodied form—at most, as a tenuous armature of the performance itself, which in its written form alone constitutes a very different and reduced experience. True, these ghosts can be animated afresh, but never in the same body (either architecture or fleshly human assembly) that hosted their genesis. In some fundamental sense, concept and material are mutually engaged, and thus mutually constitutive (Renfrew 2004). So let us momentarily envision, however imperfectly, the totality of Greek *theatron* (a performative experience) reconstituted within the *theatron* (the performative space).

For places of assembly, drama, and sport, Greek cities were the first to develop the kind of bowl architecture that still prevails today, especially in the athletic realm. Greek urban theaters, nestled in hillsides, might often have been somewhat isolated from the city core, but in certain contexts, such as late-Classical and Hellenistic Sicily, they stayed close to the city council house on account of their important roles in civic life and public identity (Marconi 2012). Like temples, they stood vacant most of the time, but when full, were densely animated by intersubjectivity (i.e. the shared subjective experience of perceptual objects: a play, a speech, actors, orators, and focal components of the building itself). This lent them an air of sacredness; dramatic performances were a kind of pilgrimage. They were also social filters, excluding certain sectors of Greek noncitizen society altogether, perhaps even women. Nothing is more object-like than a barrier, and to many urban subjects in ancient Greece, the sight of a theater implicitly conveyed the message "No entry." But as an engine of cognition for those privileged to attend, and as a powerful tool of social cohesion among this group, the theater as object was a very rich vessel for symbolic storage indeed. To the regular attendee, a theater is saturated with memories adhering to the place. Parts attached to it—a particular seat to whose occupant a famous actor tossed a lily, a graffito left by a musician, the edge of the right stage door where a comic actor broke his prosthetic phallus in a hurried exit, the spot near the left *parodos* where an ambitious choral dance fell apart—all contribute to cultural memory. This anchoring of experience in the place was enhanced by a Greco-Roman tendency to inscribe seats with the names of patrons who had bought or earned permanent occupancy (Sear 2006: 3–4; this tendency is more pronounced in the Roman period). Not only did such inscriptions attach the building by a thousand threads to real people, but they leapt out as *objecta* even to unlettered ordinary folk: move along, you don't belong here. In the Roman imperial theater, the seating hierarchy was rigid and complex, sequestering almost everyone in a particular seating sector according to social, age, and gender status (Rawson 1987).

This kind of coincident inclusion and exclusion is easy to understand; modern sports stadiums and concert halls are full of such places, segregated by rank, privilege, or bloc identity. Yet like a Fenway Park (where, on the nights Pedro Martinez pitched, nobody could displace the bloc of Dominicans in the outfield bleachers documenting each strikeout with a "K" placard attached to the back wall) or an Ebbets Field (yes, the ghosts of dead venues are real, too), few places are more intersubjective than a theater. Suppose, additionally, that the seat in which you caught the lily (perhaps memory embellishes!) was unnumbered, as most pre-Roman seating schemes probably were. You might then enlist the building itself as a reckoning tool, either (if you have sharply qualitative memories) by triangulating to a remembered vantage point by sight, or by identifying nearby habitual attendees, or (if your memory is more quantitative) by counting rows up from the orchestra and pacing off the horizontal distance from an aisle. In either case, you are relying on the theater-as-object to perform an embodied cognitive task, reinforcing or refining a memory that it helped to produce in the first place. Such problem-solving—like organizing Scrabble tiles or trying out puzzle pieces—is distributed between our minds and the material environment, and can only be realized by interaction between both (Clark 1997: 63–7). Other veteran observers around you might reinforce, modify, and supplement your recollections further (whether internally or interactively), taking cues from the surrounding building and its habitual occupants to burnish old memories even as they gather to generate new ones.

Implicitly and explicitly, the architecture of Greek theaters shaped the experience. The rigidly Euclidean conical form of the late Classical and Hellenistic theater was textured with parallel rows of curved benches. The pattern reinforced the volume; but even enlivened with the richer texture of densely arrayed bodies, its textile-like regularity deflected attention toward the seams: the radial and circumferential aisles, which became avenues of linear motion during interludes. In turn, the radial aisles drew the eye to the hub, the circular orchestra, and the rectangular stage and its colonnaded, tile-roofed scene building. Theaters were bounded objects to be sure, but they also encompassed what have been called sensorial assemblages, "a co-presence of heterogenous elements such as bodies, things, substances, affects, memories, information, and ideas" (Hamilakis 2013: 126). Sight and sound are naturally the most important senses in venues of spectacle. But other senses could play a role in generating memory, too. You might only experience the daily convection breezes of your coastal town by climbing that particular hillside at showtime, and those breezes might be intensified by the theater's design. Smells activate memories the most acutely, and Greek theaters were full of them. Food and wine, of which there was plenty (Ashby 1999: 119), body odor, offal burned on the altar by the stage during the opening ceremony—all would activate a kind of memory that, even if more generic, could be intense, like modern associations of popcorn with movie theaters or of deep-fried batter with the state fair.

Let us momentarily consider a more implicit kind of architectural cognition, what might be called connotation or secondary function (Eco 1997). Compared to analogues in many non-Western societies (Tilley 1999), metaphor hangs lightly on Greek and Roman architecture, but it nevertheless plays a significant role. To a culture so heavily invested in containers (woven, ceramic, stone) both for utility and cultural identity, the theater's form could hardly have failed to evoke a bowl or a basket. As with wine lees in an amphora, hummeled barley in a pounding mortar, ore in a washery, sediment in a cistern, or clay in a levigation vat, the theater's denser cultural layers settled toward the bottom: orchestra and stage. Contending with the fashionable aristocrats seated in the lower tiers, the stage and orchestral architecture were obviously the objects of most intent focus during the performance. As settings for the action, they intensified the theatrical experience by drawing attention downward and centripetally, filtering out the mundane and ordinary (e.g. backstage activity, city life outside, the normal movements and sounds of the audience) and highlighting the drama with the starkly geometric framing structures. The scene building, which over time acquired the aspect of palatial architecture, mimicked the cultural setting of elites and their entourages (Vitruvius, *On Architecture* 5.7). A weighted boom for airlifting *dei ex machina* over the stage also added to the shared fantasy (Ashby 1999: 81–7).

Paradoxically, these focal nodes of material embodiment, complementing the bodies and voices of the actors, conveyed the mind to a faraway, long-ago place. They did what metaphor does; literally, the Greek verbal root of the word (*metapherein*) means "to carry beyond," to transport. As such, they enacted human imagination to a degree that is rare among other kinds of architecture by collaborating with the staged action in real time. Tellingly, the word *skene* arrived at its multifarious and often abstract modern meanings by way of the builder's art: meaning, most elementally, "tent" (i.e. a lightweight, movable pavilion consisting probably of fabric stretched over a wooden frame or curtains suspended from ropes), it came to denote the stage building. In the late Hellenistic and Roman periods it developed into an elaborate, symmetrical colonnaded backdrop with three doors: the *scaenae frons*. By metonymy, the word *skene* came to represent not just stage action but almost any sequence of actions *confined within a framework of potentialities*. A scene, in all its meanings, comes with an implicit constraining architecture. We have the Greeks to thank for that.

PATTERN, ORNAMENT, AND STYLE

Art historians and anthropologists habitually discuss form and ornament as distinct entities, though obviously these domains have important interdependencies (Gombrich 1979; Gell 1998: 73–95, 155–220). This is probably because the types of objects they analyze tend to fall into two categories: (1) objects long familiar to ethnography—that is, functional objects (including tattooed human bodies) with elaborate surface patterns; and (2) architecture, ranging from the Gothic to the present, caught up in the ideological skirmishes of modernism. But it could be argued that pre-Medieval monumental architecture presents a challenge to this dichotomy, if only by blurring the boundaries between domains.

According to Alfred Gell's systematic theory of art and agency, art objects have *indexes*, which enable actions between an agent and a patient (Gell 1998: 13–14). These actions might involve the object's creation or its reception. A pattern physically applied to an object, he argues, is an index, even if it has no prototype (i.e. is abstract and does not represent anything). Any part of that pattern—what he calls a motif—can be a subordinate index nested within the governing index, acting upon another part, as when a red field "pushes" against a blue one; thus agents and patients can be things as well as persons. In patterns, these repeated acts generate the appearance of animation, by which the mind of the patient (in this case the viewer) seeks in some manner to register the characteristics of symmetry (reflection, translation, rotation, glide reflection) generating the pattern. But the mind soon finds itself entrapped by the intricacies; thus emerges a fundamental property of social relations, the state of "unfinished business," a critical component of desirability and value. This tendency to become stuck or entranced in a pattern he calls *tackiness*, or cognitive adhesiveness, and it provides the logic behind a common kind of apotropaic art: labyrinthine patterns intended to snare evil spirits like flypaper in a doorway.[4]

I choose to focus here on pattern in Classical architecture rather than form for the simple reason that the latter is far too variable, and too complex, to be addressed in a short chapter. Further, I believe that public architecture of the Classical world—what even a casual viewer would identify as characteristically Greek or Roman—has more to do with pattern than form. Columns, steps, antefixes, dentils, modillions, triglyphs, metopes, coffers—all these familiar classical features, and many more, were defined by their repetition in rows or ranks (Figure 6.6). We might notice, too, that the first two do not sit exclusively, or even comfortably, under the heading "ornament." Nor are all these features equally abstract. Antefixes often represented the heads of gods, heroes, lions, etc. And a long-standing theoretical tradition maintains that some of these elements—triglyphs in particular—are "explanatory accent" mimicking bygone structural features (Gombrich 1979: 176; Vitruvius 4.2.2). Like Doric triglyphs, modillions and dentils (features of the Ionic and Corinthian orders) can also legitimately be called ornamental vestiges in stone of the exposed ends of roof and ceiling beams drawn from an older tradition when temple exteriors displayed the terminal ends of timbers. Coffers, too, express a grid of beams set longitudinally and transversely across the ceiling (Figure 6.7).

Whereas (for example) a high English Gothic facade can be characterized as textile-like in its unrelenting richness, you might think of Classical ornament as more articulated and more indicative of architectural form. For example, it generally foregoes expansive patterns in sheets, relying instead on linear moldings to frame edges and openings. The objective is to articulate the volumes and voids of the underlying form by outlining them, a general strategy for clarifying the perceived object's essential nature; by emphasizing its general form, it accentuates its function and status (Boas 1955: 57; Gombrich 1979: 209; Swift 2009: 8). In the Roman period, this tendency effloresced into three-dimensional coffering, one of the most memorable architectural effects we have inherited from antiquity. In its simplest form, a grid of recessed squares was thrust up into a cylinder segment to articulate a barrel vault; but already by the

FIGURE 6.6 Section of entablature from the Temple of Vespasian in Rome, now displayed in the Tabularium. Photograph: R. Taylor.

FIGURE 6.7 Modern restoration of the porch ceiling of the Maison Carrée, Nîmes. Photograph: M. Kraft. Wikimedia Commons CC BY-SA 3.0. Modified. https://creativecommons.org/licenses/by-sa/3.0/deed.en.

late second century BCE, that design was elaborated into annular (ring-shaped) barrel vaults (Figure **6.8**). There followed domes, half-domes, cross vaults, etc., decked out in geometric patterns to clarify the volumes with a reticulated skin. On domes or half-domes in particular radial coffering can simulate rotary motion as the mind apprehends one radial chain of coffers and tests its sameness with its neighbor (Gombrich 1979: 137–8). The effect is especially pronounced when the chains are introduced on a bias, as with grids of hexagons or diamonds. The appraising eye urges the vault to turn like a pinwheel (Figure **6.9**).

   The colonnading of space was surely the predominant feature of Classical architectural design, advancing relentlessly over the millennium between the Archaic period and late antiquity. From the seventh century BCE onward, freestanding stoas appeared along one side of an open space in Greek cities or

FIGURE 6.8 Annular barrel vault at the Sanctuary of Fortuna Primigenia, Palestrina, Italy. Photograph: R. Taylor.

FIGURE 6.9 Semidome vault of the apse of the Temple of Venus and Roma, Rome. Photograph: Panoramio. Wikimedia Commons CC BY 3.0. Modified. https://creativecommons.org/licenses/by/3.0/deed.en.

sanctuaries. The low, rhythmic facades of stoas in the Classical period could run to remarkable lengths, sometimes exceeding 100 m. A few were amplified with a second story of lighter columns. Behind the main facade, an inner order typically ran down the building's axis. Its columns aligned with their outer correlates to support transverse beams, perhaps further articulated with coffers. On a bright Mediterranean day, the stoa's inner geometries throbbed with rhythmic striations, each varying in scale, texture, and pattern (Figure **6.10**). In the Hellenistic period, as peristyles developed around courtyards, it became the norm in public architecture to employ ranks of columns abundantly, often to define enclosures (Coulton 1976: 39–74). Roman taste carried the tendency to new extremes, not only enveloping fora, sanctuaries, bath palaestras, and gardens in colonnades, but also lining streets with them (MacDonald 1986: 32–66; Ball 2001: 256–73; Frakes 2009).

More than any other component of architecture, the colonnade embodies an ontological paradox: it is simultaneously form and ornament. Form, because it resolves into distinct structural supports; ornament, because when it is foreshortened into receding bands it ensnares the eye with its rigidly repeating pattern—sometimes white stone embellished with fluting, sometimes smooth shafts of colored marble, bases and capitals in contrasting white, and so forth.

FIGURE 6.10 Reconstructed Stoa of Attalos, Athens. Photograph: Wikimedia Commons CC BY-SA 4.0. Modified. https://creativecommons.org/licenses/by-sa/4.0/deed.en.

Theoretically, this ambiguity is significant. Few modern theories of visual or material culture—and there are many—concede that the categories of form (let alone *structural* form!) and ornament can claim the same material index. The exaggerated dichotomy seems to be inherited from Leon Battista Alberti, the Renaissance architect and architectural theorist, who famously declared that "while beauty is an intrinsic and almost natural quality which inheres in the entire structure of the organism we call beautiful, ornament has the appearance of an accessory, an adjunct, rather than a natural attribute" (*On the Art of Building* 6.2.93v; my translation). But modernist dogma, memorably expressed in Adolf Loos's equally famous 1908 manifesto, "Ornament and Crime," pried the two categories even further apart.[5] This persistent error seems to reflect a lazy dismissal of phenomenal experience simply by failing to consider the variability of effect an architectural feature can have depending on proximity and point of view. The ambiguity seems to be rooted in scale and perspective: up close, columns are formal components of their structures, but from a distance or an oblique angle they become pattern, while not necessarily losing their formal character. Consequently they do not induce what cognitive scientists call perceptual reversals, as with the famous rabbit–duck optical illusion. Colonnades are more akin to *hybrid images*, which activate a pronounced shift in the perceptual impression of an image as the viewing distance changes (Oliva et al. 2006). But even this analogy is unsatisfactory, since we are dealing with movement between two categories of perceptual response (form and ornament) rather than between two percepts within a single category (e.g. two-dimensional forms of an elephant and of a leopard). There is nothing illusional about the shift, nor does it require a jolt of conscious effort to switch modes. It is simply a matter of seeing the forest *and* the trees, either simultaneously or in succession.

Surely the colonnade in its vast diffusion can be understood, in some sense, as a critical component of *style*. Quite apart from the diverting fact that the very word is derived from the Greek *stylos*, "column" (whence the Latin *stylus*, the writing tool, and thus a manner of writing), a discourse on architecture in the Classical style would be meaningless without colonnades. In the humanities and social sciences, style is usually seen as a manner of action characteristic of a particular individual, group, or (if direct human agency seems out of reach) culturally specific time and place. In material culture, then, objects should in some sense express that manner in concrete terms (Bourdieu 1977: 72–87). I do not intend to rehearse the long and diverse debate over the meanings and instantiations of style. Suffice it to say that, with regard to *group* styles at least, I find Ian Hodder's characterization of style as a historical quality particularly compelling. "How can the individual, contextual event be linked to a general way of doing?" he asks (Hodder 1990). Hodder observes that style is a never-ending process of particular instantiations of a general class of events that encompass this "way of doing." Each event is interpretive; and by interpreting it modifies its context, thereby influencing all subsequent events and, by necessity, the whole category. Nevertheless, "style does appear to create a fixed present, an unchanging 'now.' It privileges the spatial over the temporal, appearing to halt time" (Hodder 1990: 46). Style can and does reflect wider generalities (e.g. stiletto heels reflect femininity; Western societies stand for freedom of speech), but those generalities can mask inherent contradictions (stilettos signal both delicacy and ferocity; one person's free speech can subvert another's). Interpretation may try to resolve such contradictions, but never with complete success; "the 'whole' remains partly mythical" (Hodder 1990: 48). Hodder calls on archaeologists to interpret style as social action, but with express attention to such inherent contradictions.

Could colonnades be seen as a test case for dialectic within the whole? Their sheer ubiquity, and their domination of public urban architecture over the Helleno-Roman world—some five million square kilometers of territory—and more than a millennium, challenges Hodder's notion of the "fixed present" within a style. What is confronting us, of course, is a hierarchy of styles. Within the universal columnar style, as we might call it, fall countless substyles: regional or temporal variants, individual hands, local materials, etc. Even a single block-long street colonnade could be built in several styles, each separately sponsored.[6] Moreover, the many contextual applications of columns, what we might call types, from private gardens to war memorials, tombs, baths, and streets, refract our interpretive hindsight further.

Consider colonnaded avenues, a feature of the Roman imperial period. As colonnades gradually conquered urban streetscapes, especially in eastern cities, the older, more variegated facade architecture underlying them was denatured. Individuality—and thus the rich indexicality of shopfronts and entrances as unitary and semiautonomous objects—was suppressed, creating a second paradox. As the street itself became easier to read, as its rhythms invited pedestrians forward by articulating intermediate or distant goals, the side-objects were obscured in the shadows behind a screen of columns (sometimes in the East, the street itself was roofed, but not the sidewalks, in effect forming a bazaar) (Ball 2001: 261–73). In itself the transformation of streets into colonnaded avenues seems a banality to modern analysis, a commonplace in textbooks of Roman architecture; but in fact it reflects a profound social trend. Literally and figuratively, the overlaying of a city's autonomous indexes with a vastly simplified hyper-index signals an attendant simplification of power structures and a strict consolidation of social control in many cities from the second to the fourth centuries CE, especially in the east, where street front colonnades were most common. The superrich, in their awesome munificence, found it convenient to cut off channels of agency once available to the mercantile class.

The discomfort that such patronage projects could excite is glimpsed in a speech of Dio Chrysostom, in which he bitterly condemns the resistance he met when local tradesmen learned that a colonnaded avenue he was planning to sponsor in his hometown of Prusa would displace their businesses (Oration 47). Dio's case may have been anomalous, however; most merchants and artisans were probably pleased to go upscale and grease their business potential on the gloss of opulence. Yet to judge from the evidence of inscriptions and architectural remains around the empire, once colonnades were in place, the storefront proprietors cluttered them up, devising compensatory strategies to revivify the individual agency of their shops by expanding their operations and merchandise out onto the covered sidewalk of the colonnade itself. Businesses fronting on covered walkways routinely do the same today, choking the path with furniture, partitions, and stuff, anything to slow down and draw in potential customers.[7] This blurring of purpose, along with the colonnade's formal dubiety as a liminal zone between open and enclosed spaces, lent it a metaphorical *moral* ambiguity; on the one hand it was a customary setting of social disorder, a habitual hangout of prostitutes and lowlifes, and on the other it was the highly cultured venue of refined philosophic peripatesis (Frakes 2009: 27–37).

Perhaps, then, columnar architecture does reflect a frozen moment in time, marking the rise of inequality in many parts of the eastern empire. Yet this "moment" can be said to have developed and endured over centuries, intensifying in some areas and relaxing in others.

CONCLUSION

I return momentarily to our cultural scale of physical mass, cohesion, and fixity—our Western notion that objects are things that we can, at least notionally, manipulate bodily. The need for such a cultural category is probably related to the commercial importance of physically moving, trading, and holding things of value. Buildings and constructed space, on the other hand, fall within the broader category of objects, whether physical or conceptual, that are conditioned by a property of the subject: curiosity, interest, fear, remorse, contempt, etc. Conditioned objects are far less likely to be purely incidental than simple ones: our language easily accommodates the random object, but not the random object of desire, attention, inquiry, seeking, or awe. In other words, architecture and urban space are more likely to display a relationship with their sentient subjects that goes beyond the purely casual. While it is true, as Eco remarks, that architectural discourse is experienced inattentively by most people, he also observes that architecture fluctuates between a degree of indifference to how it is used and a strong coercive streak that compels us to live in a certain way (Eco 1997: 187). The prospect of the unkempt bric-a-brac of a permanent bazaar habitually encrusting the cool and rational geometries of street colonnades in eastern Roman cities exemplifies this paradox beautifully. Whether we care or not, the built space around us, through which we walk, in whose shadows we seek relief from the sun, whose streets we perforce follow, is charged with contingency. And so it was in antiquity. Things could, and did, constantly happen between people and architecture because architecture set the scene for their everyday lives, enclosing their activities and channeling their movements. Every moment in and around buildings was, and is, an encounter.

CHAPTER SEVEN

Bodily Objects

CAROLINE VOUT

INTRODUCTION

When Vesuvius erupted in 79 CE, many of Pompeii's inhabitants fled, bags of coins, jewels, silver amulets, and saucepans with them. This was not simply about salvaging materials that could be converted into cash in the event of losing their homes, nor about preserving the memory of home, nor even, in the case of the amulets, about protecting themselves from danger and securing safe passage. It was more elemental than that. It was about not being alone, naked, bereft of the kinds of objects that had accompanied them since birth, objects that made them exceptional and normal, and connected them to a more manageable, exploitable earth, at a given time and place but also *in* time and space, than that witnessed by the intense heat and volcanic debris. In grounding them, these objects comforted them, gave them something to live for, and confirmed, by demanding that their bodies carry and covet, a very particular physicality, not just a "measure of security" in an apocalyptic moment, but an "extension of self."[1] Some of these objects may have been handed down or imported, others produced locally, possibly by their wearers. All would have qualified as *"res"* ("property," "wealth," "supplies," "matter," "facts," and "deeds"). *"Res"* is at the root of our word "reality."

Today archaeologists are well-versed in the idea of objects as active agents that have causal as well as symbolic power that helps human bodies with "embodiment" (feeding their natural appetites, focusing their gaze, and amplifying their sense of belly, limbs, digits, and skin surface and thus their place in the world) through the enactment of routines (whether eating a meal, dedicating an offering in a temple, or brushing their hair). They accept that by exercising, or interacting with, the body, objects ultimately define the body as more than a living, breathing composite made up of groups of cells, and give it a substance that cannot easily be collapsed into discourse, deflated by death, or rendered only in the present tense. As well as shaping a person's identity by assertion or obfuscation, objects, especially those worn on, handled, or consumed by the body, promise mediation. They are, in a sense, a "gift exchange" in the making—which is why ancient sanctuaries were crammed with textiles, bronzes, terracottas, *fibulae*, and so on, and why statues of Greek and Roman gods so often have attributes. These attributes give them a commensurability with humans, as much as signaling divine distinction (see also above p. 17).

The ancients, too, understood the role that such "bodily objects" played in these relationships, relationships that were the basis of the networks (social, intellectual, economic) that converted nature to culture: we will see this in their representations of humans as well as of gods, and in the grave goods that accompany the dead; we also find it in their vocabulary. The adjective "*lautus*," meaning "elegant," "well-dressed," or "splendid" in appearance or conduct, comes from the verb "*lavare*" (to wash), which might seem counterintuitive until one realizes that again this is an admission of the fact that routines such as bathing, and the objects associated with bathing, such as oil flasks and strigils, "tool" the body, converting it from its natural state to something more refined, an object, arguably, in its own right (see Olson 2008: 7). It is a reminder that cosmetics, too, are part of this chapter's material, and it preempts us exploring why strigils, and *aryballoi* and *lekythoi* (both of these containers for oil or perfume), were often buried with the deceased. When the Roman writer Petronius introduces the obscenely wealthy freedman Trimalchio to his reader as a "*lautissimus homo*" (a *very* or *excessively* "*lautus*" kind of guy), he shows us that the term signals taste, and taste signals discrimination and class (Petronius, *Satyrica* 26). Bodily objects are inevitably political. When does making an effort slide into overdoing it, and culture slide into tyranny? It should come as no surprise to discover that those objects associated most closely with the body (clothes, jewelry, and food) were policed by ancient sumptuary legislation (see above p. 145). Such is their possible affect that they have to be treated with caution.

Not that they are any more stable than the bodies they help to situate. A weapon found in a barracks is a different object, with a different remit and potential to act, from a weapon found in a tomb or sanctuary. Even if all are similar in size, material, and decoration, only in the first scenario does the weapon have the capacity to kill and to affirm the fighter's masculinity. In the others, it is arguably reduced to having only symbolic capital,[2] increasing the prestige of the deceased or the dedicator in ways that ask neither for the job description of "warrior," nor for an audience. Indeed, swords found in geometric tombs were often bent before deposition, rendering them, in the killing sense, useless (Lloyd 2015). Occasionally, as is also the case with strigils, weapons accompany female skeletons: for example in the fourth-century BCE Tomb II, the "Tomb of Philip," at Vergina (an unlooted tomb that contains an unusual wealth and variety of weapons, some of them, in all likelihood, older than the occupants were when they died), where the antechamber already houses the remains of a young woman together with a brooch, diadem, greaves, spears, a *gorytos* (combined quiver and bow holder), and pectoral (Salminen 2017).

Exceptional this may be, but it makes the idea of the object as an "extension of the self" more complex, querying the nature of the interaction that the phrase "bodily objects" implies. At our most skeptical, we might wonder whether we should expect femininity from a female corpse (or masculinity from a male), or any residual masculinity or femininity to weigh as it did in life. For all that large numbers of Greeks and Romans believed in an afterlife (blessed or enduring of punishment), exacting harsh penalties on those who desecrated corpses and going to great efforts, especially in Rome, to integrate the dead into family and civic structures, the pollution that resulted from contact with a corpse marked its othering. Does a cadaver or pile of bone or ash have any embodiment left?[3] This question is already live in Plato, when Socrates claims that his dead body is not him (that nothing of him remains in it);[4] so, too, in Aristotle, for whom a body without a soul is only homonymously a body (Aristotle, *De anima* 412b20–5). Although grave goods are regularly used to illustrate "'daily life', handicraft and art production" (Näser 2013: 643), we might do better to see bodily objects of the living and the dead as distinct, if overlapping, categories.

What follows pursues these implications, beginning neither with real bodies nor with small finds, but, unfashionably perhaps (given that scholarship regularly pits representation of the body against corporeal experience, and often sees "art" as an obfuscatory category),[5] with monumental sculpture. Starting with figurative sculptures, which derive meaning from the objects they wear and hold (cf. above p. 130 on the Prima Porta statue of Augustus), sometimes offering them out to the viewer as if to transcend the distance between them, gives us a window onto how their makers conceived of what objects do to bodies (their own and other people's) and what bodies do to objects, and at different moments in antiquity. The view provided is admittedly ideal and partial, but one that enables us nonetheless to embrace an object's aesthetics (its style and form) as part of its expansive nexus of affordances (which not only appeal to vision, but also to the panoply of sense perception),[6] and one that emphasizes that the wearing of jewelry, fabric, and perfume has the power to objectify all subjects, blurring the boundaries between object and person, representation and reality. Several of our case studies in the next section are also funerary, bridging the gap between what I have suggested might be two distinct, if not discrete, object worlds. The first of these case studies is from Archaic and Classical Greece, the next from imperial Rome, and the last from late antiquity, as we acknowledge the importance of change—that bodily objects are necessarily objects in society. Taking their lead, our second section moves inside the tomb to see how object agency operates in a closed environment.

THE CHANGING RELATIONSHIP OF BODIES AND OBJECTS

(i) Archaic and Classical Greece

In the sixth and early fifth centuries BCE, the Greek landscape was populated by an army of freestanding sculptures today known as *kouroi* (youths) and *korai* (maidens). All of them are stiff and frontal, very much part of the block from which they were hewn, yet most of them smiling as though cognizant of their liberation from the stone and their role in a transactional universe. Whereas the male figures tend to be nude,[7] their clenched fists and bulky thighs proof enough of the body modification that comes of physical exercise, the females are exquisitely coiffured and dressed (Figure **7.1**), many of them with elaborate jewels and headgear, and many clutching an animal, fruit, or flower to their chest, or presenting it in a bargaining gesture.[8] Functioning as dedications in sanctuaries or as grave markers, these statues were protagonists and, themselves, transactional objects, the aim of which was to delight mortals and immortals, easing the ontological gap between man and god, earth and Hades, by extending an arm or, in the case of *kouroi*, a left leg, as though always promising a crossing.

It is the *korai*, however, that are our focus here: their object overload does more than comment on the affective reach of objects in religious or commemorative contexts, and on the particular objectification of women (who, as they offer their gift, also offer their own bodies, sometimes drawing attention to them by tugging at their skirts). It reveals the importance of bodily objects in Greek life more generally, as markers of status, bringers of pleasure (and we think here not just of visual pleasure, but of the feel of the fabric on the skin as signaled by their skirt-tugging), and as financial and technological capital. As representations of young women, several of them showing off their belts or *zonai*, the *korai* are virgins about to be "undone": it is as though they wear their dowry. In so doing, they enforce the close connection between "good wives," paragons such as Penelope, and weaving (see above p. 92 on weaving). Are we to infer that that they have woven their clothing, and will dedicate it to Artemis or Athena before their wedding (Lee 2015: 207–11)? Entertaining this idea is important, if only to remind us that the ritual removal of bodily objects

FIGURE 7.1 Funerary statue of the kore Phrasikleia, *c.* 550–40 BCE, Merenda, Attica. National Museum of Athens inv. no. 4889. Photograph: National Archaeological Museum, Athens (V. von Eickstedt) © Hellenic Ministry of Culture and Sports/ Archaeological Receipts Fund.

was as crucial a concept as the adoption of certain attributes (we might add the dedication of a lock of hair by boys and girls to mark their coming of age, or, in Rome, a boy's removal, on reaching sexual maturity, of the *toga praetexta* and amulet or *bulla* [Sebesta 1994: 47] and the protection it provided). Certainly, their clothing is ingeniously draped, strikingly decorated with paint and buttons in anticipation almost of the finely woven, richly patterned garments worn by brides on their wedding day. Any implied effort of production is echoed in the complexities of carrying off clothes so complex as to "defy attempts to explain and categorize them" (Stieber 2004: 68) and hairstyling so sophisticated as to suggest the wearing of wigs and extensions (Stieber 2004: 63–8).

These female figures are impossibly beautiful. To treat their clothes or jewels as evidence for real *chitons* (dresses) or *himatia* (cloaks) is to miss the point.[9] They are excessive, as those *korai* found, for example, on the Athenian Acropolis or Samian Sanctuary of Hera (goddess of marriage) perhaps needed to be if they were to pay maximum honor to the goddess: real textiles are among the dedications made and commonly listed in Greek temple inventories (e.g. see Cleland 2005). They are also exotic, the elaborateness of their loose hair and the clinginess of some of their robes appearing to owe as much to Egyptian precedents as to contemporary Greek fashion (Stieber 2004: 64–5, 69–70). For the few that functioned as funerary markers, this surplus of detail not only pinpointed the honorand's individuality (only *she* wore this combination of accoutrements, all of them unique). It also assumed a productive redundancy—more summative than sensible or permissible in this life. During the Thesmophoria, a festival for married women, celebrants were expected to dress modestly, leaving their jewels and most alluring clothes at home (Parker 2005: 278): an (admittedly Hellenistic) inscription from the Peloponnese lays out careful clothing regulations for everyone involved in the mystery cult of Demeter, but with particular attention to the decoration and total monetary value of female adornment. They could wear no gold, rouge, white lead, hairband, or plaits, and no shoes except for those made of sacred leather or felt.[10]

A funerary *kore* such as that of Phrasikleia (Figure 7.1) stands defiant in a carved necklace, bracelets (each set with four stones), earrings from which hang tear-shaped pendants, and crown. Compared to many *korai*, her tunic is simply draped, an effortlessness offset by its meander design, rosettes, and ornamental belt, and by the figure's sandals that again appear to be set with stones. The fact that these and her jewelry are carved, without the drill holes necessary for the metal attachments we find on non-funerary *korai* (one of the Acropolis *korai* has its bronze bangle completely preserved), puts them, despite their similarity to actual small finds, in a different category: any enchantment of technology evidenced here is that of the sculptor, Aristion of Paros, whose name is recorded on the extant base, more than it is that of the metalworking that had born witness to prosperity and trade since at least the Homeric epics.[11] These are avowedly not smeltable assets; nor are they the kinds of jewels that were buried in tombs or hidden in hoards. They are "of the body" in a more visceral way, undetachable outcrops.[12] Phrasikleia's headdress, necklace, and earrings are made up of fruits and flowers that echo the lotus bud she holds in her left hand. The identity of this vegetation, and the symbolism that any of it brings with it, is less important than its cumulative blossoming: none of it is an attribute as the bow once held by the contemporaneous "Piraeus Apollo" statue (National Archaeological Museum, Athens, inv. no. 4645) was an attribute. Rather than signal impending action, this blossoming turns a column-like body into a self-contained visual field, unified and rarified by surface patterning.

Compared to the *korai* from the Athenian Acropolis or from Samos, which hug the object they are holding as though cherishing it or make as if to hand it over (thereby rendering it personal property of some sort), Phrasikleia's flower is delicately clasped in front of her and aligned with the center of her body in a way that has her focus not on any viewer, but on herself. Whereas it is assumed that the others' doves, hares, and so on are destined for a particular goddess, this flower, and its replication in Phrasikleia's adornment, is more enigmatic. If she is going to do anything with it, the implication is that she will sniff it (for objects stimulate smell as well as sight and touch), thereby restoring a sense of interiority, if also isolating her further. In the *Odyssey*, lotuses make one forget one's place in the world (Homer, *Odyssey* 9.91–7; Stieber 2004: 166). This distancing is entirely appropriate: as the inscription notes, the statue is a "σῆμα" or "token" of Phrasikleia, and in a far more urgent sense than any *kore* is a worshipper. For all her finery, there will be no wedding, no maturation: the inscription continues, "'*kore*' shall I always be called, having received this name from the gods in place of marriage," the verb to "receive" (λαγχάνειν) meaning really "to obtain one's portion."[13] Permanent deferral is her only rightful possession.

Might it be more accurate to talk of "transformation," and of the ways in which objects have the capacity to take people out of themselves, are themselves sometimes "out of this world?" If her necklace is made up of pomegranates, as some scholars have conjectured (e.g. Sourvinou-Inwood 1995: 249), then it supports the sense that she is no longer the Phrasikleia she was in life, but one with Demeter's daughter Persephone, also known as "Kore." According to myth, Persephone was abducted by Hades to be Queen of the Underworld, leaving her mother too bereft to do her day job and secure a good harvest. At her father Zeus' insistence, Persephone was released so as to restore the earth's fertility, but not before she had eaten pomegranate seeds that demanded that she return periodically (and here we add "taste" to our list of senses), spending part of the year on earth and the other part below.[14] As well as strengthening existing hierarchies, objects ingestible and otherwise have the capacity not just to refine who we are, but also (as sumptuary laws appreciate) to make us grow in girth and stature. In Phrasikleia's case, they press at the final frontier between life and death, mortal and immortal.

Like the *korai* who offer animals to the gods, the Persephone story reminds us that divinities also demanded objects, and not just attributes, temples, or treasuries to advertise their particular prowess, but consumables to taste and to smell as at the sacrifice. This is less obviously about verifying divine presence on earth (compare the trace elements on the Turin Shroud or Poseidon's footprints in *Iliad* 13.71–2 and Platt 2011: 58) than it is about maintaining the fiction of god's body as something more than a literary construct that then inspired sculptors to make images of Zeus and Athena; it is about giving that god, if not the physiologically entrenched urges that define Aristotle's humans, then the kind of sensory experiential knowledge attributed by Christians to God the Son. For all that Greek gods dined on a special diet of nectar and ambrosia (and we think of the nymph Calypso helping herself to these, serving them to the messenger god Hermes, but offering Odysseus, whom she must send back into society, the food "that mortals eat"; *Odyssey* 5.92–7, 195–9) and had ichor in their veins, they also derived crucial nourishment from the sacrifices offered them, angered by Prometheus' attempt to trick them into mistaking bones for meat (Hesiod, *Theogony* 535–7; Osborne 2016). From a theological perspective, Persephone's eating of the pomegranate seeds is proof that cosmic order, with its cycle of seasons, depended on object sharing.

For about fifty years after the Persian Wars (490–78 BCE), figural grave markers more or less disappear in Attica, as they, too, succumb to sumptuary legislation. Even after this legislation is relaxed, no new *korai* or *kouroi* are made: it is possible that their form's association with sixth-century BCE elites made them explosively retrograde. The stelai erected from 430 BCE onward, some of them expensive and others more modest, uphold an interest in bodily objects but outweigh the emphasis on individuals with a penchant for domestic groups. So the stele of Sostratos from *c.* 375–50 BCE, where a young man, accompanied by a slave boy with an aryballos, holds a strigil (New York, Metropolitan Museum of Art, 08.258.41), or the now well-known stele of Hegeso from the end of the fifth century BCE, who, accompanied by a servant, sits on a chair with her feet on a footstool and a jewelry box on her knee (Figure 7.2). Here, the gazes of both women (their differential positions in society revealed by the relative complexity/simplicity of their drapery and headgear, as well as by their relative size) show that the seated figure was fingering a painted necklace or garland that has since faded from the marble. Adornment is now performing a different function: far from being excessive, it is "on point," and, together with the dainty footstool, supplants the status that comes of owning objects (a status here encapsulated by the slaves)[15] with the status that comes of having the leisure to enjoy them.

Just as the oily contents of any aryballos have us think of the anointing of the corpse as well as an athlete's preparation for competition, so the chair serves to enthrone Hegeso, turning her into a deity to be adored, and her servant into the *"kore"* that offers the gift. From the start of the fifth century BCE, when sculptors began experimenting with strategies other than frontality and its direct address so as to create parallel universes and opportunities for self-conscious viewing (where does the intimate moment depicted on the Hegeso stele leave the viewer?), more nuanced visual narratives followed, and, with them, a

FIGURE 7.2 Cast of stele of Hegeso (erected *c.* 400 BCE in the Kerameikos, Athens). Cambridge, Museum of Classical Archaeology inv. no. 206. Photograph: Susanne Turner © The Museum of Classical Archaeology, University of Cambridge.

stronger sense of what it meant for a figure to perform an identity as young, old, Athenian, non-Athenian, man, woman, and, more specifically, as athlete, general, *erastes*, *eromenos*, and so on through the specifics of bodily objects and gesture (Elsner 2006). As we move into the culturally diverse Roman Empire, the affective experiences that shape these "attitudes" continue, becoming, if anything, more urgent in late antiquity when the threat of invasion combined with Christian conversion changes the relation of body (human and divine) and object forever. Throughout, and as a legacy, in part, of the Hellenistic kingdoms, we find a greater emphasis on job descriptions and the technology and ceremony associated with these, allowing us to privilege other kinds of "bodily object," the experience of tools in the hand, of food in the belly, of wine on the head.

(ii) Rome

If it is overindulgence in jewelry that excites us, we might be best looking to the female funerary reliefs of Palmyra in Syria, or the painted portraits from mummy cases in the Fayum, portraits representative of techniques that endure in Byzantine icons.[16] That attributed to the Isidora Master (Figure 7.3) from *c.* 100 CE wears "an orgy of gold and emeralds," pearl and gold earrings, a gold wreath, and a large gold pin that pokes out from behind her head, all of them of a style that owes more to Roman imperial designs than to Egyptian (Thompson 1982: 32). Here we have high fashion of a kind that makes the *korai*'s claims to Egyptomania appear half-hearted. Most of the material to survive from the Roman period is more modest, following the example of the Attic stelai in configuring bodily objects less as "bling" than as an indication of the honorand's special merits. Even, if not especially, here in a multicultural empire, the sorts of

FIGURE 7.3 Mummy Portrait of a Woman, 100 CE, attributed to the Isidora Master (Romano-Egyptian, active 100–125 CE). Los Angeles, The J. Paul Getty Museum inv. no. 81.AP.42. Photograph: The J. Paul Getty Museum, Villa Collection, Malibu, California.

summaries that claim that apples are female objects, and thus a sign of desire or fertility, and scrolls something carried by male figures to advertise their literacy and, possibly, their citizen status as well, flatten these objects' agency, rendering them symbolic, and subordinate to existing systems. Once reinflated as actors, their role in the drama of life and death is complicated by "exceptions to the rule" (e.g. that on the Romano-British tombstone of Flavia Augustina from Eboracum [York], both she and her husband carry scrolls) and by the fact that, once combined with indigenous dress (they are not clad in toga and stola, but in heavy cloaks like their two children)[17] and seen in local terms, their sphere of influence is less predictable.

While Athenian gravestones of the fifth and fourth centuries BCE do sometimes mark the person's profession (e.g. a priest with a knife and a priestess with a key), by the time we get to Rome, tools of the trade assume far more prominence, occasionally dispensing with the human figure altogether.[18] We think of the relief erected in Ivrea, Italy, between the Augustan and Flavian periods by *mensor* (land surveyor) and *sevir* (holder of minor municipal office connected with the imperial cult) Lucius Aebutius Faustus in commemoration of his own life, his spouse, his children, and freedwoman (Figure **7.4**). Rather than capture him holding hands with his wife in a typical *dextrarum iunctio* or feasting (the objects of the dinner, couches, tables, cups, garlands, and servants tapping the prestige that comes of conspicuous consumption and in hopes for a joyous afterlife),[19] the relief instead gives pride of place to a dismantled *groma* or surveying instrument, with a tiny curule chair, and fasces, insignia of a *sevir*'s office, above it (Figure **2.1**, p. 45). The *groma* is literally the star of the show, a precursor to Leonardo da Vinci's *Vitruvian Man*. It is one with Faustus; more than a gadget; man as machine and vice versa (Zimmer 1982: cat. no. 141 and, on the question of Greek precedents, 74–80; Schäfer 1989: cat. no. 62; and Cuomo 2007: 83).

All of this offers us a different emphasis from anything we have seen so far, a fascination with the material properties of the object *qua* object (Kampen 1981: 81), of technology as manual work as opposed to highfalutin theory, with theory as praxis. Whereas the objects on the Attic stelai celebrated the civilization that civic life demanded, this subset of Roman reliefs use their objects to give their owners an alternative embodiment from the traditional elite embodiment built on birth or letters. As a freedman, Faustus' practical expertise, and the invitation his stele issues to rescue the discarded *groma* and feel its weight in the hand, resists the "depersonalization and desocialization" (Joshel 1992: 165) associated with his former servile status, and finds equilibrium in symmetry. Like him, or his stonecutter, all can use *techne* to plot themselves on the landscape. Small wonder that an abacus and similar devices have been found in Italian graves of the period (Cuomo 2007: 95, fn. 72).

FIGURE 7.4 Cast of funerary stele of Lucius Aebutius Faustus, depicting tools of
a land surveyor, probably first century CE. Rome, Museo della Civiltà Romana.
Photograph: akg-images/De Agostini Picture Lib./A. Dagli Orti.

The nonappearance here of actual physical labor is striking—especially given
the scenes of working men and women to survive from cemeteries such as
Ostia's Isola Sacra, where what is emphasized is not the body of the protagonist,
its musculature, gender, or posturing, but the act of making, selling, serving,
sometimes juxtaposed with "still lives" of instruments (Kampen 1981). Instead,
labor is aestheticized, and this is the thing that "allows the object's power to spill
into the socio-political sphere." The *groma* thus "transcends its physicality" to
become, not unlike today's "consumer objects," a vehicle for desire.[20] It lends

Faustus charisma while at the same time promising closure: lying in pieces, it speaks of everyone's—everything's—lifespan (Cuomo 2007: 83).

Where does this conclusion leave the objects specific to Faustus as *sevir?* Common on the reverse of Republican coins, and seamlessly integrated into imperial imagery when issues in honor of Octavian were inscribed with the curule chair that the senate had granted his adoptive father, Julius Caesar, these symbols had long been a shorthand for public status and political office in Rome. Though they participated in a revision of this imagery, when, under the Principate, their reach extended from supporting consuls, praetors, censors, and aediles to embracing emperors and freedmen, still they were "subordinate to existing systems." They alert us to the existence not only of consumer objects, but also of brands.[21]

(iii) Late Antiquity

In the first century CE, an emperor's charisma resided in his body, and the style and pose of the body, more than in his body's paraphernalia. It is Augustus' body, its contrapposto, youth, bare feet, and intense gaze, that makes his statues impressive and paradigmatic (e.g. see Figure 5.8, p. 132, the statue of Augustus from Prima Porta), his body that is a source of curiosity for the ancient biographer Suetonius (who is more concerned with detailed corporeal description than his Greek predecessors), and this in Rome, a city that, more than Athens, liked to reflect and secure its people's hierarchies and life stages not just in clothes, but in other objects (not only the *bulla* for boys and crescent-shaped pendant for girls, but in the complex rules governing who could wear a gold as opposed to iron ring). The Roman emperor was general, priest, father, god, and might need a spear, *patera*, or scepter.

When the empire was divided into four mini-empires in the third century CE, each with its own leader, the pendulum swung to make objects more important than Polyclitan proportions. In a fracturing empire, the message was unity, these men as interchangeable effigies as opposed to competing conquerors—hence the porphyry images now in Venice and the Vatican, where the direct address and pattern of the *korai* is brought back again to divert attention from their stocky, shapeless bodies to their sword handles and the orbs that they carry.[22] As they and subsequent rulers based themselves in different capitals, increasingly delegating military operations and governance to others, they became more distanced, responding to the ongoing threat of dissolution and invasion by hiding their humanity in jeweled robes and diadems, and in lavish entourages.[23] The reverses of coins minted by eastern mints show co-rulers, Valentinian I and Valens (from 364–375 and 364–378 CE, respectively), enthroned as Pheidas' cult statue of Zeus was enthroned, waving *mappae* (consular cloths) and holding scepters. They also, as distinct from consuls, have *nimbi* (haloes of radiance) (*RIC* 9: 217, no. 29[a] and 254, no. 16[a–c] and 17).

It is not only late antique and Byzantine emperors and empresses who barricade themselves in with objects, eventually embracing impressive three-pendant brooches and heavily jeweled crowns with hanging pearls as insignia specific to imperial office (Figure 7.5).[24] Jewels generally were showier than they had been since the Hellenistic period, with many men choosing to incorporate coins and medallions into chains and bracelets or to wear large crossbow *fibulae* inscribed with the ruler's name to curry favor and advertise allegiance (Stout 1994: 79, 80). In the merger of senatorial and equestrian careers under Constantine (sole ruler from 324–337 CE), when a larger number of officials were awarded the rank and status of *clarissimus* (most distinguished) (Dillon 2015), and the shift away from Rome as primary stage, it was harder to be noticed.

FIGURE 7.5 The empress Theodora with her entourage, section of mosaic, south wall of the apse, San Vitale, Ravenna, Emilia-Romagna, Italy, sixth century CE. Photograph: akg-images/De Agostini/A. De Gregorio.

Rulers were not the only ones to have *nimbi*: first in Rome's catacombs, and then elsewhere, Christ was nimbate, and Christianity something that, though embryonic, gained imperial support. Its initial fuzziness did not stop the apologist Tertullian from penning the misogynist *De cultu feminarum* (*On Female Fashion*), a two-volume tract that intensified the criticism against luxurious fabrics, ornate hairstyles, the dyeing of hair and cloth, and the wearing of makeup (a criticism that had been live since the Republic) to query the fit of the displays of wealth that social standing required with a Christian identity. In time, some Christians withdrew from civic life to reject worldly goods and the social obligations associated with them. "Let us cast away the ornaments of this world if we truly desire those of heaven" (*De cultu feminarum* 2.13.5: *proiciamus ornamenta terrena, si caelestia optamus*).

The change that Christianity brought to the body and society cannot be underestimated (a classic is still Brown 1988): the Fall made men and women conscious of their corporality, and their gender difference, as never before. What resulted was not just a revision of attitudes to sex, nudity, and adornment, but to music, food, and so on, replacing animal sacrifice that had been a mainstay of Greek, Roman, and Jewish religious ritual for centuries, not to mention the pouring of wine and other libations,[25] with spiritual worship and with "the lamb of God who takes away the sin of the world" (John 1: 29; see Ullucci 2012, though note Conybeare 1903). Meanwhile, the centrality of the body and blood of Christ, and its re-envisioning in bread and wine, gave the sociability of sharing a meal, and the banquet's eschatological implications as long inscribed in pagan funerary art (see n. 19, p. 212), new reach. In the apse mosaics of Ravenna's Church of San Vitale (Figure 7.5), Justinian and Theodora are represented not with orbs, scepters, or *mappae*, but with a gold bread basket and Eucharistic chalice, respectively.

Some Christian groups abstained from alcohol and meat altogether, even going so far as to reject Eucharistic wine in favor of bread, water, and other foodstuffs such as honey (McGowan 1999). Others advocated fasting, not least to keep sexual appetites in check. Both were attempts to separate Christianity from pagan culture: for all that some of the philosophical schools of Greece and Rome advocated abstention from certain foods, the classic case being the Pythagoreans and beans, ritual fasting was not on the agenda (Lee 2012: 186). Food shortages also became more common as the long-distance trade that defined the high empire was subject to more interruptions (Watson 1999: 455). Yet wine remained a common denominator: like the tobacco, coffee, tea, cocoa, and sugar that would later come from the New World, it bound civilization together (Withington 2014).

Civilized drinkers took their wine watered down. In defining these drinkers, we often return to Greece, to the elite male symposium and the choreography implied by the surviving drinking vessels, water jars, and mixing jugs, many of them decorated with self-reflexive imagery, which fired imaginations, prescribed norms, and managed expectations. But we might also look to taverns in Italy with their crude graffiti and painting (e.g. Salvius' inn in Pompeii, where two men are pictured vying with one another for wine, only for the barmaid to offer it to someone else).[26] Wine was an everyday beverage for all social classes, and consistently, from the fourth century CE, in Rome, if not in Constantinople, it was part of the dole or *annona* (Vera 1999).

Wine's corporeal effects, and the need to police these effects, made it a great leveler. The wine god Dionysus (Bacchus in Latin) was the god of ecstasy and frenzy, who inspired mania in his worshippers—not just an altered state, but a loss of self that, in mythology at least, saw deluded mothers murder their sons.[27] Wine had a greater power than most objects, or at least a power that was harder for the body to handle, that changed the body's physical properties, heating its core, paralyzing its limbs, and dulling the cognition on which object/subject relations—and the sociality that is one with them—depended.[28] Using it was about using it correctly.[29] Aelian, born toward the end of the second century CE, notes how the ancient Greek law code traditionally ascribed to Zaleucus of Locri prevented anyone from drinking unmixed wine, except for medicinal purposes.[30] Undiluted wine could be used as a therapeutic agent: at that point, the person's role in society was restricted by sickness.

We have traveled a long and inevitably winding route from the Archaic Greek world of Epizephyrian Locri, a Greek colony on the tip of the toe of Italy, and Attica's *korai*, but a route that has honed our understanding of the phrase "bodily objects" by looking not only at different time periods, but also at different kinds of object (apples, tools, fasces, dress, wine) and different kinds of subject (elites and nonelites, men, women, rulers, gods). In privileging historical change over regional variation (e.g. the fact that in the Roman period, nail cleaners were a toilet instrument used almost exclusively in Britain; Eckardt 2014: 149), we have encountered continuities and discontinuities that will hopefully allow us to contextualize archaeological data and flesh out the indices of agency plotted diagrammatically by Alfred Gell—accessing a reality located in, and prompted by, the representational.[31] Building on the distinction between the healthy and the sick, we turn, in the ensuing section, to the separation of the living and the dead. In the words of the German–American writer Charles Bukowski, "The dead do not need aspirin or sorrow, I suppose. but they might need rain. not shoes but a place to walk." Although they are neither what they were, nor care for us, they "might need each other."[32]

LIVING WITH OBJECTS, DYING WITH OBJECTS

Move beyond representation and large numbers of the bodily objects that come down to us—weapons, pins, cosmetics containers, mirrors, combs, toys, strigils, necklaces, bracelets, cups, knives, spoons, scalpels—have been found not in a context of everyday usage, but in the (secondary?) context of the tomb.[33] Whereas a silver spoon's weight, taste, texture, and shine make the experience of using it different from using a bronze spoon (cf. Swift 2017: 110), supplementing the possible indulgence that lies in its economic value with something more sensory, the dead are immune to corporeal pleasures. Compare the epigrams traditionally inscribed on other kinds of Greek and Roman grave stelai to those already discussed, sepulchral epigrams such as:

> Stele and my Sirens, and, mournful urn that holds the meagre ashes belonging to Hades, tell those who pass by my tomb, be they citizens or from another town, "farewell"; and that this grave holds me, a bride. Say too, that my father called me Baucis, and my family is from Tenos, so they may know, and that my friend Erinna engraved these lines on my tombstone. (*Greek Anthology* 7.710)

The deceased is reduced to her remains, given life by the "speaking object" that is the text and the tomb it implies, and by the borrowed voice of the reader (see Platt 2018: 27–8). If there is agency here it belongs to the poet, and to the grave, which we are told "holds" Baucis (χὦτι με νύμφαν εὖσαν ἔχει τάφος). Elsewhere, the fourth-century-BCE poet Erinna, to whom this epitaph is (perhaps falsely) attributed, speaks of the "empty echo" of her poetry that penetrates to Hades, the "silence among the dead," and the "darkness" that "closes their eyes."[34] They neither see nor hear her. If there is consolation, it is that death cannot be bad for the deceased because for that to be true, they would have to exist as a subject of experience (so Lucretius, channeling Epicurus; see Edwards 2007: 81).

Needless to say, this woefully underestimates the complexities that are Greek and Roman attitudes to death. But what it does highlight is the difference between any "life" left there and the "life" in Egyptian "afterlife" (however simplified that, too, might need to be here), where despite shifts over time between life- and death-orientated grave goods (e.g. canopic jars, books of the dead), the tendency for the sand to preserve the appearance of the corpse had long since ramped up the possibilities for an embodied self in death and the potential of an ongoing personal trajectory, a selfhood dependent on the body's physical persistence (Meskell 1999; also relevant is Meskell and Joyce 2003). The Greek historian Diodorus, writing in the first century BCE, is struck by the way in which "even the hair on the eyelids and brows remains," and by their habit of gazing on those who died many generations before with a "strange enjoyment, as though they had lived" with them (Diodorus Siculus, 1.91.6–7).

In contrast to the anthropoid caskets, masks, and cartonnages of embalmed mummies, variously wrapped ready for their transport to immortality, the sarcophagi popular throughout the Roman Empire from the second century CE, and their Etruscan predecessors, were differently mimetic of the body, shielding the dead from view in an obfuscatory fashion. The warm terracotta or cold, chiseled marble signaled corporeal integrity, when eventually inside there might be none. In extreme cases, some Roman sarcophagi contained only ashes; others, more than one body, either simultaneously, or over time, in a history of recycling that destabilized the link between the deceased and the box's mythological, biographical, or more abstract decoration (see the essays by Elsner, Ewald, and Platt in Elsner and Hung 2012). In Etruria, such caskets and urns were placed in tombs designed to resemble the homes of the living, complete with furnishings, some of them (e.g. those constructed at Cerveteri from the seventh to second centuries BCE) in necropoleis with regular streets (Prayon 2000). Perhaps there, we are closer to Egyptian views of the afterlife than to those of the Greeks, whose painted pottery is found in well over half of all Etruscan tombs of the second half of the sixth and fifth centuries BCE (Reusser 2002). Certainly, it seems as though it and other Etruscan grave goods are "for the dead," in a more visceral sense than is meant by the *Iliad*'s Achilles when he asks that the dead Patroclus be provided with "everything appropriate for a dead man to have as he goes to the murky darkness." His reason? "So that unwearied fire may burn him quickly from our eyes" (*Iliad* 23.50–3). These exigencies are for Achilles' and the army's benefit.[35]

Of course, whether thrown onto the pyre or buried, grave goods (or should that be "offerings?" What is the difference?) are always also for the living, and not only during the funeral. The act of dedication alone ensures that they are that, and that the deceased remains part of the social group to which (s)he belonged in life so that memory never fades and his or her identity keeps being expressed (grave goods were always more than indices of wealth, especially once the display of wealth shifted from the tomb to the sanctuary with the emergence of the Greek city-state; Snodgrass 1986: 54). But the nature of this expression of identity depends on a whole host of factors, theological and practical, including whether the body is interred (and in a casket, pit, and so on) or cremated, practices that ebb and flow in popularity, but that prove harder (than wealth and concomitant changes in dress or diet)[36] to link to changes in philosophy or politics. As Ian Morris observes, "What was the person buried [in the late sixth-century BCE gr. 49 at Rhitsona in Boeotia] ... supposed to do with the 420 pots crammed in on top of the coffin?" (Morris 1992: 104–5).

Not that all grave goods are as crushing of the deceased as these. In the recently discovered Mycenaean "Griffin Warrior Grave" (*c.* 1500 BCE) at Pylos in the Peloponnese, for example (so-called because of an ivory plaque decorated with a mythical beast found there), weapons had been placed on the left side of the body, and gold rings and most of the seal stones in the chamber on the right, the iconography of which echoes some of the other objects found there (e.g. a bull's head staff and a mirror above the corpse's legs) (Davis & Stocker 2016). It is not only the placement of these that seems significant, although of what remains a mystery, but the fact that many of their motifs come from Minoan Crete. The implication seems to be that not unlike the Attic vessels in Etruscan tombs centuries later, these rings functioned as proof of the power that comes of cultural contact, a power that is amplified—purified even—when they are taken out of circulation. Decommissioning, if that is what this is, neither essentializes foreign culture as static, nor preserves the rings in aspic; it changes them into boundary markers that delineate the body's reach in a different way, ensuring that, though it cannot speak, it is not mute. They carry with them something of the context that created them and ensure the warrior's materiality and "the centrality of materiality to the way we understand ourselves" (Miller 2005: 2).

The quantity of jewelry and the presence of the mirror in the shaft grave are more usually associated with female burials (although already we might ask how much jewelry, or with what else, a mirror needs to be deposited to clinch the case). Gender and grave goods are not easy bedfellows. As we move through the Greek world and into the Roman, we discover time and time again that what seem like patterns (e.g. men with weapons or strigils, women with mirrors, jewelry, or hairpins) are punctured. Exceptions go some way to proving a rule, but what about "neutral" graves, some of which (e.g. the Archaic and Classical burials in the north cemetery at Corinth) have been described as "denying," even "suppressing," gender at death (Shepherd 2013: 548–9)? Part of what is at issue here is that gender binarism is no more satisfactory a model then than it is today, and gender is but one element in an aggregation of social identities. Another issue is that these identities are assumed to map onto an individual's lived identities. But how do lived identities intersect with any ideal identities that might be conferred in death, or by the "protracted collaboration" (Robb 2013: 455) between the living and the dead that comes of understanding death not as an end, but as a process, as the loosening and maintenance of binding ties? We need only think of children's burials where the grave goods can be unusually extravagant, inclusive of strigils, razors, arrowheads, and makeup, which speak not of lives lived, but of squandered potential. The paucity of *lekythoi* in infant burials in Classical Athens suggests to some that their bodies were seen as less polluted than those of adults (e.g. see Houby-Nielsen 2000: 154), but how sure are they about discriminating this order of object from one with more personal meaning?

If we return to mirrors for a moment, in particular the bronze handheld mirrors found in tombs in Etruria from around 530 BCE into the third century BCE, we find that although there is a strong link between women and mirrors, many of them engraved on the back with scenes of female adornment, some position the male body centrally as the object of the viewer's gaze, several of them (Figure 7.6) making him the object of internal gazes also.[37] In late Classical/Hellenistic Tarquinia, a few men were buried with mirrors, and many women

FIGURE 7.6 Line drawing of a bronze mirror showing a scene identified as Meleager and Atalante in the House of Oineus, third century BCE. Photograph: Gerhard, 1843–97, plate 356. © The Museum of Classical Archaeology, Cambridge.

without them (Carpino 2008: 10). Once this is acknowledged, it becomes apparent that figures of both sexes ask for scrutiny, and in a wide variety of scenes, many of which chime with the kinds of encounter and departure scenes we find on Attic grave stelai. This raises the question "what kind of bodies are these?" but with a force that might have less to say about the role of the deceased in life as measured against constructions of gender, the care of the self, and sexual desire than it does about his or her strange ontology as a proxy for the dead person. A mirror's glassy surface speaks of self-enhancement—but also of absence, of death as distortion or reversal.

ACKNOWLEDGING THE BODY'S CAPACITIES

This chapter has taken a deliberately esoteric approach to its "bodily objects" category in the hope of provoking new questions about said "reality," and the very quality of having existence or substance. It has looked at the ways in which objects convert human bodies from creatures into acculturated members of society, and at the ways in which people animate objects and capitalize on— and cope with—objects' own potentially compromising agency. By "bodily object" here, we have included everything from wigs to wine and from seeds to sarcophagi, to think about objects as markers of status, mediators, facilitators, pleasures, providers of protection and sustenance, and proofs of bodily sensation. We have also acknowledged that even early Christians, who wanted something new from objects vis-à-vis what they wanted from God, some of them going so far as to reject the comfort of possessions and foodstuffs in favor of an ascetic existence, did not dare turn their backs on wine; that some objects exert a stronger influence than others. Such influence continues into the tomb, where rather than enable someone like the "Griffin Warrior" (if a warrior is what he is or was) to be himself, they allow him to leave this world, not performing his masculinity, nor attesting his selfhood, as they would have done in life, so much as performing his passing or departure, while persuasive and delimiting of a new materiality that means he does not dissolve into nothing.

I end where I started—with objects that hold a pomegranate, apple, or other circular object as though offering it to the viewer. Rather than *korai*, these are themselves bodily objects (Figure 7.7), metal or bone hairpins, which were worn widely across the empire in the first and second centuries CE, the majority of them incorporating a right hand (for, unlike Phrasikleia, who holds the flower in her left, it is a right hand, probably because the right was seen as luckier; Lloyd 1962; Swift 2017: 190–200) with a spherical object between thumb and index finger.[38] Although other genres of object, especially votives, also shared this form, it is these pins that fit our purpose. Whatever the form's import in other contexts, it gains specificity—*reflexivity*—when sported on the body.[39]

Bodily contact makes the precise identity of the round object less important in a tiny pin than in, for example, a large healing *ex voto*. Crucial is the accentuation of touch, and of manual dexterity, a dexterity demanded of any attempt to style the hair properly. We need only think about Ovid's image of the hairpin as a hostile weapon (as one object-type bleeds into another), not to mention his displeasure at Corinna's overly styled locks: "With what patience did they yield themselves to iron and fire to form the close-curling ringlet with its winding orb! I kept crying out 'It is a crime …'" (Ovid, *Amores* 1.14.25–7). Perhaps the hand's delicate gesturing aimed at protecting the pin and its wearer from such charges. More profound than this frivolity is Cicero:

FIGURE 7.7 Silver hairpin with right hand holding a small fruit, probably a pomegranate, second century CE. London, The British Museum 1934,1210.21. Photograph: © The Trustees of the British Museum.

What clever servants for many arts are the hands which nature has given to man! For the flexibility of the joints enables the fingers to open and close with equal ease and to perform every motion without difficulty. Thus by the manipulation of the fingers the hand is fit to paint, model, carve, and elicit sounds on lyre and flute. And besides these acts of delight, there are those of utility—I mean agriculture and building, the weaving and stitching of garments, and all ways of working bronze and iron; from which it is clear that it was by applying the hands of the craftsman to the discoveries of thought and the observations of the senses that we have attained everything. (Cicero, *On the Nature of the Gods* 2.150)

Here is further justification for why the hand is privileged, but also as explicit a statement as any of the ways in which objects "maketh the man," and the woman, by having them realize their bodily capacities. It is only in tapping, as I hope we have managed, the ways in which this "realization" takes place that we get at a cultural history of objects, not object biographies.

CHAPTER EIGHT

Object Worlds

ANN KUTTNER

Thing, object, artifact: a material entity made by humans, ranging from shaped substance to shaped space. Making can be as simple and profound as taking an object not made by a human—a bone or tree or stone—and investing it with identity, with syntactical liability to being a "this," a "that," a "the"—pronouns embedded in Greek and Latin, even if not always vocalized. "Artifact" is a good word to think with, in English, for embedded in it are reverberations of artifice, facture—the processes of coming to be, the status of the material trace as a designed and crafted thing. All artifacts are tools, for all objects have their usage, the affordances that make possible planned uses.[1] The fundamental makers' urge to patterning that is observable across the range of human production of things from its earliest Paleolithic era, like the gratuitous elegance of flaking patterns for a prehistoric Clovis point, the satisfactions of cognition and sensation that the creation of such patterning desires and fills, designate those things part of whose function, affordance, is to be observed. "Art" as a category, if it is to have any applicability, the aesthetic as a domain, ranges from the fine slip and polish of a typical spindle whorl to the satisfactions posited by Greco-Roman columns' regular fluting or those of the unique Roman Laocoon (see further above pp. 125–9).

All of us in this volume have worked at some point with propositions that objects are agentive, a fruitful heuristic of anthropomorphism: that they co-create both other objects, in the inter-artifactual domain, and also their makers, users, viewers; that object can be said to swap places with subject. We perform a forensic art history and anthropology upon the infinitesimally tiny fraction now extant of the object-packed ancient designed environment in the Old World on the three continents rimming the Mediterranean. So, "What do objects want?"—the title of Gosden's elegantly compressed, seminal 2005 article[2]—is *our* question; extant texts, though intensively sampled in my piece, only go part of the way to explain ancient encounter with things. (In our cultures of study here, in fact, a millennium and a half of production essentialized the very display of text as object, compulsively filling communal space with material inscription on stones, the so-called epigraphic habit.) We do an archaeology of gaze and touch, of thought and affect, and of ancient *habitus* and the coming to be of the ancient maker and his or her world.[3] Here, the nature of objects and the nature of history-telling are mutually illuminated by Malafouris' generative formulation of objects as part of the very apparatus of cognition, constituting a "hylonoetic" domain that shapes as well as being used for shaping by mind and affect, a condition of metaplasticity.[4]

What, then, is peculiar to the ancient world of this volume, as opposed to other cultural moments covered by the whole series? And what can we get by thinking with the category "particular," my commission for this volume? This book looks at the Greek, the Roman; but it must be borne strongly in mind that multiple peoples and their object traditions populated the Greco-Roman Mediterranean, influencing Greco-Roman practices, appropriating from them, in environments of coexistence or commerce, war and colonization. To consider the so-called Greek and Roman world after the conquests of Alexander, and, in some regions, before it, is to think about proto-global conditions, polyethnic hegemonical, and imperial entities. About those, we naturally ask questions about small world/big world cognition, the formation and dissolution of identities, the indigenous and the international, and objects have rightly or wrongly been seen as key to answering those questions—if you like, themselves constitutive of such questions.

This volume makes excursions into the familiar, liable to theories of universal human habits and potentialities. In its antiquity, the fact of facture and the spectacle of making, the worth and value of expertise in making and using, were more obtrusive than to many modern persons in my own society. Far more things were directly fashioned by hand and its tools than in the Western Now. Some were, though, indeed multiples produced using another object in processes of molding, casting, stamping, from the multiplication of tiny document reliefs by seals, to mold-made pots, to plaster casts of statues. The miraculous regularity of the replication of identical forms by skilled human hands, too, made an especial appeal in the world little touched by the machine, whether the brilliant painted abstractions of the colossal pots of early Archaic Athens or the scrollwork and geometries of well-made Hellenistic and Roman mosaic floors. Replication was itself a performance, with both congruity and variation savored in various degrees and ratios. Classic for that practice is the historic Hellenistic and Roman habit, for statuary and painting, of multiplying an "original" by varied forms of emulation so that more than one community might take it in—but each city or house gave it particular character by its programmatic placement, including in regard to other art artifacts.[5] The sociability of owning the "same" thing across particular social castes is a condition of our antiquity as of any known culture, backdrop to particularity, actual or endowed. A potentially highly particular act, for instance, prayer, played out in a kind of artifact, the votive figurine, of which hundreds of thousands come down to us because they were made of durable fired clay. At a sanctuary, one can have known full well that one was buying one of a group of mass-made terracottas produced for votive gift-giving, among the shrine donatives excavated throughout the Greek and then Roman world covering a millennium of religious praxis. That sameness can have been seen as making the object more, not less, particular to the buyer/worshipper; important group solidarity between two or many persons can have been affirmed by getting and giving the same object.

Object particularity is a question about two domains: the physical characters of the artifact itself, and its identity, located in space and time, as an artifact used, thought, felt, remembered, forgotten, abandoned. It entails another singularity: that of particular persons. In this regard, the problems of understanding a human as an individual—which so much exercise all of the historical and social sciences—intersect with understanding a thing as individual, problems that bring complex issues of "identity" in their train. That singular body can be that of a maker, raising instantly the problem of authorship that troubles twentieth-century cultural criticism. But the particular body is also that of owner and/or user. The body has its own kind of memory: skill of hand can mean the thing one wields elides with one's bodily mastery, not needing conscious thought while acting. An unfamiliar tool, though, can feel "off"; two apparently identical things—hammer, spear, stylus, distaff, pan, shuttle, fibula, mantle—may feel different from one another to the person hefting and using them and, given a choice, the user will choose by preference. (Ancient-like modern "still-life" art often speaks to that condition.) The tools and elements of technology on the votive and funerary reliefs of the Roman world that Courtney Ann Roby deploys in this volume (Chapter 2) speak to an asserted personalization of a so-called standard thing. For instance, the compelling Roman "thing art" that lines up items of ritual costume and implements (Figure 8.1) that would have been held or worn by one or many persons converging in liturgical occasions constructs narratives of events because narratives are made of bodies with objects.[6]

That use and/or possession can make even a widely common thing particular to the one who has or deploys it over time, in ways that archaeology both can and cannot trace, is an operation of memory. The vast literature on the operation of memory in the Greek and Roman world is overwhelmingly concerned with cityscape and landscape, and the qualities of the monument,

FIGURE 8.1 Marble frieze slabs found near the Portico of Octavia, Rome, Augustan
(late first century CE), now Palazzo Nuovo, Museo Capitolino, fragment 100 (604)
and 104 (608), length 2.12 m and 2.47 m, height 59 m. Two of at least seven
fragments of a frieze in Luna marble depicting artifacts of religious performance, as
here, and also warship elements. Details from DAI inst. neg. 06898 and 06897; after
La Follette 2012: fig. 11.

representational and otherwise, in spaces of large congregation, civic or
religious, as well as in domestic Roman art; that conversation would do well to
speak also to those around the portable ancient object, as heirloom, memento,
souvenir, pilgrimage token. Some genres of art and artifact in the world of
the not-monumental and the small easily invite the topic of the operation of
investment by memory: the keeping and viewing of portraits of those one
knows or knew by bonds of blood or affection; personal heirlooms, as we can
read about them, like the silver cup the emperor Vespasian used for solemn and
ritual occasions because it belonged to the beloved grandmother who reared
him (Suetonius, *Life of Vespasian* 2) or discern it in archaeological contexts
(as Vespasian's cup would not likely be recognizable). Memory engages things
found rescued from damage and repaired and the object known or thought to
have been used by or have been touched by the body of a person important for
any cultural reason, like "relics." Memory and its partner, affect, co-constitute
the machine worked by the so-called souvenir, the token of a person's travels
secular or sacred. In asking about keeping things in mind, moreover (how are
they attended to?), we must recall that to own and to handle are two different
things: a Greek or Roman woman might not own what she works with in the
home, the slave owns nothing of the things whose touch is enforced on him or
her. The man who owns the oil pithos may never have touched it in his life; a
Greek or Roman adult man might go to his grave never having touched a loom
weight on the loom of his female household, though they dangled in action in
his homes from his infancy onward; a male slave might never have touched his

mistress's jewels. She and her maid might never hold a sword, or have touched some of the equipment of the male banquet.

The important gift economy of Greek and Roman cultures, both formal and informal, is about a transaction with memory, and is celebrated in that way with point and poignancy across the range of literatures from Homer onward (see Chapter 1 in this volume); the giver wishes the receiver to keep knowing from whom the thing comes, and for the quality of gift and identity of giver to endow particularity on the thing. The giver may keep memory of what has left their hands, literally or symbolically. "Who-gave-to-whom-because" is enunciated on thousands of public gifts from communities to individuals, the honorific markers and portraits of sanctuary and cityscape, whose stone bases preserve the inscriptions that aimed to keep memory of the gift alive as spectacle for generations, as well as in the mind of the person honored. In those increasingly crowded statue-scapes, location and inscription, not just finesse of workmanship, worked to make sure that one more naked athlete or heavily draped priestess or togate magistrate or cuirassed emperor (see above p. 130) might stay particular. Things for death—the gifted assemblages of grave goods from body scraper to necklace to buried sarcophagus that also yield an enormous quantity of our extant stuff, like the aboveground markers of the dead—bid for memory, too, whether that of the dead or of the living. The distinctive character of so much Greek and Roman religion is one of votive observance, the character that generates such an enormous quantity of our objects is also a gift economy that counts on a deity's memory for what is given (as for the many votives discussed in this chapter).

THINKING WITH THE THING

Almost as soon as Greeks and their written language enter documented history in the eighth century BCE, writing accompanied some important objects, as it already did in more advanced neighboring cultures (Egypt and the Middle East). Inscribed for the eyes of deity and community, on Geometric and Archaic sanctuary votives, bronze and stone, from tiny to colossal, including upon sculpture of living beings, it names the dedicant, sometimes a divine recipient, tagging the object as This One. Often words honored an object by verbal artifice, in taking poetic, metrical form; as inscription of public statuary displays shifted to their supports (though inscription onto nonrepresentational artifacts persisted), an entire poem might be commissioned, authored by a patron, an associate, or a hired poet. By the fifth century BCE, any inscription on or for objects, art, or votives was called the-writing-upon-something, *epigramma*; by the first century BCE at the latest, the term was taken up in Latin, too, for object and monument inscriptions as for short poems. These artifact texts, texts as artifacts, could circulate like any admirable poetry, orally and/or as writing; they spawned a repertoire of poets' serious or playful epigrams, not ones attached to something, discussing things both seen and imagined, actual and fictional—public objects, votives, possessions, gifts durable or ephemeral. Object epigrams that had never been inscriptions were being authored, and collected, by the early third century BCE; the practice lasted through late antiquity, its productions read in Medieval and Byzantine time–space. They have naturally attracted some of the enormous scholarly community fascinated in recent decades by Greco-Roman text–image relationships.[7]

In such poems, artifacts, persons, and transactions became things-to-think-with, things-to-feel-with; they exhorted reader/viewers, as did many actual inscriptions, to think and feel. In teasing interaction both with "high" poetry and public displays, we have already playful quotations of Homeric epic even on mediocre objects in the Archaic Period, like the "Cup of Nestor" from Ischia. By the third century BCE, ordered by authors and by anthology editors by theme (like gift, or painting, or funerary monument), compilations became an amassing of things as if books were spaces full of objects to look at. Fundamental to that project was the Macedonian poet Poseidippos of Pella writing for the early Ptolemies, the still-new rulers of Hellenistic Egypt, and their courtiers; he not only made actual monument dedications and panegyrics, but also assembled epigrams about real and invented things in distinctive response to elite amassing in the first generations of Hellenistic "collecting."

The third- or second-century BCE papyrus book roll of Poseidippos, discovered in Egypt, has 112 poems (few known previously from ancient anthologies) in a thematic order that seems to be the poet's; objects, monuments, and images recur across the categories. I use the now conventional section labels, most not in the scroll.[8] Some grouped standard epigram categories (votive things, 36–41, here for the new temple of queen Arsinoe-Aphrodite; tomb poems, 42–61). But novel were two assembling things *qua* things. One "masterpiece gallery" (62–70) orders actual statues from around the Greek world (*andriantopoiika*) by famous artists. This finds context in real royal collections (e.g. the textually documented displays of Ptolemy II's dining pavilion; Athenaios, *Deipnophistae* 5.196a–197c, citing Kallixeinos of Rhodes' book on Alexandria). For officers and courtiers, the king crammed it with masterpiece statues and paintings, as well as dramatic tableaux, animal skins, tapestry cloaks with political imagery, and astoundingly copious displays of precious metal banquet apparatus.

Poseidippos' serio-comic set about gemstone and stone objects (*lithika*, 1–21) ranges from regal cups to historic or invented gem jewelry to perfume containers, from trophies from Persia to remarkable boulders, things for women and for men, made for Greeks and not-Greeks, purchases and gifts. Named artisans, real or not real, as well as anonymous artisans are praised for skill; named and anonymous users, owners, and donors see and are seen with the objects described, like the women whose erotic aura is enhanced by gem bracelet, ring, earring, necklace (4–7). There are even some particular persons depicted (like King Darius of Persia). Names and descriptions particularize objects even of a generic sort like ringstones or earrings: the poet says "look at this one," as he awakes desire to see objects of attributed value. The *lithika* are famously an imperialist map of a world of gems reaching to India and the Red Sea by new trade and conquest, where Ptolemaic luxury, *tryphē*, embodies power and culture, as it could, too, for nonroyal persons (Bing 2005; Kuttner 2005). It is also a tour, from in and out of aristocratic banquet halls into lovers' bedrooms where possession is self-augmentation and self-description, the using and wearing of artifacts a performance for others. Many objects are for handling, sometimes touched at the very moment described. Things are transactional of affect, from simple pleasure in substances' light and color to a sense of catered luxury, from savoring artifice and interesting things to philosophical and scientific reflections, from lust to piety.

These are not objects of the poor; but Poseidippos' potential audience at Alexandria and beyond reached deep into the nameless elite, to anyone who could afford at least one pair of fine earrings or sealing stone. And some may have been for real objects. Clearly, Poseidippos estimated that his audience already thought and felt about and by means of things possessed, artifact-scapes surveyed; to read him thoughtfully was to meditate on human engagement with the world as humanly shaped from natural substance, and on artisanship as a fundamental human practice. Any one object-epigram triggered visualization and haptic imagination; their amassing turned them into assemblages for readers to link things by similarity and variegation. Poseidippos' epigram scroll gives the originary phases of a way of writing, reading, hearing, seeing, and touching that echoes through time and space to, most notably, the influential work of the first-century CE poet Martial at Rome. Thing-poems, from adulatory to satirical, crowd his epigram corpus, not least the poetry of gifts as they negotiate social relations. Of interest here is Book 14, the *Apophoreta*, things, each with a label header, sent to or taken from a feast as gifts, on the putative occasion of the annual Saturnalia; that was traditionally a time of both big and little gifts to kin, friends, clients, patrons.

Martial's thing-poems make a serio-comic tour of the Roman social economy, up and down the vertical axis of worth and use, from peasant to the emperor Domitian. They move in cityscape and countryside as the reader locates what she reads in place of use, often spelled out—wheatfield or kitchen, forum or street, bedroom or dining room, modest dwelling or palace. Copious textile and costume references gesture also to multiple occasions, from practical to ceremonious to erotic. Martial creates an implied task-scape, from wool's implied weaving room, to cups' dining rooms where things construct status. That any one category (they are largely grouped in categories) contains both costly and cheap material invites reflection on what "worth" is worth, a classic

Roman satirical gambit; it also highlights things good of their kind in material, craftsmanship, and use. The set is embedded in a capitalist economy where anything is for judicious purchase, even as its frame is a gift economy that need not always seek recompense. Desire and need are counterpoised. Amassing becomes assemblage and even, for aestheticized things, collection.[9]

The poems teasingly and seriously point to ordering of things, like poems, into constellations that make sense, and could be recombined in congeries to define persons with tools for living among other people as well as with ourselves. Stuff comes from both Martial's thriving Rome and Italy and, reflecting a voracious Roman economic and political imperial hegemony, from around the empire, too, now an enormous world of circulating raw materials and finished goods. A similar dynamism, with the formation of a common visual material culture inflected by intense localisms, had characterized the pre-Roman Hellenistic-era world as well, its empires, cities, and kingdoms; the rise of the Roman Empire as a singular bounded entity across much of this territory nurtured both the local and the proto-global object world, and these poems embody that.[10] Within it lie choices, particular ones: writing tablets use notoriously costly (North African) citron wood (3), but ordinary writing papyrus (11, from Egypt) is great stuff of its kind. Particular knowledge is appealed to in interesting ways (just like the assessments in Pliny the Elder's contemporary *Natural History* of grades of this and that from various places),[11] like that of good rain-cloaks of different kinds from Italy or the provinces, even a fine British basket.

The artifacts span most of this volume's categories: a toothpick of wood or quill (22) is just a few lines away from a silk-clad girl's gold hairpin (24, "Gold hairpin": "Lest damp hair harm bright silks, let a pin fix and hold up the twisted locks"; on pins, see also above p. 181); hunting spear, sword, and belt and dagger of manly elite activities of hunting and warfare (31–3) are followed by peasant's scythe, a hatchet, then barbers' tools (34–6); a well-ordered domestic assemblage has gone nuts, to take in corsets, couches, an architect's measuring rod, a child's toy, a golden Victory for the emperor himself, as well as a little (cheap) terracotta figurine of Hercules, books by famous Roman poets with puppies and hunting horses, cooking spits and bird-catchers' rods. Martial's posture of knowing a great deal about his culture's stuff, its codes and practicalities, emerges very clearly in the set 85–121, which stock a dining room from couch to silver spoon. Side by side are the costliest of cups, made of gold or gemstone, and earthenware jugs, plates, and cups (98, 100–2, 106, 108, 114, 119). Those, fascinatingly for archaeologists, are broken down by type and source city and described as appreciated for their workmanship and the appeal of smooth surface and red color, whether fine wheel-thrown Sorrentine cups or (mold-made) Arretine ware (98, "Arretine ware": "I advise you not to be too scornful of Arretine ware. Porsenna was luxurious with Tuscan cookery"). The poet is both joking and serious that elites as well as sub-elites might use good "ordinary" stuff, artifacts for which gemmed gold is ideologically coded hypertrophy, and that range from ceramic to more precious materials recurs in real Roman vessel assemblages.

Such attributed particularity that exemplifies kinds is contingent on knowledge and memory. It can be connoisseur's knowledge of artistic pedigree, as for a statuette of a lovely youth supposedly once treasured by the (tyrannicide) Brutus (171). It can also be the sensation of donor or recipient in whose consciousness a gifted or possessed thing might surface, with the thought of the other human in gift transaction particularizing even a common thing. Above all, that each poem strives to be a particular, original formulation focuses in imagination our eyes and minds on this one thing, here, and notionally entire, in our hands or sightline, even if we own enough that this and that thing has slipped our mind.

Poseidippos and Martial gloss the world of makers, as do so many ancient texts. Relations between buyer and maker were far more often direct than in our world, in encounters of commission and purchase from workshops—and that world fascinated onlookers. Telling artifacts of the consciousness both of elites and of sub-elite artisans of the spectacle of making are those ancient objects that themselves discourse on authorship, reception, skill, the gaze, parallel to the surviving elite texts about the spectacle of facture. Chapter 6 in this volume refers to public Roman monuments with labor scenes of, especially, architecture. Archaic Homer has Thetis take us into the workshop of master-smith Hephaistos in the *Iliad*, and Classical Plato's Socrates has us amble into carpenter shops; in the Roman Empire, Ovid's *Metamorphoses* (6.1–144 at 1–23) pulls us into the weaver shop of Arachne where local nymphs watch her talented fingers, Virgil's *Aeneid* (I.418–37) takes us to the cliff edge from which his Aeneas watches Dido's Carthage being built, a panorama riveting his fascinated gaze and inspiring him to build a city himself. Not only fictions, but actualities remain in ancient texts, whose authors presumed that such tellings would amuse or awe or interest: Republican Cicero's letters to his brother Quintus (*Ep. ad Qu.* 2.5, 3.1, 3.3) take us into the minutiae of supervision of domestic building contractors, just as the Hellenistic and Roman sources of Imperial-era Pliny the Elder's accounts of painters (*Natural History* 35) repeatedly stage visits to their workrooms by kings and commoners alike. But makers and designers meditated, too, on making and assembling, and sometimes archaeology preserves a visual trace of that, even very far down the social scale.

For Romanists, a classic visual entertainment about shops and workshops, complete with visiting customers, are the miniaturist shop scenes staffed by busy Cupids with visiting Psyches in the reception room q of Pompeii's House of the Vettii; mythical makers show up in room m where customer Pasiphae watches Daedalus and assistant work on the hollow cow statue in which she would copulate with her husband's prize bull.[12] Cutting back in time, a fascinating subset of fifth-century BCE Athenian red-figure pottery takes cups' owners to eye the making both of painted pottery itself and also very-high-status cultural objects such as statues. Most famous is the now-anonymous Foundry Painter's Berlin cup, his name-cup (Figure 8.2):[13] in the run of fifth-century BCE Athenian pots, known in thousands, workshop scenes are rare but recurrent, and this painter made several. Here, in a foundry for statuary, gentlemen in elegant body wrappings lean on fashionable walking sticks to watch the manufacture of bronze/naked men; we and they can see the furnace with its fires carefully watched, master craftsmen and helpers near-naked or naked at their task, in postures vividly lifelike in their not-elegant character—squatting, crouching, scraping. By the forge, little images of guardian gods watch over the work; spare models for feet hang on the wall along with tools. The statues are of generic kinds; they will become particular, named beings, someone's inscribed dedication. There is visual wit in the assembly of a statue of a jumping or running athlete, bespoke by someone in that highly prestigious social position, victor in a Panathenaic or pan-Hellenic competition (or, to be more accurate, by the wealthy head of household of the young victor): in a comic echo of heroic combat, the sculptor, with the separately cast head gaping between his feet, hammers on the sprawled body reaching its arms toward him like a suppliant loser in battle. Elsewhere, an assembled statue of an epic young warrior in combat receives its final polish from diminutive workmen, dwarfed both by the visitors and the statue. Such statues will have bases signed as "X made it," meaning the master hands of the workshop; the watchers belong either to the commissioning class or just as likely to the ordinary sub-elite taking in the *thauma* (marvel of workmanship) with a gossipy or cultured interest in what goes up where and how fun it is to watch. And, at banquet, elite or sub-elite persons enjoy the spectacle of spectacle—and the Foundry Painter himself praises by comparisons his own skill at painting, his own workshop's art of clay, for clay statue is where bronze cast statue starts. Both simple and profound is the matching of interior to exterior: the tondo, an epic domain, shows the makers' god, the god-smith Hephaistos, visited by Thetis checking out the panoply being made for her son Achilles, with the god showing off the helmet, hammer in his hand, the nymph hefting the shield (cf. p. 4, and Homer, *Iliad* 18.368–617).

The human workmen look ignoble, even the master sculptor—but he knows, as his spectators and customers do not, how to make enduring high art. In making this piece, and in visiting a statuary workshop himself for details, the humble ceramic craftsman has to have compared his own lot. To please a customer, ephemeral fashion generated the inscriptions in added red, common on Attic red-figure pots: inside "The Boy Is Beautiful," on either side a *kalos* inscription also—"Diogenes Is Beautiful Too," "The Boy Is Beautiful Also." The stylized homoeroticism of the Athenian elites is served by such "*kalos* cups." The kinds of statues of beautiful young men

FIGURE 8.2 Terracotta drinking cup made at Athens, *c.* 490–80 BCE, red-figure technique, painted by the so-called Foundry Painter. Berlin, Antikensammlung F 2294. Height 12 cm, diameter 30.5 cm; from an Etruscan tomb at Vulci. Exterior: (a, b) Bronze sculptors' workshop and the making of bronze statues. Interior (c): Sea-nymph Thetis in the workshop of Hephaistos with the helmet and shield being made for Thetis' son Achilles (cf. *Iliad* 18). With the permission of the Antikensammlung, Staatliche Museen zu Berlin—Preussischer Kulturbesitz; photograph: Johannes Laurentius.

shown here served it, too; their depicted bodies seem to invite the words inscribed as if the spectators voiced them. Body as both agent and object is meditated with and upon here, as is acute consciousness of the clash between class structure and skill—a salutary reminder that conceptual consciousness, ethical and philosophical, is not the genetic privilege of elites. We have no artisan's own poetry in texts: here is a telling document. It ended up deposited by an Etruscan buyer in a tomb at Vulci, part of the massive export trade of fifth-century BCE Athenian fine wares to the Etruscan market; there, too, naturalistic bronze sculpture flourished, and the cup can have kept its particular appeal.

A BELIEVING WORLD IN A PARTICULAR PEARL

Archaeologists have very few scenes of ancient Greco-Roman making; most of them come from the public and private art of the Roman world. (Its funerary reliefs are especially rich [see Chapter 2] with images of the deceased's craft, tools, or shop.) But for the marvel of the well-made thing we must usually work out from artifacts themselves, and, in constructing narratives for them as the conscious historian must, outline the wide worlds in which they, and makers, patrons, and users circulate. I have just mentioned grave goods, so major a piece of the ancient gift economy, in which family give to kin, in a communal ritual and spectacle—a category that yields an innumerable quantity of the artifacts of the Greek and Roman world, including that of subject and neighbor peoples. I have also here just gestured to the votive thing—the gift to god and, because happy gods help everyone, to society, too—and its economic and social circulation. I close with the exploration of a votive object once documentably very particular to someone, curated for several centuries after her death, and a miniature by contrast to the monumental images we have just observed being made.

Upright in its British Museum case,[14] the second-century BCE object (Figure 8.3) takes its notional orientation—the shape in the mind of designer, user, viewer: a very thin, tapering, pointed shaft below a compaction of elaborately worked gold (the soft metal is supported on a bronze matrix), channeling light and shadow, setting off the large white mass above cradled and capped in gold, topped by a bead of like substance. What are its affordances? Patently, it is made to be handled, and to be joined to another substance; it cannot stand alone, but being upright is the point of that multisided head, with its animal elements on the object axis. The discernable function for metal so thin and pointed is to be a pin, temporarily piercing a substance to hold it in firm place: in the source culture, it is a kind of thing to be worn by a woman, fastening her clothing. The enormous white bead atop the shiny golden mass also claims the right to fascinate by contour and color; it once shone, too, as

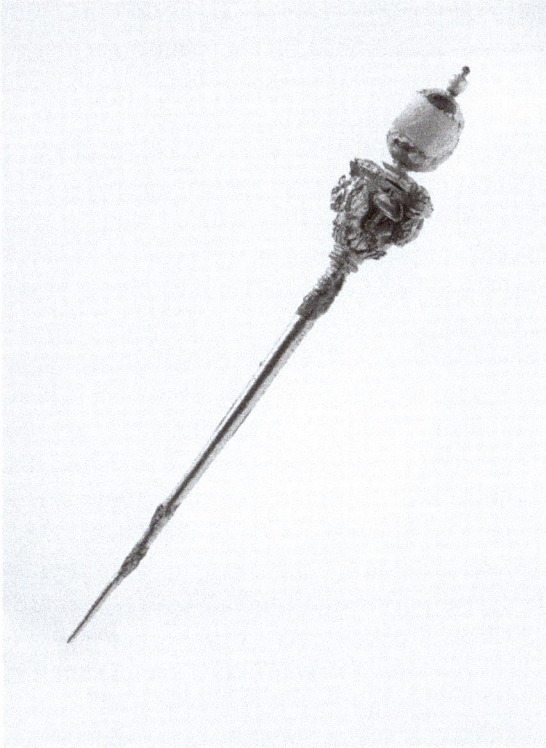

FIGURE 8.3 Dress pin of bronze, gold, and pearl, second century BCE, length 17.8 cm, excavated within the temple of Aphrodite at Old Paphos in Cyprus; inscribed on the shaft: "To the Paphian Aphrodite Eubola vowed this, wife of Aratas the Kinsman, and Tamisa." London, British Museum GR 1888,1115.2. Photograph: © The Trustees of the British Museum.

did the little pearl at the top. This pin is, then, made to catch the eye, whether in bright sunlight outdoors or lamplight within.

That compaction is, to trained modern viewers, as to ancient ones, a playful variation on column capitals, as on analogous pins, "Corinthian" ones: from turned rings and spool at the upper shank of the shaft, as visual and tactile transition to the relatively enormous mass of ornament, spring ripple-edged acanthus leaves; in place of corner leaves there curvet prick-eared horned goats' heads, as if in pasture springing at vegetation. A large lotus blossom, a flared bowl on a stiff stalk, rises between each animal protome, under the rosette of a standard capital crown. This is sculpture of sculpture, monumental stone or bronze reimagined; overhead sits the "real," doves just alit as on any monumental eminence, and, in facing pairs, dipping heads toward the lotus blossom cups, as if those were real, too. The realm of natural movement is playfully choreographed so that four busy birds are perfectly aligned to the capital's surface as to one another. Between them rises the elaborately molded plinth for the crowning bead—ovoid played against inverted pyramid, curves against straight lines. The imagery is of and about desire (those birds are thirsty, bending toward sweet moisture), because doves, and sometimes male goats in their randiness, are emblems of Aphrodite. An object of this kind, in being brought into and out of use, talks about penetration and unfastening, in ways that can seem either lyrically or crudely sexual. Its white crowning ornaments trope flesh, with pearly substances worn on them (Greek pearl jewelry arrives in the Hellenistic age). The large bead, if pearl it is, would be the largest to survive from antiquity—a fine dedication.

This object is caught complexly between female and male gaze and touch, the persistent peculiar condition of the decoration of women in historic societies.[15] Its context was eventually Roman, but in origin "Greek" from before the Roman expansion into the east Mediterranean, at a site originally not-Greek but Cypriote, in Cyprus: the temple building of the internationally renowned sanctuary of Aphrodite at Old Paphos. Its inscription, pricked on the shaft, reads "To the Paphian Aphrodite Eubola vowed this, wife of Aratas the Kinsman [a court office of Ptolemaic Egypt], and Tamisa." In Greek culture, such pins had, in the Archaic and Classical periods, been worn to fasten garments, classically in pairs, one for each shoulder of a woman in a peplos. The Hellenistic era in the Greek east sees a different costume, voluminous body-swathing mantle over chiton; from that time–space era do we find ornamentalized single pins, some with gem finials related to this one. The object stakes a claim to a certain kind of user—one who knows to handle it carefully—and to a certain kind of viewer— one who has a taste for the miniature, for intricacy of artifice (which, as both texts and objects tell us, fascinated Greeks and Romans of all classes), for the discerning and decoding of representations, and for making small speak to big in intermedial transactions. It draws on visual education in the monumental world, where fine single-column shafts rise with important statues at their crown, white marble here become white bead. It works of itself to produce the viewer it needs and desires. Desire is its very project: not just the visceral body-matching of hand sensing how to hold this object, but desire to hold intimately and examine, optic/haptic, with eye and careful finger—or as carefully not-touching some of it—and to see very, very closely. The shine of gold and glow of lustrous white can catch eyes far off: closer scrutiny means more privileged access both to body and thing.

There are things I know as a historian of visual culture that the maker and viewers may have known, too: that images of doves descended to shiny metal bowls to drink were a fashionable Hellenistic artistic conceit, given form in a famous mosaic known textually to us, Sosos' "Drinking Doves" at Pergamon (Pliny, *Natural History* 36.184), which set off a flurry of related images in mosaics from Delos to Pompeii (see Figure **8.4**, center, for a Late Antique

FIGURE 8.4 Ceiling vault mosaic, one of two pendent panels, from the ambulatory of the fourth-century CE Mausoleum of Santa Costanza, Rome, an imperial foundation for Constantina, daughter of Emperor Constantine (d. 354): silver and silver-gilt vessels and implements, fruited and flowering branches, and birds (Wikimedia Commons: Pitichinaccio).

version). Other extant Hellenistic body ornaments also miniaturize masterpieces of high culture, visual paideia to be conveyed orally between makers, patrons, and owners, by goldsmiths who had somewhere seen the statuary types referenced. See, for instance, an unprovenanced gold pin in the Benaki Museum in Athens,[16] of similar format to ours with Corinthian capital; on it, kneeling naked, Aphrodite wrings her wet hair, arisen from the sea ("Anadyomene"). That tropes a type known in multiple media, playful Erotes holding items of toilette like unguent flasks seated about her.

But who is the user for such an object? The shadow to a thing like this, ornamentalized in such a way as to complicate its use, is the pin of more ordinary substance, less fragile elaboration. One ought to be able to grip the solid head of such an object without fear of breaking or deforming it; ours and pins like it represent the luxurious hypertrophy of the usefully shaped, requiring extra care, fingers pinched around those rings under the head proper. The woman who owns a pin like this owns service, too; an enslaved female body servant would handle this, in tidying the owner's possessions, bringing her items of dress, helping her arrange her hair and clothing. This object needs a container to protect or store it, a box or pouch, and so a table or shelf, a room; does an owner leave it out on a table to please the sight or store the covered thing in memory? Touch of such an object was something enforced on a servant, not chosen; whether also pleased in handling such a thing or bleak at holding what she would never wear, her servile status was instantiated by the yawning abyss between handling, "using," and "using" as "owning/wearing." Body ornament serves always the body as spectacle and stage, as Chapter 7 explores in this volume: Who sees it on, when the owner cannot see it easily or at all but rather is framed by it? Is this a viewer whose admiration or satisfaction she wishes, as she imagines herself seen—admiring or covetous female gazes, or also a male gaze, admiring the grace, *charis*, the object lends her, as of the husband (the last and perhaps first owner had one; see below), the son or father approving, within a household occasion? Or the passersby on the street? Just how male or female is this object, when carefully considered? Men were constructed as admirably masculine and acquired status by the adorned bodies of the women of their kin or their other affections. Insofar as female bodies usually belonged to men, and the money to buy fine things and the legal right to own them may have often been male in Hellenistic Egypt and Cyprus, the "user" of this thing could be a man who wants his woman splendid to please his sight, confirm his status, and within an affectional or passionate bond give pleasure. A man, not a woman, may have chosen this thing at a shop, or inherited it from his own mother. And the imagery makes clear that qualities of beauty are tied to desire of male for female, and to the female duty, wife to husband, to heighten that desire. At the same time, in societies that closeted women often with other women and permitted female friendships, women's interested and admiring gazes, permission to see closely or to hold, could matter to a female user, too, along both lateral and vertical axes of socialization within kin and outside them. (Of course, such items also served as transactions of artifact and desire between men and female sex workers.) Only the more intimate would be able, or allowed, to come very close to this thing while it was being worn. The user in this sense is any viewer who takes satisfaction: the maker of such objects sketches as shadow the touch of a man who removes a fastener to make a woman more naked to him. This one stimulates the thought of sexual and affectional hunger: it putatively lives in, as well as discusses, the domain of affect—a character of Greek and Roman jewelry that countless texts attest from Homer and Hesiod onward, and that could be derived from the artifact record itself even without texts. Moreover, this piece, and so much else of Late Classical and Hellenistic female metal body ornament that alludes to the domain of Aphrodite, Eros, and Isis, is open to being invested very seriously by an owner/user with talismanic force, in bringing and maintaining desire or "love" between male and female (e.g. see Faraone 1999).

So how do we have this pin? It has a vivid life in the popular imagination and popular scholarship. Unlike the bulk of ancient Greek goldwork extant from the Mediterranean, it has a known archeological context, discovered in 1888 at the Aphrodite sanctuary at Palaiopaphos, legally and scientifically excavated. It lay in the temple's central chamber near the foundation level of the walls, "in the last inch of soil above the rock."[17] This was beneath the level of a later pavement of the Roman Imperial period that carefully fitted slabs including older votives' fragments. This chamber would have originally been full of precious and/or significant votives and votive tokens: when the Imperial-era floor was laid, this pin was lost in the clearing of the divine hoard or deliberately left behind as an auspicious foundation deposit.

Its inscribing donor Eubola was a (wealthy) aristocrat, for her husband Aratas' title "Kinsman" (*syngenes*, i.e. of the king) was the highest rank in the court bureaucracy of the Ptolemaic dynasty as instituted by Ptolemy Epiphanes (205–180 BCE), dating our artifact to the second century BCE. From the late 290s BCE on, the Ptolemies directly administered Cyprus, having killed or displaced the seven Cypriot city kings; this object is, among other things, a telling sociopolitical document, entangling sex with power in an artifact of empire, from a land key to Ptolemaic maritime power and economic prosperity. Both men and women of the colonizing power prayed at the extant sanctuaries of the conquered island, already rich with aristocratic and royal as well as commoners' dedications, and these sites were thick with dedications for and from Ptolemaic civic and military officials; the indigenous Cypriote elites had an interest in that sacro-political investment as a way to configure themselves as important in the structure of empire. The female kin of the important conquerors, identified as such, could occupy dedicatory space as well, as we know from numerous statue bases, including at our Aphrodite sanctuary.[18]

OBJECTS OF PRAYER

What is a votive? An enormous amount of ancient Mediterranean artifacts extant or textually documented, of architectures and designed spaces, is for contexts specifically religious, where matter has discourse with the immaterial, intentionality of placement is unquestionable, and at least a moment's attention to an object once it left its makers' hands can be inferred with certainty. God wants stuff. In Greek religious practice as it emerged in the Dark Ages, and in much of Etruscan and Roman practice, as for some other peoples of this Old World between Central Asia and the Atlantic, giving material things to a deity was a significant technology for bringing about personal and communal wellbeing (see above p. 17). It was a tool wielded with affect—in fear or despair or hope or gratitude—and in social competition—to mediate relationships with the not-human through the artifactual. It had complex symmetries and asymmetries with amassing, ownership, and gifting by humans among humans. In Christian Late Antiquity, votive habits still retained force, with donors competing to give vessels, implements, textiles, lamps, and candelabra to the celebration and celebrants of ritual, the housing of relics, and the splendor of sacred interior space,[19] even donating entire shrines and their decoration. The Christian sacred object at shrines comes into focus only with the first generation of state-sanctioned Christianity under Constantine, with the wide establishment of public Christian sanctuaries for the first time; God wanted stuff in those, too. A classic visual commentary is given by the ceiling vault mosaics of the fourth-century CE imperial mausoleum of Santa Costanza in Rome (Figure 8.4) that show what would ordinarily have been banquet silver decoratively spread out, to echo the now-lost fine precious metal vessels this church surely saw on the altar, as we know them from inventories of Constantine's own donations at Rome and so many elsewhere, as well as archaeologically. The fourth-century CE image follows an ancient tradition of sanctuary art that glossed its votive landscape, as in the Flavian or Trajanic temple friezes in the same city, at the Temple of Venus Genetrix; lively Amores bustle, heaving and arranging in her Olympian house fine metal objects, from bathwater or wine urn to her lover Mars' shield, to gloss the votive cluster in her splendor-packed earthly house (Figure 8.5).

Some things were purpose-made for display in religious space; of these, some had no cognate use in the lived world other than votive character, like tripods, or many kinds of terracotta figurines. Others were fine versions of things from the world of personal use, of tool or costume. Yet other objects derived their force from having been in the possession of the dedicator and used by the dedicator before being gifted. Our pin is a classic example of an object conceived for personal usage and individual ownership that was moved with will and thought, and with some sort of emotion (even the irony of agnostics) into sacred space, and the possession of an entity to whom the giver hoped the memory of the donor would recur for good effect. One of the performances of piety was to look not only at ritual actions by living persons, but also at ritual action instantiated in these mediating things. It was of enormous importance that the god be known to have stores and treasures,[20] and that some of these at least should be on show, in any case to the privileged, inside sanctuary structures, as well as around them. (Numerous texts detail elite and sub-elite visits to see things at shrines.) Communal identities in their construction by ritual played out in sacred space, hence monuments and artifacts desiring communal gaze accumulated there: these were in every sense sites for memory, hoped for by individuals and communities. Even the small and not very visible—or not visible at all—was powerful in the memory of at least two cognizant beings, particular to the giver and the god. The object is itself the prayer, and it is, at the same time, the pray-er. And words very powerfully activated donation and commemoration, though of course god knew givers anyway: they were

FIGURE 8.5 Marble relief from the Temple of Venus Genetrix in the Forum Julium at Rome, from its restoration in the late first or early second century CE, Museo dei Fori Imperiali (Palazzo Conservatori inv. 2398); height 1.45 m, length 1.92 m, depth 1.39 m. Entablature fragment with a frieze of Amores arranging decorative and functional fine objects (here, filling a water or wine basin from an amphora, moving an incense stand, and propping up a shield) (Wikimedia Commons: Sailko).

important speech acts, whether or not much on show. In being inscribed by a metalsmith at its donors' behest and passed to the goddess, the Paphian pin entered a field of force, a condition of entanglement, radically different from that of the artifact's notional status as possession of an individual or her family, yet also permanently entangled with them. Could you see the pin as a visitor? Perhaps its enormous outsized pearl can have made it as intriguing then as now; so fragile it would have had a box, a stand, a shelf. Certainly, it was looked after until its late first-century CE burial, and, in its origin period, notated, we can be sure, by sanctuary official in typical temple inventory.[21] Note well that this pin was given privileged space, because of its donor's standing, at the very temple cella in a sanctuary where the real estate of piety was at a premium. Eubola could hope her name, and that of her listed kin, would be read and reread down the centuries by more than gods, even if only by a harried clerk.

That the pin with Aphrodite's doves on it moved from the domain of the body, an extension of flesh, to a goddess of the body was very much its point, as we know from the rich record of costuming passed from female donors to Aphrodite in particular. Dress pin votives by the thousand are archeologically documented in the Greek world in the Archaic and early Classical periods (Brøns 2016: on pins at 191–3). Did Eubola know that—or did she simply pick "pin" in following Greek female custom of giving to goddesses rich costume elements, particularly those meant to wrap the body and to hold clothing and coiffure together, whose removal meant sexual congress? A human woman as wife, perhaps as mother, greets in prayer the goddess, for having or wishing a husband's love, a matron's fertility, or her human charm: if Eubola did not "believe," which is a modern way of assessing ritual aims, she still walked at least notionally the motions of enacted piety, a worshipper from Egypt across the sea, as if there were an Aphrodite to be pleased at global domain. Inscribed, the husband (who may have given it to her and/or seen it on her) is sanctified, too, in an aristocratic echo of the typical cultic role of Eubola's queen in serving the wellbeing and memory of her royal husband and the important cults of Aphrodite-in-Egypt that were royal foundations and/or tied to the queens.

For anything gifted to the sanctuary, humble or grand, there are questions archaeology cannot answer easily, if at all, for any single artifact, though we can speak in generalities. Did the donor actually come here, and pass the pin from her own hands to a sanctuary attendant? Is this the instantiation of pious pilgrimage? Or did the donor give someone else instructions to dedicate an object for her, so that it journeyed in her stead? If so, did she ever actually see or touch it herself, or was the maker/buyer instructed verbally, even in writing, to cause the object to come into being and to get it to the sanctuary? Historic elite votives have such gift histories in our ancient texts. Was this pin perhaps even dispatched from Egypt at the return of Eubola there, or did Eubola stay in Egypt while her husband came to Cyprus and send a prayer to the goddess of the seas on his behalf? We have little or no idea, in fact, of the Greco-Roman ritual of votive deposition, save to guess that at least some of the time there has to have been a place to take things by custom, and/or a priest or other sacred official to hand them to. Surely all portable votive objects were notionally felt to pass from the hands of the giver, and body objects above all. We need more work on the votive thing's situation in the Greco-Roman world to map its place in the meshwork of affect, memory, politics, religion, and identity tying these transactional gifts to individual and community, human and supernal; perhaps this little object chapter and its citations can be a spur for scholars and enrich the responses of any reader viewing the Greco-Roman object.

NOTES

Preface

1 Foucault himself had a hand in the English title, since he would have preferred to call the French book *L'Ordre des choses*.

Introduction

1 French theorists: Baudrillard 1996, Latour 1993; anthropologists: Strathern 1988, Gell 1992, 1998; literary critics: Brown 2001, 2003; sociologists: Preda 1999; archaeologists: Lemonnier 1993, Schiffer 1999, DeMarrais, Gosden, and Renfrew 2004, Meskell 2005, Boivin 2008, Skibo and Schiffer 2008, Miller 2010, Olsen 2010, Hodder 2012.
2 Works on material culture of particular periods: Perry 2001, O'Malley and Welch 2007; survey: Bennett and Joyce 2010; history of the world: MacGregor 2012.
3 The anonymous poem *Aetna* from the first century CE becomes a description of human theories of the causes of volcanic activity rather than simply a description of Etna itself and ends up with a story of two brothers rescuing their parents; Philostratos' Scamander is really about Homer, not about landscape (*Imagines* 1.1).
4 On this tradition, see Pavlovskis 1973; on Statius and Ausonius' *Mosella*, see also Kenney 1984. Statius' famous description of the road of Domitian in *Silvae* 4.17 (on which see Chapter 2) is particularly important here.
5 Fragmentation and connectivity are the key terms in Horden and Purcell's classic analysis of Mediterranean history (2000).
6 On the role of objects in the late Bronze Age world see Steel 2013.
7 See further Lloyd 1973, Cuomo 2007, and Chapter 2.
8 Coulton 1977: 53–73. Senseney 2011 traces the development of architectural drawing ("ichnography") and its practical role; see Senseney 2011: 26 n.1 for a summary of the debate on the role of scale drawing.
9 For objects made by gods in Pausanias see Osborne 2010; for epiphany see Platt 2011.

Chapter 1

1 This is a view particularly associated with Moses Finley. See Finley (1965)1981, 1973; for recent revisions, see Greene 2000, Wilson 2002.
2 For swords, see Snodgrass 1964: 103–4; for plows and scythes, see Margaritis and Jones 2008: 168–71; for jewelry, see Ogden 1998.
3 On pre-Socratic theories, see Graham 2006; Warren 2007.
4 See the classic discussion of Lloyd 1979. On magic and materiality, see Boschung and Bremmer 2015. Objects characteristically manifest their supernatural agency in magic through human physical acts with regard to them; see Glucklich 1997: 230–1.
5 See in general Wilson 2008. On the earliest use of the block and tackle and its consequences, see Coulton 1974.
6 For an introduction to Parmenides and reactions to Parmenides, see Warren 2007: 73–118.
7 For a helpful account of Plato's epistemology, see Wolfsdorf 2014.
8 For a helpful account of Aristotle's epistemology, see Lorenz 2014.
9 For helpful introductions to Roman property law, see Crook 1967: 139–78; Du Plessis 2015.
10 See further the discussion in Chapter 2.
11 Compare Aristotle's history of coinage, *Politics* 1275a.
12 The absence of small change had been asserted by Kraay 1964; the contrary was demonstrated first by Kim (2001, 2002), whose findings have been subsequently reinforced; see Van Alfen 2006: 49–85.
13 On lending and borrowing in classical Athens, see Millett 1991.
14 Simmel (1907)1978: 227. For the alleged opposition to coinage and the monetary economy in late archaic Greece, see Kurke 1999.
15 Wilson 2000 on choregic monuments; Ma 2013 on saying thank you with a statue.

Chapter 2

1 Hero's dates have historically been the subject of controversy, though he is now most commonly dated to the first century CE (Keyser 1988; Asper 2001; Sidoli 2011).
2 It may be noted that Hero is advertising for the *dioptra*, a competing technology. But my own experiences using a *groma* in the wind certify the fairness of Hero's critique.
3 Museo Archeologico Nazionale di Napoli, inv. 109982. In her analysis of the mosaic, Cuomo argues that the carpenter's square, signifying that death makes everyone equal, becomes a potent polemical image when displayed by a wealthy freedman (Cuomo 2007: 99–102).
4 Philo's *Syntaxis* originally comprised nine books: an introduction, μοχλικά (On Levers), λιμενοποιικά (Harbor-Making), βελοποιικά (Artillery-Making), πνευματικά (Pneumatics), αὐτοματοποιητικά (Automaton-Making), παρασκευαστικά (Siege Preparation), πολιορκητικά (Siegecraft), and a ninth volume probably on stratagems. Many of these books are now lost; only the "Artillery-Making," the "Siege Preparation," and the "Siegecraft" are extant in Greek, while the "Pneumatics" survives primarily in Arabic and Latin.
5 Cuomo provides a nuanced overview of the cautionary notes Plato, Aristotle, and other elite authors offered on *technē*'s role in society (2007: 22–40). Rather

than taking their judgments at face value, Cuomo shows how "distaste for the banausic technician channeled wider disquiet about non-traditional power groups" (2007: 37).

6 Medical authors provide some information on technical training that might serve as comparison, heavily slanted though it is toward the textual and theoretical rather than the practical (Oser-Grote 1998). Pilar Pérez Cañizares (2017) focuses more closely on the extent to which a reader might learn practical procedures from Hippocratic texts.

7 https://www.topoi.org/project/d-5-6/. (Accessed June 05 2020).

8 Molly Swetnam-Burland explains that Pliny conflates different obelisks (2010).

9 Jones notes that the grant application written by Derek de Solla Price to fund the first studies of the Antikythera Mechanism indeed references the device made by Archimedes (2017: 41).

10 http://www.antikythera-mechanism.gr/faq (accessed November 3, 2017). The answer given is negative.

Chapter 3

1 See, for example, the series of studies published by the Oxford Roman Economy Project (OXREP), including Bowman and Wilson (2009, 2011, 2013, 2017). See also Scheidel and Von Reden 2002; Manning and Morris 2005; Scheidel, Morris, and Saller 2007.

2 Zuniga 1999: 299, in conversation with Menger's *Principles of Economics* (1871, 1951).

3 Ossandon 2015 draws on Mol 2002 for the concept of enactment. Mol uses the term, broadly, to refer to the way that objects are meaningfully constituted through interactions. See also Thomas 1991 and Strathern 1999.

4 Appadurai 1986. See also discussion in Caple 2006.

5 See discussion in Papadopoulos and Urton 2012 on the concept of *value*, in its broadest sense.

6 See Dewald's discussion of the variable ways that knowing or not knowing about an object's meaning plays out in the *Histories*, esp. 1993: 64ff.

7 In a recent handbook to ancient Greek and Roman numismatics, the editor rather dryly observes that "for the Greek world discussion of economic history is surprisingly free of references to coinage." Metcalf 2012: 9. For a corrective, see Von Reden 2010; Bresson 2016.

8 For a discussion of the range of terms used in ancient sources to connote value, money, coinage, and related concepts, see Von Reden 2010: 6–8.

9 Burnett 2012: 302–4, fig. 16.11–12 for the third-century examples and fig. 16.13 for the earlier, likely Etruscan, bars.

10 See Papadopoulos 2012: 268–70 for the distribution of these early coin types, especially in sanctuary contexts. See also Kim 2001; Kurke 1999: 10; Von Reden 2010: 21–5.

11 For example studies, see Stevens 1991; Haselgrove and Wigg-Wolf 2005; Sauer 2005; Wellington 2006; Von Kaenel and Kemmers 2009; Ciric 2013; Kemmers 2018.

12 See Van Oyen's recent study (2016: 3–7) for a discussion of this tendency and in general for a reconsideration of *terra sigillata*'s potential to support more dynamic object–agent narratives.

13   The reuse of amphorae in maritime commerce and other scenarios is well-documented in antiquity, providing some context for the phenomenon of mass dumping described above. See Abdelhamid 2013.

Chapter 5

1   Stewart 2007: 162; Platt 2011; Myrup Kristensen 2013: ch. 1. I am most grateful to Robin Osborne, Michael Squire, Caroline Van Eck, and the Leiden "Innovating objects" team for their critical feedback, as well as to Troels Kristensen, Eric Moorman, and David Rijser.
2   Gell 1998; Van Eck 2015a; see also Chapter 8 of this volume.
3   For instance, Pliny, *NH* 36.21: "A certain individual, it is said, became enamoured of this statue, and, concealing himself in the temple during the night, gratified his lustful passion upon it, traces of which are to be seen in a stain left upon the marble."
4   Important still Gordon 1979; see recently Frontisi-Ducroux 2016.
5   Livy 29.14.10–14 and Ovid, *Fasti* 4.343–7, see Gruen 1990: 5–33 also for the episode more generally.
6   See Trentmann 2009: 288 for a similar observation regarding historical studies in general ("In short, historical material culture studies have been more about culture than about material. Objects are 'bundles of meaning'. But are they only that?") and Versluys 2017b for a brief evaluation of the material turn within Roman archaeology in particular. For a history of the scholarly conceptualization of objects, see Miller 2017.
7   Good and theoretically sophisticated recent collections that provide an overview of the field are Bielfeldt 2014; Van Oyen and Pitts 2017; and the special issue of *Art History* entitled *The Embodied Object in Classical Antiquity* (41[3] 2018).
8   There are many (wonderful) examples of such human–thing entanglements in the chapters of this book: the Sidonian silver mixing bowl with a gold rim that binds Menelaos and Telemachos together (Chapter 1); the interactions between individual technological objects and their "devoted users, obsessive designers, proud patrons, or inspired admirers" (Chapter 2); the encounters between the architecture of Greek Classical theaters and their humans that would shape Euripides and his plays (Chapter 6); or the objects taken by the inhabitants of Pompeii, fleeing away from the eruption in 79 CE, as extensions of their selves (Chapter 7).
9   See Chapter 1 of this volume, as well as Gosden 2006 more generally.
10 Showing how the change from polytheism to Christianity is connected to a change in religious focus from object to text/book (Chapter 1); how sundials instigated the contraction of time and space in the ancient world, thus being important protagonists in a story of ancient globalization (Chapter 2); how colonnades and "the colonnading of space" were central actants in the processes of change we call Hellenization and Romanization (Chapter 6); or how changes in the available repertoire of jewelry and other bodily objects resulted in profoundly different conceptions of the cosmos (Chapter 7). For an attempt to materialize the history of Roman religion from such a perspective, see Versluys and Woolf forthcoming.
11 For the concept of *object-scape* as a hermeneutic tool to try and document material agency from a long-term perspective, see Versluys 2017b, Pitts and Versluys forthcoming. In Chapter 8 of this volume, Kuttner uses the ideas of statue-scapes and artifact-scapes.
12 I will not deal with the Roman word (or concept) for object, which, if they really had one that is comparable to ours, is *res*. This can mean very many things, especially in

a legal sense. *Res* is at the root of our word "reality" (see Chapter 7 of this volume; Daremberg-Saglio IV. 2.840–4 sv. *res*). Although this is a very important element of the discussion, I will also not deal with philosophical understandings of concepts like object, matter, and materiality in antiquity, for which see the splendid volume Porter 2010; Bielfeldt 2014; and some remarks on the concept of aesthetics further below.

13 Throughout this article I will use the concepts "things" and "objects" indiscriminately, as if they are the same thing, and not deal with the important debate on the (conceptual) difference between objects and things, for which see recently Domínguez Rubio 2016 (with earlier literature).

14 Fundamental is Squire 2009. For Homer, see Becker 1995; Crielaard 2003; Grethlein 2008.

15 Translation after R. Lattimore, who indeed translated *"tetugmenon"* as "work of art." *Odyssey* book 4 presents us with a comparable story regarding a similar bowl made by Hephaistos and coming from the king of the Sidonians; see Chapter 1 of this volume.

16 Maran and Stockhammer 2012. For the concept of social exoticism, see Helms 1988.

17 See Kistler 2010; Crielaard 2015. For (repertoires of) objects in motion making up new cultural figurations in general, see Van Eck et al. 2015.

18 See Gosden 2006; Versluys 2014 for theoretical background and more examples of "impact repertoires."

19 For this interpretation as well as the monument and its historical context in general, see Versluys 2017a (with all earlier bibliography), on which this section is based.

20 For the impact and agency of semantic elements and repertoires, see Hölscher 1987, 2018. For the "haunting character" of certain object repertoires and their material presence, see Versluys 2015.

21 Gawlikowski 2008; Myrup Kristensen 2013: 211–18. Allat was a goddess of Semitic origin that could be associated with Athena.

22 See Harmansah 2015 for a pertaining analysis, although not so much concerned with object agency. Apparently our statue of Allat Athena was part of this and has again been violated (Troels Kristensen, personal communication).

23 I will not deal with the Greek and Roman words describing what we call art, which are *technē* and *ars*, respectively, but only note that the ancient world had no word that translates as our concept of art, as these terms mean "craft," "skill," or "expertise" and can refer to any activity that can be learned or that involves a body of knowledge. The articles in Platt and Squire 2010 provide a fine overview of the debate. See also the introductions to recent companions on Greek and Roman art, respectively: Smith and Plantzos 2012; Hallett 2015. The latter proposes to do away with the concept of art for the Roman world altogether and to talk about visual culture instead.

24 Squire 2012; see also the introductory chapters to Squire 2009 and 2011. That there had been no chapters on art in the first edition of the *Classical Archaeology* volume for the Blackwell series *Studies in Global Archaeology* is illustrative of the difficulty scholars have had (and still have) with finding a place for the concept of art in their study of material culture. Within Classical archaeology, two attitudes—both extremist—seem to pertain: uncritical embrace versus ideological neglect. In his article, Squire explicitly deals with this most unfruitful dichotomy and its history, as do Scott 2006; Versluys 2010/11; Marlowe 2013.

25 Kinney 2006; Boschung 2017 for a "morphomatic" reading of such objects traveling through time.
26 For these questions, see Mitchell 1996; Gosden 2005; Grethlein 2017.
27 Cf. Morphy 2010: 265: "I have come to believe in the utility of the concept of art and that the practice and performance of art reflects particular ways of knowing and acting in the world."
28 As Gell 1996 in the first volume of the *Journal of Material Culture*.
29 Garrow and Gosden 2012; Meyer 2013, respectively. These books deal with very different object repertoires but have a very similar subject.
30 Bahrani 2014. Although this is an important topic, I will not deal with "the aesthetic of the sublime" as the strongest experience of objects. For relations between art, agency, and the sublime, see Porter 2010: pt. III, the overview provided by Costelloe 2012 and Porter 2016.
31 Summers 2010: 11. Cf. also the introductions to Sluiter and Rosen 2012; Destrée and Murray 2015.
32 Many examples of such sensory appeal can be found in Sluiter and Rosen 2012; Destrée and Murray 2015: does the material turn in Classics takes place through an interest in the concept of aesthetics as well?
33 Porter 2010: 11; cf. Platt 2016; the special issue of *Art History* entitled *The Embodied Object in Classical Antiquity* (41[3] 2018); as well as, more generally, the Routledge series *The Senses in Antiquity*.
34 As Chris Gosden (2004: 31) put it: "... our relationship with the object world through our senses can be best understood in terms of aesthetics, the sets of discriminations of taste that we apply to the sensory qualities of objects and people." Cf. also Gosden 2000.
35 Segalen 2002. For introductions to his work and ideas, see Forsdick 2000; Van Alphen 2016, both with earlier bibliographies. Jean Baudrillard referred to these ideas when discussing "singular objects" with the architect Jean Nouvel toward the end of his life (see the epigraph in this chapter, from Baudrillard and Nouvel 2002).
36 Quotes from Forsdick 2000: 185; Baudrillard and Nouvel 2002: 9–10, respectively.
37 For "impact repertoires," see above. Versluys 2017c discusses Egyptian-looking objects as such an "impact repertoire" worldwide and throughout time.
38 Segalen's ideas might also help in explaining why, in terms of stylistics, cultures always need the radical exoticism of "the primitive" next to the Archaic, the Classical, etc.; see Hallett 2012; Schmidt-Linsenhoff 2014; Van Eck et al. 2015.
39 See Hölscher 2006; Squire 2013. I refer to these articles for their immense bibliographies on the Prima Porta Augustus and for many observations on the statue that follow.

Chapter 6

1 Coarelli 1983. As the notional center of city life, the Forum brought together important buildings and people; government, judicial, and financial functions; converging streets; and a staggering number of toponyms and associated stories.
2 Leroi-Gourhan 1943; Gibson 1979; Gell 1998; Hodder 2012. Knappett 2004 observes usefully that affordances do not actually inhere in objects but rather are situational; for example, a chair is not inherently sittable to all agents, such as children.

3   Arafat 2009. The principal literary sources on the treasuries are of course Pausanias and Plutarch, both of whom speak with precision about the circumstances and personalities surrounding the founding of treasuries many centuries earlier.

4   This view might seem antithetical to Gombrich's well-known cognitive hypothesis (1979)—derived from Karl Popper's "tenet of exclusion"—that the mind is far more attentive to breaks in a pattern than in the pattern itself, selecting discontinuities because of their greater explanatory value in our phenomenal world. But the two are not really so incompatible; the result of surveying a mass of ornament without the help of intelligible discontinuities that would cue our "break spotters" is confusion—a state comparable, perhaps, to Gell's trance-like fascination.

5   Loos 1998. I am grateful to Natsumi Nonaka and Richard Etlin for their insights into the influence of Alberti and Loos on contemporary perceptions of architectural ornament. Ironically, Loos's own architecture is exquisitely ornamented, at least in its obsessive attention to materials and detailing.

6   Frakes 2009: 87–8, 258–63. For the example of Volubilis in Morocco, in which a bricolage of abutting facades of arcaded pillars, trabeated pillars, and columns appeared in sequence along the *decumanus maximus*, see Crowther 2019.

7   I owe these and other observations on Roman colonnaded streets to Crowther 2019.

Chapter 7

1   https://friendsofclassics.wordpress.com/2013/03/29/pompeii-again/ (accessed August 18, 2017).

2   Although note the "Living with objects, dying with objects" section of this essay (*infra*) and Chapter 8 in this volume on the "bid for memory" made by burial assemblages.

3   Raising the agency of the corpse is Robb 2013.

4   Plato, *Phaedo* 115c–e. Although qualifying this, note *Gorgias* 524b–d. Also relevant here is *Apology* 40C. I thank Franco Basso for help on this point.

5   For more on this, see "Object agency and the concept of art" in Chapter 5 of this volume.

6   Important here is Routledge's *Senses in Antiquity* series; Toner 2014; Betts 2017.

7   On clothed *kouroi*, see Barletta 1987.

8   For *korai*, see Karakasi 2003; Stieber 2004. Note that although Acropolis Museum, inv. no. 680 (530–20 BCE) extends her hand toward the viewer to offer an apple, the Peplos Kore (Acropolis Museum, inv. no. 679) may originally have held a bow and been intended as Artemis; Neer 2012: 157.

9   That said, they still give meaning to dress. For Greek dress, see e.g. Sebesta and Bonfante 1994; Lee 2015; and for the agency of clothes beyond Greece and Rome, see Miller 2010: 12–41.

10 Ogden 2002: 203–4; and, for a sense of the longer tradition of which the Hellenistic Andania inscription is a part, see Parker 1983: 83, fn. 36.

11 Karakasi 2003: 121. On the Acropolis *kore*, see Acropolis Museum, inv. no. 670.

12 On objects as an extension of the body, see Gaifman and Platt 2018.

13 For the full inscription, see Stieber 2004: 146. Also critical here is Svenbro 1993.

14 An early, formative version of the myth is the *Homeric Hymn to Demeter*; see Warren 2017.

15 On slave as object, see duBois 2003; Bielfeldt 2018.

16   Although note, too, occasional Fayum portraits of jeweled men and children; Borg 1996: 167–72.

17   *Roman Inscriptions of Britain* 685, Yorkshire Museum, inv. no. 1998.18; see also Mattingly 2006: 209. The dearth of comparanda makes stelai like these difficult to date; it could be first to fourth century CE.

18   On the glimpses these Roman reliefs offer on the subject–object relations between "craftsman, their tools, and their products," and for the range of representational choices they play with even in a given period, see Chapter 2 of this volume.

19   For these feasting or "Totenmahl" scenes, see Dunbabin 2003: 103–10.

20   I am influenced here by, and owe the quotes to, McQueston 2013: 76.

21   I think here, in particular, of the red-slipped and burnished tablewares of the first and second centuries CE ("*terra sigillata*") often stamped with their maker's name. On "*terra sigillata*" as "a standardized and homogenous product" (Allison and Pitts 2018), see Van Oyen 2016.

22   For a basic picture of the "Tetrarchs" in relation to prior imperial portraiture, see Kleiner 1992: 400–7.

23   On the increased importance of imperial ceremonial, see MacCormack 1981.

24   See also the carved ivory panels of a Byzantine empress (Ariadne?), *c.* 500 CE, now in the Museo Nazionale del Bargello, Florence, and the Kunsthistorisches Museum, Vienna, and Stout 1994: 83.

25   For an experiential approach to the Classical Greek libation bowl as handheld object, see Gaifman 2018.

26   For the symposium, see Hobden 2013; and for the Inn (Pompeii, VI.14.35–6), see Clarke 2003: 161–8.

27   I am thinking here of the story of Pentheus (e.g. see Euripides' *Bacchae*).

28   For cognition and sociality, with particular reference to Alfred Gell's work, see Chua and Elliott 2013.

29   For example, see fourth-century BCE Athenian doctor Mnesitheus (as discussed in Jouanna 2012: 193) on wine for mortals as "the greatest blessing for those who use it correctly, for those who use it unregulated, the opposite."

30   Aelian, *Historical Miscellany* 2.37. See also 2.38 on the restrictions imposed on the women of Massilia and Miletus, and women and slaves of Rome.

31   For an introduction to the "Gellogram" and its uses, see Gell 1998; Osborne and Tanner 2007.

32   From the poem "Everything" in *The Roominghouse Madrigals: Early Selected Poems (1946–1966)*.

33   See Chapter 4 in this volume for what was and was not left behind at Pompeii and the curious dearth in houses there of objects such as knives, spoons, loom weights, spindles, mirrors, and strigils, some of which must have been taken with them by the fleeing residents.

34   As cited in Stobaeus 4.51.4 (*Suppl. Hell.* no. 402). For the poem and further discussion, see Rayor 2005: 67–8.

35   Morris, 1992: 104, 106 on how few burials included a coin for Charon, the ferryman to Hades.

36   On, for example, the link between fish and philosophy, see Davidson 1997.

37   This discussion is dependent on, but departs from, Izzet 1998, 2007, whose emphasis is gender. Compare Gerhard 1843–97: pl. 175, now in the Louvre. Also important here is the *Corpus Speculorum Etruscorum* series.

38 Eckardt 2014: 153–76. These are themselves a subset of a much larger corpus of Roman
    hairpins representing human hands, some also jet, shale, or glass: e.g. see Cool 1990.
39 Also important on pins and hairpins is Chapter 8 in this volume.

Chapter 8

1 For the concept of affordances—what an object permits, constrains, and enjoins as
   its handling—see recently, for example, Swift 2017; my discussion can be framed in
   the words of her title.
2 Alfred Gell (1994) gives a related but differently constructed argument about the
   entrancements of the well-made thing. He famously enunciated in 1998 a complex
   analytic system about relationships between objects and humans, including makers
   and viewers; he explored how art artifacts have agency, probing the mechanisms
   for how they signal or mean something; for attempts to cope with Gell in a range
   of disciplines engaged with antiquity as of modernity, see, for example, Tanner and
   Osborne 2007 and Chua and Elliott 2013.
3 *Habitus* is the social phenomenon mapped seminally by Pierre Bourdieu; for its
   application to a sociology of artists and their art, see in compressed form his elegant
   essay of 1993. What is applied by him to "high" arts can translate to any artisanry,
   that particular link along the anthro-archaeologists' model of the *chaîne opératoire*
   of substance acquisition, shaping, and positioning.
4 Malafouris writes copiously; see, for example, 2013 and 2015. Important for
   archaeologists of the post-prehistoric as well is Malafouris and Renfrew 2010.
5 For "art," replica studies have an enormous bibliography: a fine recent work of the
   particularizing of the same replica in different houses at Rome is Trimble 2018, on
   a statue type of powerful aesthetic, sensual, and sexual appeal as well as an emotive
   and intellectual one.
6 La Follette 2012.
7 The bibliography is too large to cite: see, for instance, the references in n. 9.
   Classical studies of object poems would do well to engage the "new materialism" in
   literary criticism of modern-era thing text, as in, for example, Brown 2003, 2015.
   Productive for object epigram and collectionism is Stewart 1993, famous especially
   for its discussion of the miniature.
8 In general on Poseidippos, see, for example, Gutzwiller 2005 and Acosta-Hughes et
   al. 2004: bibliography; see also Magnelli 2009.
9 Bounia 2004: 231–9; Stroup 2005; Macdonald 2017. For commoditization, still
   useful to think with is Kopytoff 1986, in a volume broadly relevant here.
10 For "Romanization" in the larger empire as such a dynamic universe of "object in
   motion," see, for example, Versluys 2014, and, in the same journal issue, responses
   to his project. See Chapter 5 in this volume for further object-based approaches,
   including Versluys' own work on a "Roman global." For a lovely exploration of the
   ramifying production and consumption of the everyday tool across social strata and
   its aestheticization across multiple large Roman regions, see, for example, Eckardt
   2017 (e.g. on decorated metal inkwells).
11 Cf. Blake 2011 on Martial and Pliny; on the imperial reach of Pliny himself, see, for
   example, Carey 2003.
12 On the House of the Vettii, see Clarke 1991: 208–35, pl. 12 and figs. 124–8, 132;
   on power dynamics in this and the Roman house generally, see Severy Hoven
   2012.

13 Berlin, Antikensammlung F 2294, *c*. 490–80 BCE, diameter 30.5 cm, height 12 cm. Mattusch 1980, 1988: fig. 5.7, 106–7; Neer 2002: 78–85, figs. 37–9; Lee 2015: 49, fig. 2.7. On art and craft workshop scenes on Athenian red-figure ware generally, see, for example, Lewis 2011; this painter made more.

14 British Museum GR 1888, 1115.2; length 17.8 cm, bronze, gold, and pearl. Excavated at the Sanctuary of Aphrodite at Old Paphos. https://www.britishmuseum. org/collection/object/G_1888-1115-2 (accessed June 05 2020).

15 All studies of what ornamented women's bodies (including costume and coiffure) can benefit both from considering the complex engagement with such things by both genders and from contextualizing themselves in a self-conscious archaeology of gender: besides Chapters 4 and 7 in this volume, exemplary, for instance, is the compilation by Nelson 2006—also an outstanding resource for object and thing studies broadly speaking.

16 On this, and other pins with Aphrodite/Eros, see Havelock 2007: 89; Jackson 2006 (on Eros jewelry of all kinds): 53.

17 See Hogarth et al. 1888: pl. XI and 161, 165 and 222–3, no. 11 with a drawing of the inscription for details of the findspot, along with Hogarth 1888: 186–7; the British Museum database (see n. 14) gives additional bibliography. Most recently in (semi-) popular form, see Lapatin 2015: 268–9, pl. 170. The two crowning beads were found separately near it; their reattachment is modern.

18 On the sanctuary, base for the contemporary second-century BCE Polykrateia, daughter of another royal Kinsman, Theodoros the *strategos* of Cyprus, see Connelly 2007: 140; on Aratas' mission, see Papantoniou 2012: 399.

19 On church "treasures" and possessions in inventories, see Caseau 2007, and in the same volume see Fiema 2007 and Michel 2007 on archaeological traces.

20 Most recently, see Shaya 2015; for further on Greek temple interiors (applicable also to Roman ones) and the evidence for their votive displays, both the what and the how, see Miles 2016. One of the very few method essays on the votive, in anthropological as well as archaeological comparative terms, is Osborne 2004 (and see other papers in that journal volume).

21 On temple inventories, which survive as epigraphic commemorative versions on stone of papyrus records, see, for example, the overview of Shaya 2015, and also see Hamilton 2000 discussing the inventories for the temples of Artemis and of Apollo at Delos (rich with jewelry).

BIBLIOGRAPHY

Abdelhamid, S. 2013. "Against the throw-away-mentality: The reuse of amphoras in ancient maritime transport." In H. P. Hahn and H. Weiss (ed.), *Mobility, Meanings and Transformations of Things*. Oxford: Oxbow, 91–106.

Abry, J.-H. 1993. "Les diptyques de Grand, noms et images des décans." In J.-H. Abry (ed.), *Les tablettes astrologiques de Grand (Vosges): et l'astrologie en Gaule romaine: actes de la Table-Ronde du 18 mars 1992 organisée au Centre d'études romaines et gallo-romaines de l'Université Lyon III*. Centre d'études romaines et gallo-romaines. Lyon: Université Jean Moulin, 77–112.

Acosta-Hughes, Benjamin, Elizabeth Kosmetatou and Manuel Baumbach (eds.). 2004. *Labored in Papyrus Leaves: Perspectives on an Epigram Collection Attributed to Posidippus (P.Mil.Vogl. VIII 309)*. Hellenic Studies Series 2. Washington, DC: Center for Hellenic Studies. Available online: http://nrs.harvard.edu/urn-3:hul. ebook:CHS_AcostaHughesB_etal_eds.Labored_in_Papyrus_Leaves.2004 (accessed June 05/2020).

Alcock, Susan E. 2002. *Archaeologies of the Greek Past: Landscape, Monuments, and Memories*. Cambridge and New York: Cambridge University Press.

Allison, Penelope. 2004. *Pompeian Households: An Analysis of Material Culture*. Los Angeles: Cotsen Institute of Archaeology, UCLA.

Allison, Penelope M. 2006. *The Insula of the Menander at Pompeii. Vol. III: The Finds: A Contextual Study*. Oxford: Clarendon Press. Online database to accompany the publication: https://www.le.ac.uk/ar/menander/databasefields.html (accessed June 05 2020).

Allison, Penelope and Martin Pitts. 2018. "Roman Tablewares: Some Notes on Definitions and Terminology." *InternetArchaeology* 50. https://doi.org/10.11141/ ia.50.21.

Almeida, Emilio R. 1984. *Il Monte Testaccio: Ambiente, storia, materiali*. Rome: Quasar.

Andrianou, D. 2009. *The Furniture and Furnishings of Ancient Greek Houses and Tombs*. Cambridge: Cambridge University Press.

Appadurai, Arjun (ed.). 1986. *The Social Life of Things: Commodities in Cultural Perspective*. Cambridge: Cambridge University Press.

Arafat, Karim W. 2009. "Treasure, Treasuries, and Value in Pausanias." *The Classical Quarterly* 59: 578–92.

Arthur, P. 2007. "Form, function and technology in pottery production from late
    antiquity to the early middle ages." In L. Lavan et al. (ed.), *Technology in Transition
    A.D. 300–650*. Leiden: Brill, 159–86.
Ashby, Clifford. 1999. *Classical Greek Theatre: New Views of an Old Subject*. Iowa
    City, IA: University of Iowa Press.
Asper, M. 2001. "Dionysios (Heron, Def. 14. 3) und die Datierung Herons von
    Alexandria." *Hermes*, 129(1): 135–37.
Asper, M. 2007. *Griechische Wissenschaftstexte: Formen, Funktionen,
    Differenzierungsgeschichten*. Stuttgart: Steiner.
Ault, Bradley. 1994. *Classical Houses and Households: An Archaeological and
    Artifactual Case Study from Halieis, Greece*. PhD thesis. University of Indiana,
    Bloomington, IN.
Ault, Bradley. 2005. *Excavations at Ancient Halieis*. Bloomington, IN: Indiana
    University Press.
Bahrani, Z. 2014. *The Infinite Image: Art, Time and Aesthetic Dimension in Antiquity*.
    London: Reaktion Books.
Baird, D. 2004. *Thing Knowledge: A Philosophy of Scientific Instruments*. Berkeley:
    University of California Press.
Ball, Warwick. 2001. *Rome in the East: The Transformation of an Empire*. London and
    New York: Routledge.
Barletta, Barbara A. 1987. "The Draped Kouros Type and the Work of the Syracuse
    Youth." *American Journal of Archaeology* 91: 223–46.
Bassi, Karen. 2016. *Traces of the Past: Classics between History and Archaeology*. Ann
    Arbor: University of Michigan Press.
Baudrillard, Jean. 1996. *The System of Objects*. London: Verso.
Baudrillard, Jean and Jean Nouvel. 2000. *Les objects singuliers. Architecture et
    philosophie*. Paris 2000 (quoted after the English translation by R. Bononno, *The
    singular objects of architecture*, Minnesota: University of Minnesota Press, 2002).
Béal, J.-C. 1993. "Les tablettes astrologiques de Grand: étude des planches d'ivoire."
    In J.-H. Abry (ed.), *Les tablettes astrologiques de Grand (Vosges): et l'astrologie
    en Gaule romaine: actes de la Table-Ronde du 18 mars 1992 organisée au Centre
    d'études romaines et gallo-romaines de l'Université Lyon III*. Centre d'études
    romaines et gallo-romaines. Lyon: Université Jean Moulin, 53–62.
Becker, Andrew Sprague. 1995. *The Shield of Achilles and the Poetics of* Ekphrasis.
    Lanham: Rowan and Littlefield.
Beetham, David. 2013. *The Legitimation of Power*, 2nd edn. Basingstoke: Palgrave
    Macmillan.
Bémont, C. and J.-P. Jacob. 1986. *La Terre sigillée gallo-romaine. Lieux de production
    du Haut Empire: implantations, produits, relations, Documents d'archéologie
    française 6*. Paris: Editions de la Maison des sciences de l'homme.
Bennett, Tony and Patrick Joyce (eds.). 2010. *Material Powers: Cultural Studies,
    History and the Material Turn*. London: Routledge.
Berryman, S. 2009. *The Mechanical Hypothesis in Ancient Greek Natural Philosophy*.
    Cambridge and New York: Cambridge University Press.
Bertaux, J.-P. 1993. "La découverte des tablettes: les données archéologiques." In J.-H.
    Abry (ed.), *Les tablettes astrologiques de Grand (Vosges): et l'astrologie en Gaule
    romaine: actes de la Table-Ronde du 18 mars 1992 organisée au Centre d'études
    romaines et gallo-romaines de l'Université Lyon III*. Centre d'études romaines et
    gallo-romaines. Lyon: Université Jean Moulin, 39–47.

Betts, Eleanor. 2017. *Senses of the Empire: Multisensory Approaches to Roman Culture*. London and New York: Routledge.

Betz, H. D. 1986. *The Greek Magical Papyri in Translation, Including the Demotic Spells*. Chicago, IL: University of Chicago Press.

Bielfeldt, Ruth (ed.). 2014. *Ding und Mensch in der Antike. Gegenwart und Vergegenwärtigung*. Heidelberg: Universitätsverlag Winter.

Bielfeldt, Ruth. 2018. "*Candelabrus* and Trimalchio: Embodied Histories of Roman Lampstands and the Slaves." *Art History* 41(3) (*The Embodied Object in Classical Antiquity*): 420–43. Available online: https://onlinelibrary.wiley.com/doi/abs/10.1111/1467-8365.12382?af=R (accessed June 5, 2020).

Bing, Peter. 2005. "The Politics and Poetics of Geography in the Milan Posidippus, Section One: On Stones (AB 1-20)." In Kathryn Gutzwiller (ed.), *The New Posidippus: A Hellenistic Poetry Book*. Oxford: Oxford University Press, 119–40.

Blake, Sarah. 2011. "Martial's Natural History: The *Xenia* and *Apophoreta* and Pliny's Encyclopedia." *Arethusa* 44: 353–77.

Boardman, J. 2001. *Greek Gems and Finger Rings*. London: Thames and Hudson.

Boas, Frans. 1955. *Primitive Art*. New York: Dover.

Boatwright, Mary T. 2013. "Hadrian and the Pantheon Inscription." In Thorsten Opper (ed.), *Hadrian: Art, Politics and Economy*. London: British Museum, 19–30.

Boivin, Nicole. 2008. *Material Culture, Material Minds*. Cambridge: Cambridge University Press.

Bolton, R. 2012. "Science and Scientific Enquire in Aristotle: A Platonic Provenance." In C. Shields (ed.), *The Oxford Handbook of Aristotle*. Oxford: Oxford University Press, 46–60.

Bonifay, Michel. 2004. *Etudes sur la Céramique Romaine Tardive d'Afrique*, BAR international series 1301. Oxford: Archaeopress.

Bonifay, Michel. 2007. "Ceramic production in Africa during late antiquity: continuity and change." In L. Lavan et al. (eds.), *Technology in Transition A.D. 300–650*. Leiden: Brill, 143–86.

Borg, Barbara. 1996. *Mumienporträts: Chronologie und kultureller Kontext*. Mainz am Rhein: von Zabern.

Boschung, Dietrich. 2017. *Werke und Wirkmacht. Morphomatische Reflexionen zu archäologischen Fallstudien*. Paderborn: Verlag Wilhelm Fink.

Boschung, Dietrich and Jan N. Bremmer (eds.). 2015. *The Materiality of Magic*. Paderborn: Verlag Wilhelm Fink.

Bounia, Alexandra. 2004. *The Nature of Classical Collecting: Collectors and Collections, 100 BCE–100 CE*. Aldershot and Burlington, VT: Ashgate.

Bourdieu, Pierre. 1977. *Outline of a Theory of Practice*. Cambridge: Cambridge University Press.

Bourdieu, Pierre. 1993. "Who Created the Creators?" Trans. in Jeremy Tanner (ed.), *Sociology of Art*. London: Routledge, 96–103.

Bowman, Alan K. and Andrew Wilson. 2009. *Quantifying the Roman Economy: Methods and Problems*. Oxford: Oxford University Press.

Bowman, Alan K. and Andrew Wilson. 2011. *Settlement, Urbanization, and Population*. Oxford: Oxford University Press.

Bowman, Alan K. and Andrew Wilson. 2013. *The Roman Agricultural Economy: Organisation, Investment, and Production*. Oxford: Oxford University Press.

Bowman, Alan K. and Andrew Wilson. 2017. *Trade, Commerce, and the State in the Roman World*. Oxford: Oxford University Press.

Bresson, Alain. 2005. "La machine d'Héron et le coût de l'énergie dans le monde antique." In Elio Lo Cascio (ed.), *Innovazione tecnica e progresso economico nel mondo romano: atti degli incontri capresi di storia dell'economia antica (Capri 13–16 aprile 2003*. Bari: Edipuglia, 55–80.

Bresson, Alain. 2016. *The Making of the Ancient Greek Economy: Institutions, Markets, and Growth in the City-States*. Trans. Steven Rendall. Princeton, NJ: Princeton University Press.

Brøns, Cecilie. 2016. *Gods and Garments: Textiles in Greek Sanctuaries in the 7th to the 1st Centuries BC*. Oxford and Philadelphia, PA: Oxbow Books.

Broodbank, Cyprian. 2013. *The Making of the Middle Sea: A History of the Mediterranean from the Beinning to the Emergence of the Classical World*. London: Thames and Hudson.

Brown, Bill. 2001. "Thing Theory." *Critical Inquiry* 28(1): 1–22.

Brown, Bill. 2003. *A Sense of Things: The Object Matter of American Literature*. Chicago, IL: University of Chicago Press.

Brown, Bill. 2015. *Other Things*. Chicago, IL: University of Chicago Press.

Brown, Peter. 1988. *The Body and Society. Men, Women, and Sexual Renunciation in Early Christianity* (republished with a new introduction, 2008). New York: Columbia University Press.

Bruhn, Jutta-Annette. 1993. *Coins and Costume in Late Antiquity*. Washington, DC: Dumbarton Oaks Research Library and Collection.

Bruno, Vincent and Russell Scott. 1993. *Cosa IV: The Houses. Memoirs of the American Academy in Rome* 38. University Park: Pennsylvania State University Press.

Bussels, S. 2012. *The Animated Image: Roman Theory on Naturalism, Vividness and Divine Power*. Leiden: Akademie Verlag/Leiden University Press.

Burnett, A. 2012. "Early Roman coinage and its Italian context." In W. Metcalf (ed.), *The Oxford Handbook of Greek and Roman Coinage*. Oxford: Oxford University Press, 297–14.

Burrell, Barbara. 2006. "False Fronts: Separating the Aedicular Facade from the Imperial Cult in Asia Minor." *American Journal of Archaeology* 110: 437–69.

Cahill, Nicholas. 2002. *Household and City Organization at Olynthus*. New Haven, CT: Yale University Press.

Cahill, Nicholas and John Kroll. 2005. "New archaic coin finds at Sardis." *AJA* 109(4): 589–617.

Caple, Chris. 2006. *Objects: Reluctant Witnesses to the Past*. London: Routledge.

Carey, Sorcha. 2003. *Pliny's Catalogue of Culture: Art and Empire in the Natural History*. Oxford and New York: Oxford University Press.

Carpino, Alexandra, A. 2008. "Reflections from the Tomb: Mirrors as Grave Goods in Late Classical and Hellenistic Tarquinia." *Etruscan Studies* 11: 1–33.

Caseau, Béatrice. 2007. "Objects in Churches: The Testimony of Inventories." In Luke Lavan, Ellen Swift and Toon Putzeys (eds.), *Objects in Context, Objects in Use: Material Spatiality in Late Antiquity*. Leiden: Brill, 551–79.

Chouquer, G. and F. Favory. 2001. *L'arpentage romain: histoire des textes, droit, techniques*. Paris: Errance.

Chua, Liana and Mark Elliott (eds.). 2013. *Distributed Objects: Meaning and Mattering after Alfred Gell*. New York: Berghahn.

Ciric, G. 2013. "A secondary use of Roman coins? Possibilities and limitations of object biography." In H. P. Hahn and H. Weiss (eds.), *Mobility, Meaning and the Transformations of Things*. Oxford: Oxbow, 107–19.

Clark, Andy. 1997. *Being There: Putting Brain, Body, and World Together Again*. Cambridge, MA: MIT Press.

Clarke, John. 1991. *The Houses of Roman Italy, 100 B.C.–A.D. 250: Ritual, Space and Decoration*. Berkeley: University of California Press.

Clarke, John. 2003. *Art in the Lives of Ordinary Romans: Visual Representation and Non-Elite Viewers in Italy, 100 B.C.–A.D. 315*. Berkeley: University of California Press.

Clarke, K. 1999. *Between Geography and History: Hellenistic Constructions of the Roman World*. Oxford: Oxford University Press.

Clay, Jenny Strauss. 2003. *Hesiod's Cosmos*. Cambridge: Cambridge University Press.

Cleland, Liza. 2005. *The Brauron Clothing Catalogues: Text, Analysis, Glossary, and Translation*. Oxford: John and Erica Hedges Ltd.

Coarelli, Filippo. 1983. *Il foro romano*. 2 vols. Rome: Quasar.

Collins, H. M. 2010. *Tacit and Explicit Knowledge*. Chicago, IL and London: University of Chicago Press.

Connelly, Joan Breton. 2007: *Portrait of a Priestess: Women and Ritual in Ancient Greece*. Princeton, NJ: Princeton University Press.

Conybeare, Fred C. 1903. "The Survival of Animal Sacrifices inside the Christian Church." *The American Journal of Theology* 7(1): 62–90.

Cool, Hilary E. M. 1990. "Roman Metal Hairpins from Southern Britain." *Archaeological Journal* 147: 148–82.

Coote, Jeremy (ed.). 1994. *Anthropology, Art and Aesthetics*. Oxford: Clarendon Press.

Costelloe, Timothy M. (ed.). 2012. *The Sublime: From Antiquity to the Present*. Cambridge: Cambridge University Press.

Coulton, J. J. 1974. "Lifting in early Greek architecture." *Journal of Hellenic Studies* 94: 1–19.

Coulton, J. J. 1976. *The Architectural Development of the Greek Stoa*. Oxford: Clarendon Press.

Coulton, J. J. 1977. *Greek Architects at Work*. London: Elek

Cova, E. 2013. "Cupboards, closets and shelves: storage in the Pompeian household." *Phoenix* 67: 373–91.

Creese, D. E. 2010. *The Monochord in Ancient Greek Harmonic Science*. Cambridge: Cambridge University Press.

Crielaard, Jan Paul. 2003. "The Cultural Biography of Material Goods in Homer's Epics." *GAIA* 7: 49–62.

Crielaard, Jan Paul. 2015. "Powerful things in motion. A biographical approach to eastern elite goods in Greek sanctuaries." In E. Kistler, B. Öhlinger, M. Mohr and M. Hoernes (eds.), *Sanctuaries and the Power of Consumption. Networking and the Formation of Elites in the Archaic Western Mediterranean World*. Wiesbaden: Harrassowitz Verlag, 351–72.

Crook, John A. 1967. *Law and Life of Rome*. London: Thames & Hudson.

Crowther, B. 2019. "Life on the Streets: Architecture and Community along the Colonnaded Streets of the Roman Empire (1st–4th Centuries CE)." PhD diss., University of Texas at Austin.

Cuomo, Serafina. 2007. *Technology and Culture in Greek and Roman Antiquity*. Cambridge: Cambridge University Press.

Cuomo, Serafina. 2011. "A Roman Engineer's Tales." *The Journal of Roman Studies* 101: 143–65.

Davidson, James N. 1997. *Courtesans and Fishcakes: The Consuming Passions of Classical Athens*. London: Harper Collins.

Davis, Jack. L. and Sharon R. Stocker. 2016. "The Lord of the Gold Rings: The Griffin Warrior of Pylos." *Hesperia* 85: 627–55.

Degryse, Patrick (ed.). 2015. *Glass Making in the Greco-Roman World*. Leuven: Leuven University Press.

DeMarrais, Elizabeth, Chris Gosden and Colin Renfrew (eds.). 2004. *Rethinking Materiality: The Engagements of Mind with the Material World*. Cambridge: McDonald Institute Monographs.

Destrée, Pierre and Penelope Murray (eds.). 2015. *A Companion to Ancient Aesthetics*. Malden, MA: Wiley-Blackwell.

Dewald, Carolyn. 1993. "Reading the world: the interpretation of objects in Herodotus' *Histories*." In Ralph Rosen and Joseph Farrell (eds.), *Nomodeiktes. Festschrift for Martin Ostwald*. Ann Arbor: University of Michigan Press, 55–70.

Dewald, Carolyn. 2006. "Humour and danger in Herodotus." In C. Dewald and J. Marincola (eds.), *The Cambridge Companion to Herodotus*. Cambridge: Cambridge University Press, 145–64.

Dilke, O. A. W. 1971. *The Roman Land Surveyors: An Introduction to the Agrimensores*. Newton Abbot: David and Charles.

Dillon, John Noël. 2015. "The Inflation of Rank and Privilege: Regulating Precedence in the Fourth Century AD." In Johannes Wienand (ed.), *Contested Monarchy: Integrating the Roman Empire in the Fourth Century AD*. Oxford: Oxford University Press, 42–66.

Domergue, C. and J.-L. Bordes. 2005. "Quelques nouveautés tèchniques dans les mines et la métallurgie à l'époque romaine: leur efficacité et leurs effets sur la production." In Elio Lo Cascio (ed.), *Innovazione tecnica e progresso economico nel mondo romano: atti degli incontri capresi di storia dell'economia antica (Capri 13–16 aprile 2003)*. Bari: Edipuglia, 197–223.

Domínguez Rubio, Fernando. 2016. "On the discrepancy between object and things: An ecological approach." *Journal of Material Culture* 21(1): 59–86.

Donald, Merlin. 1991. *Origins of the Modern Mind: Three Stages in the Evolution of Culture and Cognition*. Cambridge, MA: Harvard University Press.

Donald, Merlin. 2001. *A Mind So Rare: The Evolution of Human Consciousness*. New York: Norton.

Du Plessis, P. 2015. "Property." In David Johnston (ed.), *The Cambridge Companion to Roman Law*. Cambridge: Cambridge University Press, 175–98.

duBois, Page. 2003. *Slaves and Other Objects*. Chicago, IL: University of Chicago Press.

Dunbabin, Katherine M. D. 2003. *The Roman Banquet: Images of Conviviality*. Cambridge: Cambridge University Press.

Eckardt, Hella. 2014. *Objects and Identities: Roman Britain and the North-Western Provinces*. Oxford: Oxford University Press.

Eckhardt, Hella. 2017. *Writing and Power in the Roman World: Literacies and Material Culture*. New York: Cambridge University Press.

Eco, Umberto. 1997. "Function and Sign: The Semiotics of Architecture." In Neil Leach (ed.), *Rethinking Architecture: A Reader in Cultural Theory*. London: Routledge, 173–86.

Edwards, Catharine. 2007. *Death in Ancient Rome*. New Haven, CT: Yale University Press.

Elsner, Jaś. 2006. "Reflections on the 'Greek Revolution': From Changes in Viewing to the Transformation of Subjectivity." In Simon Goldhill and Robin Osborne (eds.),

Rethinking Revolutions through Ancient Greece. Cambridge: Cambridge University Press, 68–95.

Elsner, Jaś and Hung Wu (eds.). 2012. Editorial. *Res: Anthropology and Aesthetics*, 61–2: 5–21.

Evans, J. 1999. "The material culture of Greek astronomy." *Journal for the History of Astronomy*, 30: 237–307.

Evans, J. 2004. "The astrologer's apparatus: a picture of professional practice in Greco-Roman Egypt." *Journal for the History of Astronomy*, 35: 1–44.

Faraone, Christopher. 1999. *Ancient Greek Love Magic*. Cambridge, MA: Harvard University Press.

Favro, Diane G. 1998. *The Urban Image of Augustan Rome*. Cambridge: Cambridge University Press.

Fentress, Lisa and Philip Perkins. 1988. "Counting African Red Slip Ware." In A. Mastino (ed.), *L'Africa Romana: Atti del V Convegno di Studio, Sassari, 11–13 dicembre 1987*. Sassari: Dipartimento di storia, Università degli studi di Sassari, 205–14.

Ferrari, Gloria. 2002. "The Ancient Temple on the Acropolis at Athens." *American Journal of Archaeology* 106: 11–35.

Fiema, Zbigniew. 2007. "Storing in the Church: Artefacts in Room I of the Petra Church." In Luke Lavan, Ellen Swift and Toon Putzeys (eds.), *Objects in Context, Objects in Use: Material Spatiality in Late Antiquity*. Leiden: Brill, 607–23.

Finley, Moses I. (1965)1981. "Technical innovation and economic progress in the ancient world." *Economic History Review*, 18: 29–45. Reprinted in M. I. Finley *Economy and Society in Ancient Greece*. Edited by R. Saller and B. Shaw. London: Chatto and Windus, 176–95.

Finley, Moses I. 1973. *The Ancient Economy*. 1st edn. Berkeley: University of California Press.

Finley, Moses I. 1985. *The Ancient Economy*. 2nd edn. Berkeley: University of California Press.

Finley, Moses I. 1999. *The Ancient Economy*. With an Introduction by Ian Morris. Berkeley: University of California Press.

Fitch, C. and N. Goldman. 1994. *Cosa: The Lamps. Memoirs of the American Academy in Rome* 39. Ann Arbor: University of Michigan Press.

Fleury, P. 1993. *La mécanique de Vitruve*. Caen: Université de Caen, Centre d'études et de recherche sur l'antiquité.

Flower, Richard. 2015. "Tamquam figmentum hominis: Ammianus, Constantius II and the portrayal of imperial ritual." *Classical Quarterly*, 65: 822–35.

Forsdick, Charles. 2000. *Victor Segalen and the Aesthetics of Diversity*. Oxford: Oxford University Press.

Foucault, Michel. (1970)2002. *The Order of Things*, 2nd edn. (trans. of *Les mots et les choses*, Paris, 1966). London: Routledge.

Fowler, Robert. 1996. "Herodotos and his contemporaries." *JHS* 116: 62–87.

Foxhall, Lin. 2007. *Olive Cultivation in Ancient Greece: The Ancient Economy Revisited*. Oxford: Oxford University Press.

Foxhall, Lin. 2011. "Loom Weights." In J. C. Carter and A. Prieto (eds.), *The Chora of Metaponto 3. The Survey I. Bradano to Basento*. Austin, TX: Institute of Classical Archaeology, 539–54.

Foxhall, Lin. 2012. "Family time: temporality, materiality and women's networks in ancient Greece." In J. Marincola, L. Llewellyn-Jones and C. Maciver (eds.), *Greek*

Notions of the Past in the Archaic and Classical Eras. History without Historians. Edinburgh: Edinburgh University Press, 183–206.

Foxhall, Lin. 2018. "Loom Weights." In J. C. Carter and K. Swift (eds.), *The Chora of Metaponto 7. The Greek Sanctuary at Pantanello.* Austin, TX: Institute of Classical Archaeology, 609–69.

Foxhall, Lin and A. Quercia. 2016. "Loom Weights." In F. Silvestrelli and I. Edlund-Berry (eds.), *The Chora of Metaponto 6. A Greek Settlement at Sant'Angelo Vecchio.* Austin, TX: Institute of Classical Archaeology, 455–68.

Frakes, James F. D. 2009. *Framing Public Life: The Portico in Roman Gaul.* Vienna: Phoibos.

Freeth, T. and A. Jones. 2012. "The cosmos in the Antikythera mechanism." *ISAW Papers*, 4.

Freeth, T., Y. Bitsakis, X. Moussas, J. H. Seiradakis, A. Tselikas, M. Zafeiropoulou et al. 2006. "Decoding the ancient Greek astronomical calculator known as the Antikythera Mechanism." *Nature*, 444(7119): 587–91.

Freeth, T., Y. Bitsakis, A. Jones and J. M. Steele. 2008. "Calendars with Olympiad display and eclipse prediction on the Antikythera Mechanism." *Nature*, 454(7204): 614–17.

Fritsch, B., E. Rinner and G. Graßhoff. 2013. "3D Models of Ancient Sundials: A Comparison." *International Journal of Heritage in the Digital Era*, 2(3): 361–73.

Frontisi-Ducroux, Françoise. 2016. "Visages invisibles: retour à Cyrène." *Mètis* 14: 245–65.

Fulford, Michael. 2013. "Gallo-Roman sigillata: fresh approaches, fresh challenges, fresh questions." In M. Fulford and E. Durham (eds.), *Seeing Red: New Economic and Social Perspectives on Terra Sigillata.* London: Institute of Classical Studies, 1–17.

Gahtan, Maia and Donatella Pegazzano (eds.). 2015. *Museum Archetypes and Collecting in the Ancient World.* Leiden: Brill.

Gaifman, Milette. 2018. "The Greek Libation Bowl as Embodied Object." *Art History* 41(3) (*The Embodied Object in Classical Antiquity*): 444–65.

Gaifman, Milette and Verity Platt. 2018. "Introduction: From Grecian Urn to Embodied Object." *Art History* 41(3) (*The Embodied Object in Classical Antiquity*): 402–19.

Garrow, Duncan and Chris Gosden. 2012. *Technologies of Enchantment? Exploring Celtic Art: 400 BC to AD 100.* Oxford: Oxford University Press.

Gates-Foster, Jennifer. 2016. "Finley and Archaeology." In D. Jew, R. Osborne and M. Scott (eds.), *The Impact of Moses Finley.* Cambridge: Cambridge University Press, 250–69.

Gawlikowski, Michael. 2008. "The statues of the sanctuary of Allat in Palmyra." In Y. Z. Eliav, E. A. Friedland and S. Herbert (eds.), *The Sculptural Environment of the Roman Near East: Reflections on Culture, Ideology and Power.* Leuven: University of Leuven Press, 397–411.

Gell, Alfred. 1992. "The Technology of Enchantment and the Enchantment of Technology." In J. Coote and A. Shelton (eds.), *Art and Aesthetics.* Oxford: Clarendon Press, 40–63.

Gell, Alfred. 1994. "The Technology of Enchantment and the Enchantment of Technology." In Jeremy Coote (ed.), *Anthropology, Art and Aesthetics.* Oxford: Clarendon Press, 40–63.

Gell, Alfred. 1996. "Vogel's Net. Traps as Artwork and Artwork as Traps." *Journal of Material Culture*, 1(1): 15–38.

Gell, Alfred. 1998. *Art and Agency: An Anthropological Theory*. Oxford: Clarendon Press.

Gerhard, Eduard. 1843–97. *Etruskische Spiegel*. Berlin: G. Reimer.

Gibbs, S. L. 1976. *Greek and Roman Sundials*. New Haven, CT: Yale University Press.

Gibson, James J. 1979. *The Ecological Approach to Visual Perception*. Boston, MA: Houghton Mifflin.

Glucklich, A. 1997. *The End of Magic*. New York: Oxford University Press.

Gombrich, Ernst H. 1979. *The Sense of Order: A Study in the Psychology of Decorative Art*. Oxford: Phaidon.

Gordon, Richard. 1979. "The real and the imaginary. Production and religion in the Graeco-Roman world," *Art History*, 2: 5–34

Gordon, Richard. 1990. "The Veil of Power: Emperors, Sacrificers and Benefactors." In Mary Beard and John North (eds.), *Pagan Priests: Religion and Power in the Ancient World*. Ithaca, NY: Cornell University Press, 199–231.

Gosden, Chris. 2000. "Making Sense: Archaeology and Aesthetics." *World Archaeology*, 33: 163–7.

Gosden, Chris. 2004. "Shaping life in the Late Prehistoric and Romano-British periods." In R. M. Rosen (ed.), *Time and Temporality in the Ancient World*. Philadelphia: University of Pennsylvania Museum of Archaeology and Anthropology, 29–44.

Gosden, Chris. 2005. "What do objects want?" *Journal of Archaeological Method and Theory*, 12: 193–211.

Gosden, Chris. 2006. "Material culture and long-term change." C. Tilley et al. (eds.), *Handbook of Material Culture*. London: Sage, 425–42.

Graham, Daniel W. 2006. *Explaining the Cosmos: The Ionian Tradition of Scientific Philosophy*. Princeton, NJ: Princeton University Press.

Greene, Kevin. 1992. *Roman Pottery*. London: British Museum Press.

Greene, Kevin. 2000. "Technological innovation and economic progress in the ancient world: M. I. Finley reconsidered." *Economic History Review*, 53: 29–59.

Greene, Kevin. 2006. "Archaeology and Technology." In J. Bintliff (ed.), *A Companion to Archaeology*. Malden, MA: Wiley-Blackwell, 155–73.

Grethlein, Johannes. 2008. "Memory and material objects in the *Iliad* and the *Odyssey*." *Journal of Hellenic Studies*, 128: 27–51.

Grethlein, Johannes. 2017. *Aesthetic Experience and Classical Antiquity. The Significance of Form in Narratives and Pictures*. Cambridge: Cambridge University Press.

Griffiths, D. 2016. *The Social and Economic Impact of Artificial Lighting at Pompeii*. PhD thesis. University of Leicester, Leicester.

Gruen, Erich. 1990. *Studies in Greek Culture and Roman Policy*. Berkeley: University of California Press.

Gutzwiller, Kathryn (ed.). 2005: *The New Posidippus. A Hellenistic Poetry Book*. New York: Oxford University Press.

Hahn, H. P. and H. Weiss. 2013. *Mobility, Meaning and Transformations of Things*. Oxford: Oxbow.

Hahn, Johannes, Stephen Emmel and Ulrich Gotter (eds.). 2008. *From Temple to Church: Destruction and renewal of Local Cultic Topography in Late Antiquity*. Leiden: Brill.

Hallett, Christopher H. 2012. "The archaic style in sculpture in the eyes of ancient and modern viewers." In V. Coltman (ed.), *Making Sense of Greek Art*. Exeter: Exeter University Press, 70–100.

Hallett, Christopher H. 2015. "Defining Roman Art." In B. Borg (ed.), *A Companion to Roman Art*. Malden, MA: Wiley-Blackwell, 11–33.

Hamilakis, Yannis. 2013. *Archaeology and the Senses: Human Experience, Memory, and Affect*. Cambridge: Cambridge University Press.

Hamilton, Richard. 2000: *Treasure Map: A Guide to the Delian Inventories*. Ann Arbor: University of Michigan Press.

Hansen, Maria Fabricius. 2003. *The Eloquence of Appropriation: Prolegomena to an Understanding of Spolia in Early Christian Rome*. Rome: L'Erma di Bretschneider.

Harmansah, Omur. 2015. "ISIS, Heritage, and the Spectacles of Destruction in the Global Media." *Near Eastern Archaeology*, 78: 170–7.

Harris, E. M. 2002. "Workshop, marketplace and household: the nature of technical specialization in classical Athens and its influence on economy and society." In Paul Cartledge, Edward Cohen and Lin Foxhall (eds.), *Money, Labour and Land: Approaches to the Economies of Ancient Greece*. London: Routledge, 67–99.

Harrison, A. R. W. 1968. *The Law of Athens. Vol. 1. The Family and Property*. Oxford: Clarendon Press.

Haselgrove, Colin and D. Wigg-Wolf (eds.). 2005. *Iron Age Coinage and Ritual Practices*. Mainz: von Zabern.

Havelock, Christine. 2007. *The Aphrodite of Knidos and Her Successors: A Historical Review of the Female Nude in Greek Art*. Ann Arbor: University of Michigan Press.

Hayes, John W. 1972. *Late Roman Pottery*. London: British School at Rome.

Hayes, John W. 1980. *A Supplement to Late Roman Pottery*. London: British School at Rome.

Hayes, John W. 1985. "Sigillate Orientali." In *Enciclopedia dell'arte antica classica e orientale. Atlante delle Forme Ceramiche II, Ceramica Fine Romana nel Bacino Mediterraneo (Tardo Ellenismo e Primo Impero)*. Rome: Istituto della Enciclopedia Italiana, 1–96.

Hayes, John W. 1997. *Handbook of Mediterranean Roman Pottery*. London: British Museum Press.

Hayes, John W. 2008. *Roman Pottery: Fine-Ware Imports. Vol. 32, The Athenian Agora: Results of Excavations Conducted by the American School of Classical Studies at Athens*. Princeton, NJ: American School of Classical Studies.

Heidegger, Martin. 1953. *Sein und zeit*. 7th edn. Tübingen: Neomarius Verlag.

Heidegger, Martin. 1971. *Poetry, Language, Thought*. Trans. A. Hofstadter. New York: Harper & Row.

Heidegger, Martin. 1996. *Being and Time*. Trans. Joan Stambaught. Albany: Stante University of New York Press.

Helms, Mary W. 1988. *Ulysses' Sail. An Ethnographic Odyssey of Power, Knowledge and Geographical Distance*. Princeton, NJ: Princeton University Press.

Hermet, F. 1979. *La Graufesenque (Condatomago): I. Vases sigilles–II. Graffites*. Marseille: Laffitte Reprints.

Hobden, Fiona. 2013. *The Symposion in Ancient Greek Society and Thought*. Cambridge: Cambridge University Press.

Hodder, Ian. 1990. "Style as Historical Quality." In Margaret W. Conkey and Christine A. Hastorf (eds.), *The Uses of Style in Archaeology*. Cambridge: Cambridge University Press, 44–51.

Hodder, Ian. 2012. *Entangled: An Archaeology of the Relationships between Humans and Things*. Malden, MA: Wiley-Blackwell.

Hogarth, David. 1888. "The Recent Excavation at Paphos." *Classical Review*, 2(6): 186–8.

Hogarth, David, M. R. James, R. Elsey Smith and E. A. Gardner. 1888. "Excavations in Cyprus, 1887–88. Paphos, Leontari, Amargetti." *Journal of Hellenic Studies*, 9: 147–271.

Holland, L. 1944. "Colophon." *Hesperia*, 13: 91–171.

Hollmann, A. 2011. *The Master of Signs: Signs and the Interpretation of Signs in Herodotus' Histories*. Washington, DC: Center for Hellenic Studies.

Hölscher, Tonio. 1987. *Römische Bildsprache als semantisches System*. Heidelberg: Winter; trans. A. Snodgrass-Künzl and A. M. Snodgrass, 2004. *The Language of Images in Roman Art*. Cambridge: Cambridge University Press.

Hölscher, Tonio. 2006. "Greek styles and Greek art in Augustan Rome: issues of the present versus records of the past." In J. I. Porter (ed.), *Classical Pasts: The Classical Traditions of Greece and Rome*. Princeton, NJ: Princeton University Press, 237–59.

Hölscher, Tonio. 2018. *Visual Power in Ancient Greece and Rome: Between Art and Social Reality*. Berkeley: University of California Press.

Horden, Peregine and Nicholas Purcell. 2000. *The Corrupting Sea: A Study of Mediterranean History*. Oxford: Blackwell.

Houby-Nielsen, Sanne. 2000. "Child Burials in Ancient Athens." In Joanna Sofaer Derevenski (ed.), *Children and Material Culture*. London: Routledge, 151–65.

Hulme, E. W. 1896. "The History of the Patent System under the Prerogative and at Common Law." *Law Quarterly Review*, 46: 141–54.

Humphrey, John H. (ed.). 2009. *Studies on Roman Pottery of the Provinces of Africa Proconsularis and Byzacena (Tunisia): Homage à Michael Bonifay*. Journal of Roman Archaeology Supplementary series 76. Portsmouth, RI: Journal of Roman Archaeology.

Ihde, D. 1990. *Technology and the Lifeworld: From Garden to Earth*. Bloomington: Indiana University Press.

Izzet, Vedia. 1998. "Holding a Mirror to Etruscan Gender." In Ruth Whitehouse (ed.), *Gender and Italian Archaeology: Challenging the Stereotypes*. London: Accordia Research Institute, Institute of Archaeology, University College, London, 209–27.

Izzet, Vedia. 2007. *The Archaeology of Etruscan Society*. Cambridge: Cambridge University Press.

Jackson, Monica. 2006: *Hellenistic Gold Eros Jewelry: Technique, Style and Chronology*. BAR International Series 1510. Oxford: Archaeopress.

Jaeger, M. 2008. *Archimedes and the Roman Imagination*. Ann Arbor: University of Michigan Press.

Jones, Alexander. 2017. *A Portable Cosmos: Revealing the Antikythera Mechanism, Scientific Wonder of the Ancient World*. New York: Oxford University Press.

Jones, John Ellis, L. H. Sackett and A. John Graham. 1962. "The Dema House in Attica." *Annual of the British School at Athens*, 57: 75–114.

Jones, John Ellis, A. John Graham, L. H. Sackett and M. J. Geroulanos. 1973. "An Attic Country House Below the Cave of Pan at Vari." *Annual of the British School at Athens*, 68: 355–452.

Jordon, David and Susan Rotroff. 1999. "A Curse in a Chytridion: A Contribution to the Study of Athenian Pyres." *Hesperia*, 68: 147–54.

Joshel, Sandra. 1992. *Work, Identity and Legal Status at Rome: A Study of the Occupational Inscriptions*. Norman: University of Oklahoma Press.

Jouanna, Jacques. 2012. "Wine and Medicine in Ancient Greece." In Philip van der Eijk (ed.), *Greek Medicine from Hippocrates to Galen*. Leiden: Brill, 173–93.

Kampen, Natalie. 1981. *Image and Status: Roman Working Women in Ostia*. Berlin: Gebr. Mann.

Karakasi, Katerina. 2003. *Archaic Korai*. Los Angeles: J. Paul Getty Museum.

Kehoe, Dennis P. 1997. *Investment, Profit, and Tenancy: The Jurists and the Roman Agrarian Economy*. Ann Arbor: University of Michigan Press.

Kemmers, F. 2018. "Worthless? The practice of depositing counterfeit coins in Roman votive contexts." In B. Myrberg Burström and G. Ingvardson (eds.), *Divina Moneta: Coins in Religion and Ritual*. London: Routledge, 193–208.

Kemmers, F. and N. Myrberg. 2011. "Rethinking numismatics. The archaeology of coins." *Archaeological Dialogues*, 18(1): 87–108.

Kenney, Edward J. 1984. "The *Mosella* of Ausonius." *Greece and Rome*, 31: 190–202.

Keyser, P. 1988. "Suetonius *Nero* 41.2 and the date of Heron Mechanicus of Alexandria." *Classical Philology*, 83: 218–20.

Keyser, P. 1992. "A New Look at Heron's 'Steam Engine'." *Archive for History of Exact Sciences*, 44(2): 107–24.

Kim, Henry S. 2001. "Archaic coinage as evidence for the use of money." In Andrew Meadows and Kirsty Shipton (eds.), *Money and Its Uses in the Ancient Greek World*. Oxford: Oxford University Press, 7–21.

Kim, Henry S. 2002. "Small change and the moneyed economy." In Paul Cartledge, Edward Cohen and Lin Foxhall (eds.), *Money, Labour and Land: Approaches to the Economies of Ancient Greece*. London: Routledge, 44–51.

Kinney, Dale. 2001. "Roman Architectural Spolia." *Proceedings of the American Philosophical Society*, 145(2): 138–61.

Kinney, Dale. 2006. "The concept of *spolia*." In C. Rudolph (ed.), *A Companion to Medieval Art. Romanesque and Gothic in Northern Europe*. Malden, MA: Wiley-Blackwell, 233–52.

Kistler, Erich. 2010. "Großkönigliches *symbolon* im Osten – exotisches Luxusgut im Westen: zur Objektbiographie der achämenidischen Glasschale aus Ihringen." In R. Rollinger et al. (eds.), *Interkulturalität in der alten Welt. Vorderasien, Hellas, Ägypten und die vielfältigen Ebenen des Kontakts*. Wiesbaden: Harrassowitz, 63–95.

Kleiner, Diana E. E. 1992. *Roman Sculpture*. New Haven, CT: Yale University Press.

Knappett, Carl. 2004. "The Affordances of Things: A Post-Gibsonian Perspective on the Relationship of Mind and Matter." In Elizabeth DeMarrais, Chris Gosden and Colin Renfrew (eds.), *Rethinking Materiality: The Engagement of Mind with the Material World*. Cambridge: McDonald Institute for Archaeological Research, 43–51.

Kogge, W. 2012. "Empeiría. Vom Verlust der Erfahrungshaltigkeit des 'Wissens' und vom Versuch, sie als 'implizites Wissen' wieder zu gewinnen." In J. Loenhoff (ed.), *Implizites Wissen: epistemologische und handlungstheoretische Perspektiven*. Weilerswist: Velbrück Wissenschaft, 31–48.

Konuk, Koray. 2012. "Asia Minor to the Ionian Revolt." In W. Metcalf (ed.), *The Oxford Handbook of Greek and Roman Coinage*. Oxford: Oxford University Press, 43–60.

Kopytoff, Igor. 1986. "The cultural biography of things: Commoditization as Process." In Arjan Appadurai (ed.), *The Social Life of Things: Commodities in Cultural Perspective*. Cambridge: Cambridge University Press, 64–91.

Kraay, Colin M. 1964. "Hoards, small change and the origin of coinage." *Journal of Hellenic Studies*, 84: 76–91.

Kroll, John H. 2008. "The monetary use of weighed bullion in archaic Greece." In W. V. Harris (ed.), *The Monetary Systems of the Greeks and the Romans*. Oxford: Oxford University Press, 12–37.

Kroll, John H. 2012. "The Monetary background of early coinage." In W. Metcalf (ed.), *The Oxford Handbook of Greek and Roman Coinage*. Oxford: Oxford University Press, 34–42.

Kurke, Leslie. 1999. *Coins, Bodies, Games and Gold: The Politics of Meaning in Archaic Greece*. Princeton, NJ: Princeton University Press.

Kuttner, Ann. 2005. "Cabinet Fit for a Queen: The *Lithika* as Posidippus' Gem Museum." In Kathryn Gutzwiller (ed.), *The New Posidippus: A Hellenistic Poetry Book*. Oxford: Oxford University Press, 141–63.

La Follette, Laetitia. 2012. "Parsing Piety: The Sacred Still Life in Roman Relief Sculpture." *Memoirs of the American Academy in Rome*, 56–7: 15–35.

Lamm, Susanne. 2012. "Einige beispiele der einheimishchen grauen feinen keramik der villa rustica von grünau (Steiermark)." In C. Reinhold and W. Wohlmayer (eds.), *Akten d. 13. Österreichischen Archäologentages*. Vienna: Phoibos, 345–52.

Lapatin, Kenneth. 2015. *Luxus: The Sumptuous Arts of Greece and Rome*. Los Angeles: J. Paul Getty Museum.

Lateiner, Donald. 1989. *The Historical Method of Herodotus*. Toronto: Toronto University Press.

Lateiner, Donald. 1990. "Deceptions and delusions in Herodotus." *Classical Antiquity*, 9(2): 230–46.

Latour, Bruno. 1991. *Nous n'avons jamais été modernes. Essai d'antropologie symétrique*. Paris: La Découverte.

Latour, Bruno. 1993. *We Have Never Been Modern*. Cambridge, MA: Harvard University Press.

Lavan, Luke, Ellen Swift and Toon Putzeys (eds.). 2007. *Objects in Context, Objects in Use: Material Spatiality in Late Antiquity = Late Antique Archaeology 5*. Leiden: Brill.

Lee, Christina. 2012. "Reluctant Appetites: Anglo-Saxon Attitudes towards Fasting." In Stuart McWilliams (ed.), *Saints and Scholars: New Perspectives on Anglo-Saxon Literature and Culture*. Cambridge: D. S. Brewer.

Lee, Mireille M. 2015. *Body, Dress and Identity in Ancient Greece*. New York: Cambridge University Press.

Lemley, M. A. 2012. "The myth of the sole inventor." *Michigan Law Review*, 110(5): 709–60.

Lemonnier, P. (ed.). 1993. *Technological Choices: Transformation in Material Cultures since the Neolithic*. London: Routledge.

Leroi-Gourhan, André. 1943. *L'homme et la matière*. Paris: Albin Michel.

Lewis, David M. 1997. "After the profanation of the Mysteries." In P. J. Rhodes (ed.), *Selected Papers in Greek and Near Eastern History*. Cambridge: Cambridge University Press, 158–72.

Lewis, M. J. T. 2001. *Surveying Instruments of Greece and Rome*. Cambridge: Cambridge University Press.

Lewis, Sian. 2011. "Images of Craft on Athenian Pottery: Context and Interpretation." *Bollettino di Archeologia* online I 2010/Volume speciale = XVII International Congress of Classical Archaeology, Roma Sept. 22–26, 2008 Session: Greek Vases, Etruscan Contexts 12-26. http://151.12.58.75/archeologia/bao_document/articoli/3_LEWIS.pdf.

Lloyd, Geoffrey E. R. 1962. "Right and Left in Greek Philosophy." *Journal of Hellenic Studies*, 82: 56–66.

Lloyd, Geoffrey E. R. 1973. *Greek Science after Aristotle*. London: Chatto and Windus.

Lloyd, Geoffrey E. R. 1979. *Magic, Reason and Experience: Studies in the Origin and Development of Greek Science*. Cambridge: Cambridge University Press.

Lloyd, Matthew. 2015. "Death of a Swordsman, Death of a Sword: the Killing of Swords in the Early Iron Age Aegean (ca. 1050 to 690 B.C.E)." In Geoff Lee, Helen Whittaker and Graham Wrightson (eds.), *Ancient Warfare: Introducing Current Research, Volume I*. Newcastle Upon Tyne: Cambridge Scholars Press.

Loison, L. 2016. "Forms of presentism in the history of science. Rethinking the project of historical epistemology." *Studies in History and Philosophy of Science Part A*, 60: 29–37.

Longfellow, Brenda and Ellen Perry (eds.). 2018. *Roman Artists, Patrons and Public Consumption: Familiar Works Reconsidered*. Ann Arbor: University of Michigan Press.

Loos, Adolf. 1998. *Ornament and Crime: Selected Essays*. Trans. Michael Mitchell. Riverside, CA: Ariadne Press.

Lorenz, Hendrik 2014. "Understanding, knowledge, and inquiry in Aristotle." In James Warren and Frisbee Sheffield (ed.), *The Routledge Companion to Ancient Philosophy*. London: Routledge, 290–303.

Lynch, Kathleen. 2011. *The Symposium in Context: Pottery from a Late Archaic House near the Athenian Agora*. Hesperia suppl. 46. Princeton, NJ: American School of Classical Studies at Athens.

Ma, John. 2013. *Statues and Cities: Honorific Portraits and Civic Identity in the Hellenistic World*. Oxford: Oxford University Press.

MacCormack, Sabine, G. 1981. *Art and Ceremony in Late Antiquity*. Berkeley: University of California Press.

MacDonald, Carolyn. 2017. "Take-Away Art: Ekphrasis and Appropriation in Martial's *Apophoreta* 170–82." *Classical Antiquity*, 36: 288–316.

MacDonald, William L. 1986. *The Architecture of the Roman Empire, Vol. 2: An Urban Appraisal*. New Haven, CT: Yale University Press.

MacGregor, Neil. 2012. *A History of the World in 100 Objects*. London: Penguin Books.

MacLeod, C. 2002. *Inventing the Industrial Revolution: The English Patent System, 1660–1800*. Cambridge: Cambridge University Press.

Maffi, Alberto. 2005. "Family and Property Law." In Michael Gagarin and David Cohen (eds.), *The Cambridge Companion to Ancient Greek Law*. Cambridge: Cambridge University Press, 254–66.

Magnelli, Enrico. 2009. "Posidippus of Pella." *Oxford Bibliographies. Classics*. Oxford: Oxford University Press.

Malafouris, Lambros. 2013. *How Things Shape the Mind: A Theory of Material Engagement*. Boston, MA: MIT Press.

Malafouris, Lambros. 2015. "Metaplasticity and the Primacy of Material Engagement." *Time & Mind*, 8(4): 351–71.

Malafouris, Lambros and Colin Renfrew (eds.). 2010: *The Cognitive Life of Things: Recasting the Boundaries of Mind*. Cambridge: McDonald Institute for Archaeological Research, University of Cambridge.

Manning, Joseph G. and Ian Morris (eds.). 2005. *The Ancient Economy: Evidence and Models*. Stanford, CA: Stanford University Press.

Maran, Josef and P. W. Stockhammer (eds). 2012: *Materiality and Social Practice: Transformative Capacities of Intercultural Encounters*, Oxford: Oxbow.

Marconi, Clemente. 2012. "Between Performance and Identity: The Social and Cultural Context of Theaters in Late Classical and Hellenistic Sicily." In K. Bosher (ed.), *Theater Outside Athens: Drama in Greek Sicity and South Italy*. Cambridge and New York: Cambridge University Press, 175–207.

Margaritis, Evi and Martin K. Jones. 2008. "Greek and Roman Agriculture." In J. P. Oleson (ed.), *The Oxford Handbook of Engineering and Technology in the Classical World*. Oxford: Oxford Univeristy Press, 158–74.

Marlowe, Elizabeth. 2013. *Shaky Ground: Context, Connoisseurship and the History of Roman Art*. London: Bloomsbury.

Mattingly, David. 2004. "Being Roman: expressing identity in a provincial setting." *JRA*, 17: 5–25.

Mattingly, David. 2006. *An Imperial Possession: Britain in the Roman Empire, 54 BC–AD 409*. London and New York: Penguin Books Ltd.

Mattingly, David. 2010. *Imperialism, Power, and Identity: Experiencing the Roman Empire*. Princeton, NJ: Princeton University Press.

Mattusch, Carol. 1980. "The Berlin Foundry Cup: The Casting of Greek Bronze Statuary in the Early Fifth Century BC." *American Journal of Archaeology*, 84: 435–44.

Mattusch, Carol. 1988. *Greek Bronze Statuary: From the Beginnings Through the Fifth Century B.C.* Ithaca, NY: Cornell University Press.

Mauss, Marcel. 1990. *The Gift: The Form and Reason for Exchange in Archaic Societies*. Trans. W. D. Halls. London: Routledge.

McGowan, Andrew. 1999. *Ascetic Eucharists: Food and Drink in Early Christian Ritual Meals*. Oxford and New York: Clarendon Press.

McQueston, Kaitlynn. 2013. "Pornaganda and the Felt Machine." In Stephanie Anderson and Cierra Webster (eds.), *Objects in Context: Theorizing Material Culture*. London, Ontario, 73–84.

Meadows, Andrew R. 2011. "Athenian coin dies from Egypt: the new discovery at Heracleion." *Revue Belge de Numismatique et de Sigillographie*, 147: 95–116.

Meißner, B. 1999. *Die technologische Fachliteratur der Antike: Struktur, Uberlieferung und Wirkung technischen Wissens in der Antike (ca. 400 v. Chr.–ca. 500 n. Chr.)*. Berlin: Akademie Verlag.

Meister, Jan Bernhard. 2012. *Der Körper des Princeps. Zur Problematik eines monarchischen Körpers ohne Monarchie*. Stuttgart: Steiner.

Menger, C. 1950. *Principles of Economics*. Glencoe, IL: Free Press.

Merleau-Ponty, Jacques. 2005. *Phenomenology of Perception*. Trans. Colin Smith. London and New York: Routledge.

Meskell, Lynn M. 1999. "Archaeologies of Life and Death." *American Journal of Archaeology*, 103: 181–99.

Meskell, Lynn M. (ed.). 2005. *Archaeologies of Materiality*. Malden, MA: Wiley-Blackwell.

Meskell, Lynn M. and A. Joyce Rosemary (eds.), 2003. *Embodied Lives: Figuring Ancient Maya and Egyptian Experience*. London and New York: Routledge.

Metcalf, W. 2012. "Introduction." In W. Metcalf (ed.), *The Oxford Handbook of Greek and Roman Coinage*. Oxford: Oxford University Press.

Meyer, Caspar. 2013. *Greco-Scythian Art and the Birth of Eurasia: From Classical Antiquity to Russian Modernity*. Oxford: Oxford University Press.

Michel, Vincent. 2007. "Furniture, Fixtures and Fittings in Churches: Archaeological Evidence from Palestine (4th–8th c.) and the Role of the Diakonikon." In Luke Lavan, Ellen Swift and Toon Putzeys (eds.), *Objects in Context, Objects in Use: Material Spatiality in Late Antiquity*. Leiden: Brill, 581–606.

Miles, Margaret. 2016. "The Interiors of Greek Temples." In M. Miles (ed.),
    Companion to Greek Architecture. Malden, MA: Wiley-Blackwell, 360–85.
Miller, Daniel. 1987. *Material Culture and Mass Consumption*. Oxford: Blackwell.
Miller, Daniel. 1998. "Why some things matter." In Daniel Miller (ed.), *Material
    Cultures: Why Some Things Matter*. Chicago, IL: University of Chicago Press, 3–24.
Miller, Daniel. 2005. "Materiality: An Introduction." In Daniel Miller (ed.),
    Materiality. Durham, NC, and London: Duke University Press.
Miller, Daniel. 2010. *Stuff*. Cambridge and Malden, MA: Polity.
Miller, Peter N. 2017. *History and Its Objects: Antiquarianism and Material Culture
    Since 1500*. Ithaca, NY: Cornell University Press.
Millett, M. 1990. *The Romanization of Britain: An Essay in Archaeological
    Interpretation*. Cambridge: Cambridge University Press.
Millett, P. C. 1991. *Lending and Borrowing in Ancient Athens*. Cambridge: Cambridge
    University Press.
Mitchell, W. J. T. 1996. "What do pictures 'really' want." *October*, 77: 71–82.
Mol, A. 2002. *The Body Multiple: Ontology in Medical Practice*. Durham, NC: Duke
    University Press.
Morphy, Howard. 2010. "Art as action, art as evidence." In D. Hicks and M. Beaudry
    (eds.), *The Oxford Handbook of Material Culture Studies*. Oxford: Oxford
    University Press, 265–90.
Morris, Ian. 1992. *Death Ritual and Social Structure in Classical Antiquity*. Cambridge:
    Cambridge University Press.
Morris, I., R. P. Saller and W. Scheidel. 2007. *The Cambridge Economic History of the
    Greco-Roman World*. Cambridge: Cambridge University Press.
Müller, Miriam (ed.). 2015. *Household Studies in Complex Societies: (Micro)
    Archaeological and Textual Approaches. Papers from the Oriental Institute Seminar
    Household Studies in Complex Societies Held at the Oriental Institute of the
    University of Chicago 15–16 March 2013*. Oriental Institute Seminars 10. Chicago,
    IL: The Oriental Institute of the University of Chicago.
Mumford, L. 1934. *Technics and Civilization*. New York: Harcourt, Brace and Company.
Mumford, L. 1952. *Art and Technics*. New York: Columbia University Press.
Mumford, L. 1967. *The Myth of the Machine*, 1st edn. New York: Harcourt, Brace and
    World.
Murray, Oswyn. 2018. *The Symposion—Drinking Greek Style: Essays on Greek
    Pleasure, 1983–2017* (ed. V. Cazzato). Oxford: Oxford University Press.
Myrup Kristensen, Troels. 2013. *Making and Breaking the Gods: Christian Responses
    to Pagan Sculpture in Late Antiquity*. Aarhus: Aarhus University Press.
Näser, Claudia. 2013. "Equipping and Stripping the Dead: A Case Study on the
    Procurement, Compilation, Arrangement, and Fragmentation of Grave Inventories
    in New Kingdom Thebes." In Sarah Tarlow and Liv Nilsson Stutz (eds.), *The
    Oxford Handbook of the Archaeology in Death and Burial*. Oxford: Oxford
    University Press, 643–63.
Neer, Richard. 2002. *Style and Politics in Athenian Vase Painting: The Craft of
    Democracy, ca. 530-460 B.C.E.* Cambridge and New York: Cambridge University
    Press.
Neer, Richard. 2012. *Art and Archaeology of the Greek World: A New History,
    c.2500–c.150 BCE*. London: Thames and Hudson.
Nelson, Sarah Milledge. 2006: *Handbook of Gender in Archaeology*. Lanham, MD:
    AltaMira Press.

Nevett, Lisa C. 1999. *House and Society in the Ancient Greek World*. Cambridge: Cambridge University Press.

Nevett, Lisa C. 2010. *Domestic Space in Classical Antiquity*. Cambridge: Cambridge University Press.

Nevett, Lisa C. 2015: "Artifact Assemblages in Classical Greek Domestic Contexts: Toward a New Approach." In C. Müller (ed.), *Household Studies in Complex Societies*. Chicago, IL: The Oriental Institute of the University of Chicago, 101–16.

Newlands, Carol E. 2002. *Statius' Silvae and the Poetics of Empire*. Cambridge: Cambridge University Press.

Nightingale, P. 2009. "Tacit Knowledge and Engineering Design." In A. Meijers (ed.), *Philosophy of Technology and Engineering Sciences*. Amsterdam, London and Boston, MA: Elsevier/North Holland, 351–74.

Nisbet, Robin G. M. and Niall Rudd (eds.). 2004. *A Commentary on Horace* Odes *Book III*. Oxford: Oxford University Press.

Noble, Joseph V. and Derek J. de Solla Price. 1968. "The Water Clock in the Tower of the Winds." *American Journal of Archaeology*, 72(4), 345–55.

O'Malley, Michelle and Evelyn Welch (eds.). 2007. *The Material Renaissance*. Manchester: Manchester University Press.

Ogden, Daniel. 2002. "Controlling Women's Dess: *Gynaikonomoi*." In Lloyd Llewellyn-Jones (ed.), *Women's Dress in the Ancient Greek World*. London: Duckworth, 209–25.

Ogden, Jack. 1998. "The jewellery of Dark Age Greece: construction and cultural connections." In Dyfri Williams (ed.), *The Art of the Greek Goldsmith*. London: British Museum Press, 14–21.

Oleson, J. P. 2005. "Design, materials, and the process of innovation for Roman force pumps." In J. Pollini (ed.), *Terra Marique: Studies in Art History and Marine Archaeology in Honor of Anna Marguerite McCann on the Receipt of the Gold Medal of the Archaeological Institute of America*. Oxford and Oakville: Oxbow Books and David Brown Book Co., 211–31.

Oliva, Aude, Antonio Torralba and Philippe G. Schyns. 2006. *Hybrid Images*. Association for Computing Machinery. Available online: https://dl.acm.org/doi/10.1145/1141911.1141919 (accessed June 05 2020).

Olsen, Bjorn. 2010. *In Defence of Things*. Walnut Creek, CA: Altemira Press.

Olson, Kelly. 2008. *Dress and the Roman Woman: Self-Presentation and Society*. Abingdon and New York: Routledge.

Osborne, Robin. 1996. "Pots, trade and the archaic Greek economy." *Antiquity*, 70: 31–44.

Osborne, Robin. 2004. "Hoards, votives, offerings: the archaeology of the dedicated object." *World Archeology*, 36(1) (*The Object of Dedication*): 1–10.

Osborne, Robin. 2010. "Relics and Remains in a world of anthropomorphic gods." In Alexandra Walsham (ed.), *Relics and Remains, Past & Present Supplement 5*, Oxford: Oxford University Press, 56–72.

Osborne, Robin. 2011. *The History Written on the Classical Greek Body*. Cambridge: Cambridge University Press.

Osborne, Robin. 2016. "Sacrificial Theologies." In Esther Eidinow, Julia Kindt and Robin Osborne (eds.), *Theologies of Ancient Greek Religion*. Cambridge: Cambridge University Press, 233–48.

Osborne, Robin and Jeremy Tanner (eds.). 2007. *Art's Agency and Art History*. Malden, MA: Blackwell.

Oser-Grote, C. 1998. "Einführung in das Studium der Medizin: Eisagogische Schriften des Galen in ihrem Verhältnis zum *Corpus Hippocraticum.*" In W. Kullmann, J. Althoff and M. Asper (eds.), *Gattungen wissenschaftlicher Literatur in der Antike.* Tübingen: G. Narr, 95–117.

Ossandon, J. 2015. "The enactment of economic things." In M. Kornberger et al. (eds.), *Making Things Valuable.* Oxford: Oxford University Press, 187–208.

Panvini, R. 2001 "La nave greca arcaica di Gela. Analisi della tecnica costruttiva e del carico commerciale." In Lezioni Fabio Faccenna (ed.), *Conferenze di archeologia subacquea, I e II ciclo.* Bari: Edipuglia, 139–51.

Papadopoulos, John. 2002. "Minting identity: Coinage, ideology and the economics of colonization in Akhaian Magna Graecia." *CAJ*, 12(1): 21–55.

Papadopoulos, John. 2012. "Money, art and the construction of value in the ancient Mediterranean." In John Papadopoulos and G. Urton (eds.), *The Construction of Value in the Ancient World.* Los Angeles, CA: Cotsen Institute of Archaeology, 261–87.

Papadopoulos, John and G. Urton. 2012. "Introduction: the construction of value in the ancient world." In John Papadopoulos and G. Urton (eds.), *The Construction of Value in the Ancient World.* Los Angeles, CA: Cotsen Institute of Archaeology, 1–47.

Papantoniou, Giorgos. 2012: *Religion and Social Transformations in Cyprus: From the Cypriot Basileis to the Hellenistic Strategos.* Leiden: Brill.

Parker, Robert. 1983. *Miasma: Pollution and Purification in Early Greek Religion.* Oxford: Clarendon Press.

Parker, Robert. 2005. *Polytheism and Society at Athens.* Oxford: Oxford University Press.

Pavlovskis, Zoja. 1973. *Man in an Artificial Landscape: The Marvels of Civilization in Imperial Roman Literature.* Leiden: Brill.

Peña, J. Theodore. 2007a. *Roman Pottery in the Archaeological Record.* Cambridge and New York: Cambridge University Press.

Peña, T. 2007b. "The quantitative analysis of roman pottery: general problems, the methods employed at the palatine east, and the supply of African sigillata to Rome." In E. Papi (ed.), *Supplying Rome and the Empire: The Proceedings of an International Seminar held at Siena-Certosa di Pontignano on May 2–4, 2004, on Rome, the Provinces, Production and Distribution.* Portsmouth, RI: Journal of Roman Archaeology, 153–72.

Pérez Cañizares, P. 2017. "From words to acts: on the applicability of Hippocratic therapy." In M. Formisano and P. van der Eijk (eds.), *Knowledge, Text and Practice in Ancient Technical Writing.* Cambridge: Cambridge University Press, 93–111.

Perry, Curtis (ed.). 2001. *Material Culture and Cultural Materialisms in the Middle Ages and Renaissance.* Turnhout: Brepols.

Pitts, Martin & Miguel John Versluys. Forthcoming. "Objectscapes. A manifesto for investigating the impacts of object flows on past societies." *Antiquity.*

Platt, Verity J. 2011. *Facing the Gods: Epiphany and Representation in Graeco-Roman Art, Literature and Religion.* Cambridge: Cambridge University Press.

Platt, Verity. 2016. "The Matter of Classical Art History." *Daedalus*, 145(2): 69–78.

Platt, Verity J. 2018. "Silent Bones and Singing Stones: Materializing the Poetic Corpus in Hellenistic Greece." In Nora Goldschmidt and Barbara Graziosi (eds.), *Tombs of the Ancient Poets: Between Literary Reception and Material Culture.* Oxford: Oxford University Press, 21–50.

Platt, Verity J. & Michael Squire (eds.). 2010. *The Art of Art History in Graeco-Roman Antiquity*. Arethusa 43(2): 133–63.

Plattner, S. 1989. *Economic Anthropology*. Stanford, CA: Stanford University Press.

Pomey, P. and A. Tchernia. 2005. "Les inventions entre l'anonymat et l'exploit." In E. Lo Cascio (ed.), *Innovazione tecnica e progresso economico nel mondo romano: atti degli incontri capresi di storia dell'economia antica (Capri 13–16 aprile 2003)*. Bari: Edipuglia, 81–99.

Porter, James. 2010. *The Origins of Aesthetic Thought in Ancient Greece: Matter, Sensation, Experience*. Cambridge: Cambridge University Press.

Porter, James. 2012. "The value of aesthetic value." In J. K. Papadopoulos and J. Urton (eds.), *The Construction of Value in the Ancient World*. Los Angeles, CA: Cotsen Institute of Archaeology, 336–53.

Porter, James. 2016. *The Sublime in Antiquity*. Cambridge: Cambridge University Press.

Prayon, Friedhelm. 2000. "Tomb Architecture." In M. Torelli (ed.), *The Etruscans*. Milan: Bompiani.

Preda, A. 1999. "The turn to things: arguments for a sociological theory of things." *The Sociological Quarterly*, 40(2): 347–66.

Price, D. J. de S. 1974. *Gears from the Greeks: The Antikythera Mechanism, a Calendar Computer from ca. 80 B.C.* Philadelphia, PA: American Philosophical Society.

Prusac, M. 2011. *From Face to Face: Recarving of Roman Portraits and the Late-Antique Portrait Arts*. Leiden: Brill.

Prusac Lindhagen, M. 2017. "The Constantinian Bronze Colossus. Nero's Hairstyle and the Beard of Commodus." *Acta ad archaeologiam et artium historiam pertinentia*, 29: 113–30.

Purcell, Nicholas. 1983. "The Apparitores: A Study in Social Mobility." *Papers of the British School at Rome*, 51: 125–73.

Purves, Alex. 2010: *Space and Time in Ancient Greek Narrative*. New York: Cambridge University Press.

Rathje, W. L. and C. Murphy. 1992. *Rubbish! The Archaeology of Garbage*. New York: Harper Collins.

Rawson, Elizabeth. 1987. "Discrimina Ordinum: The Lex Julia Theatralis." *Papers of the British School at Rome*, 55: 83–114.

Rayor, Diane J. 2005. "The Power of Memory in Sappho and Erinna." In Ellen Greene (ed.), *Women Poets in Ancient Greece and Rome*. Norman: University of Oklahoma Press.

Renfrew, Colin. 1986. "Varna and the Emergence of Wealth in Prehistoric Europe." In Arjun Appadurai (ed.), *The Social Life of Things: Commodities in Cultural Perspective*. Cambridge: Cambridge University Press, 141–68.

Renfrew, Colin. 2004. "Towards a Theory of Material Engagement." In Elizabeth DeMarrais, Chris Gosden and Colin Renfrew (eds.), *Rethinking Materiality: The Engagement of Mind with the Material World*. Cambridge: McDonald Institute for Archaeological Research, 23–31.

Reusser, Christoph. 2002. *Vasen für Etrurien. Verbreitung und Funktionen attischer Keramik im Etrurien des 6. und 5. Jahrhunderts v. Chr.* Zurich: Akanthus.

Revell, Louise. 2009. *Roman Imperialism and Local Identities*. Cambridge and New York: Cambridge University Press.

Rhodes, Peter J. and Robin Osborne. 2003. *Greek Historical Inscriptions 404–323 B.C.* Oxford: Oxford University Press.

Richter, Gisela M. A. 1968. *The Furniture of the Greeks, Etruscans and Romans*. London: Phaidon.

Rihll, Tracy E. 2007. *The Catapult: A History*. Yardley, PA: Westholme Publishing.

Rihll, Tracy E. and J. V. Tucker. 2002. "Practice makes perfect: knowledge of materials in classical Athens." In Christopher Tuplin and Tracy E. Rihll (eds.), *Science and Mathematics in Ancient Greek Culture*. Oxford: Oxford University Press, 274–305.

Robb, John. 2013. "Creating Death: An Archaeology of Dying." In Sarah Tarlow and Liv Nilsson Stutz (eds.), *The Oxford Handbook of the Archaeology in Death and Burial*. Oxford: Oxford University Press.

Robinson, David M. 1941. *Metal and Minor Miscellaneous Finds. Olynthus X*. Baltimore, MD: Johns Hopkins University Press.

Robinson, David M. 1942. *Necrolynthia. Olynthus XI*. Baltimore, MD: Johns Hopkins University Press.

Robinson, David M. and W. Graham. 1938. *The Hellenic House. Olynthus VIII*. Baltimore, MD: Johns Hopkins University Press.

Roby, Courtney. 2016. "Embodiment in Latin technical texts." In W. M. Short (ed.), *Embodiment in Latin Semantics*. Studies in language companion series. Amsterdam: John Benjamins, 211–38.

Rotroff, Susan and M. Ntinou. 2013. *Industrial Religion: The Saucer Pyres of the Athenian Agora. Hesperia Supplement* 47. Princeton, NJ: American School of Classical Studies at Athens.

Ruck, B. 2007. *Die Grossen dieser Welt: Kolossalporträts im antiken Rom*. Heidelberg: Verlag Archäologie und Geschichte.

Russell, Ben. 2013. *The Economics of the Roman Stone Trade*. Oxford and New York: Oxford University Press.

Salminen, Elina. 2017. "The Tomb Doth Protest too Much? Constructed Identity in Tomb II at Vergina." In Lisa C. Nevett (ed.), *Theoretical Approaches to the Archaeology of Ancient Greece*. Ann Arbor: University of Michigan Press.

Sauer, Eberhard. 2005. *Coins, Cult and Cultural Identity: Augustan Coins, Hot Springs and the Early Roman Baths at Bourbonne-les-Bains*. Leicester: University of Leicester, School of Archaeology and Ancient History.

Schäfer, Thomas. 1989. *Imperii Insignia: Sella Curulis und Fasces*. Mainz: von Zabern.

Schiffer, Michael B. 1999. *The Material Life of Human Beings: Artifacts, Behavior, and Communication*. London and New York: Routledge.

Schmidt-Linsenhoff, Viktoria. 2014. *Ästhetik der Differenz. Postkoloniale Perspektiven vom 16. Bis zum 21. Jahrhundert*. Marburg: Jonas.

Scott, Sarah. 2006. "Art and the archaeologist." *World Archaeology*, 38(4): 628–43.

Seaford, Richard A. S. 2004. *Money and the Early Greek Mind: Homer, Philosophy, Tragedy*. Cambridge: Cambridge University Press.

Seaford, Richard A. S. 2012. *Cosmology and the Polis*. Cambridge: Cambridge University Press.

Sear, Frank. 2006. *Roman Theatres: An Architectural Study*. Oxford: Oxford University Press.

Sebesta, Judith Lynn. 1994. "Symbolism in the Costume of the Roman Woman." In Judith Lynn Sebesta and Larissa Bonfante (eds.), *The World of Roman Costume*. Madison: University of Wisconsin Press.

Segalen, Victor. 2002. *Essay on Exoticism: An Aesthetics of Diversity*. Durham, NC: Duke University Press.

Senseney, J. R. 2011. *The Art of Building in the Classical World: Vision, Craftsmanship, and Linear Perspective in Greek and Roman Architecture*. Cambridge: Cambridge University Press.

Severy Hoven, Beth. 2012. "Master Narratives and the Wall Painting of the House of the Vettii, Pompeii." *Gender & History*, 24(3): 540–80.

Shaya, Josephine. 2015. "Greek Temple Treasures and the Invention of Collecting." In M. W. Gahtan and D. Pegazzano (eds.), *Museum Archetypes and Collecting in the Ancient World*. Leiden: Brill, 24–32.

Shepherd, Gillian. 2013. "Ancient Identities: Age, Gender, and Ethnicity in Ancient Greek Burials." In Sarah Tarlow and Liv Nilsson Stutz (eds.), *The Oxford Handbook of the Archaeology in Death and Burial*. Oxford: Oxford University Press, 543–58.

Sidoli, N. 2011. "Heron of Alexandria's Date." *Centaurus*, 53(1): 55–61.

Simmel, G. (1907)1978. *The Philosophy of Money*. (Eng. trans. of *Die Phlosophie des Geldes*, 2nd edn.). London: Routledge and Kegan Paul.

Skibo, J. M. and Michael B. Schiffer. 2008. *People and Things: A Behavioral Approach to Material Culture*. New York: Springer.

Sluiter, Ineke and Ralph M. Rosen (eds.). 2012. *Aesthetic Value in Antiquity*. Leiden: Brill.

Smith, Tylor Jo and Dimitris Plantzos (eds.). 2012. "The Greeks and their art." In *A Companion to Greek Art*. Malden, MA: Wiley-Blackwell, 1–14.

Snodgrass, Anthony M. 1964. *Early Greek Armour and Weapons*. Edinburgh: Edinburgh University Press.

Snodgrass, Anthony. 1986. "Interaction by Design: The Greek City State." In Colin Renfrew and John F. Cherry (eds.), *Peer Polity and Socio-Political Change*. Cambridge: Cambridge University Press.

Sourvinou-Inwood, Christiane. 1995. *"Reading" Greek Death: To the End of the Classical Period*. Oxford: Clarendon Press.

Sparkes, Brian and Lucy Talcott. 1970. *Black and Plain Pottery of the 6th, 5th and 4th centuries BC. Agora XII*. Princeton, NJ: American School of Classical Studies at Athens.

Spawforth, Antony J. S. 2011. *Greece and the Augustan Cultural Revolution*. Cambridge: Cambridge University Press.

Squire, Michael. 2009. *Image and Text in Graeco-Roman Antiquity*. Cambridge: Cambridge University Press.

Squire, Michael. 2011. *The Iliad in a Nutshell: Visualizing Epic on the Tabulae Iliacae*. Oxford: Oxford University Press.

Squire, Michael. 2012. "Classical Archaeology and the Contexts of Art History." In Susan E. Alcock and Robin Osborne (eds.), *Classical Archaeology* (Blackwell Studies in Global Archaeology, 2nd edn.). Malden, MA: Wiley-Blackwell, 468–99.

Squire, Michael. 2013. "Embodied ambiguities on the Prima Porta Augustus." *Art History*, 36(2): 242–79.

Squire, Michael. 2015. "Conceptualizing the visual 'arts'." In Pierre Destrée and Penelope Murray (eds.), 2015. *A Companion to Ancient Aesthetics*. Malden, MA: Wiley-Blackwell, 307–26.

Steel, Louise. 2013. *Materiality and Consumption in the Bronze Age Mediterranean*. London: Routledge.

Stevens, S. 1991. "Charon's obol and other coins in ancient funerary practice." *Phoenix*, 45(3): 215–29.

Stewart, Peter. 2003. *Statues in Roman Society: Representation and Response*. Oxford: Oxford University Press.

Stewart, Peter. 2007. "Gell's idols and Roman cult." In R. Osborne and J. Tanner (eds.), *Art's agency and Art History*. Malden, MA: Wiley-Blackwell, 158–78.

Stewart, Susan. 1993. *On Longing: Narratives of the Miniature, the Gigantic, the Souvenir, the Collection*. Durham, NC: Duke University Press.

Stieber, Mary C. 2004. *The Poetics of Appearance in the Attic Korai*. Austin: University of Texas Press.

Stout, Ann M. 1994. "Jewelry as a Symbol of Status in the Roman Empire." In Judith Lynn Sebesta and Larissa Bonfante (eds.), *The World of Roman Costume*. Madison: University of Wisconsin Press.

Strathern, Marilyn. 1988. *The Gender of the Gift*. Berkeley: University of California Press.

Strathern, Marilyn. 1999. *Property, Substance and Effect: Anthropological Essays on Persons and Things*. New Brunswick, NJ: Athlone Press.

Strootman, Rolf and Miguel John Versluys (eds.). 2017. *Persianism in Antiquity*. Stuttgart: Steiner.

Stroup, Sarah Culpepper 2005. "Invaluable Collections: The Illusion of Poetic Presence in Martial's *Xenia* and *Apophoreta*." In Ruud Nauta, Johannes Smolenaars and Harm-Jan Dam (eds.), *Flavian Poetry*. Mnemosyne Suppl. 270. Leiden: Brill, 299–313.

Summers, David. 2010. "Aesthetics." In A. Grafton, G. W. Most and S. Settis (eds.), *The Classical Tradition*. Cambridge, MA: Harvard University Press, 11–18.

Svenbro, Jesper. 1993. *Phrasikleia: An Anthropology of Reading in Ancient Greece*. Trans. from French edn. of 1988 by Janet Lloyd. Ithaca, NY: Cornell University Press.

Swetnam-Burland, M. 2010. "Aegyptus Redacta: The Egyptian Obelisk in the Augustan Campus Martius." *Art Bulletin*, 92(3): 135–53.

Swift, Ellen. 2009. *Style and Function in Roman Decoration: Living with Objects and Interiors*. Aldershot: Ashgate.

Swift, Ellen. 2014. "Design, function and use wear in spoons: reconstructing everyday Roman social practice." *Journal of Roman Studies*, 27: 203–37.

Swift, Ellen. 2017. *Roman Artefacts and Society: Design, Behaviour and Society*. Oxford: Oxford University Press.

Tanner, Jeremy (ed.). 2003: *Sociology of Art: A Reader*. London: Routledge.

Tanner, Jeremy. 2006. *The Invention of Art History in Ancient Greece*. Cambridge: Cambridge University Press.

Tanner, Jeremy and Robin Osborne (ed.). 2007. *Art's Agency and Art History*. Malden, MA: Blackwell.

Taplin, Oliver. 1992. *Homeric Soundings: The Shaping of the* Iliad. Oxford: Clarendon Press.

Tarrant, Richard. 2012. *Virgil* Aeneid *Book XII*. Cambridge: Cambridge University Press.

Taylor, Rabun. 2003. *Roman Builders: A Study in Architectural Process*. Cambridge and New York: Cambridge University Press.

Taylor, Rabun. 2017. "Pagan Sanctuaries." In *The Eerdmans Encyclopedia of Early Christian Art and Architecture, Vol. 2*. Grand Rapids, MI: Eerdmans, 274–7.

Taylor, Rabun, Katherine Rinne and Spiro Kostof. 2016. *Rome: An Urban History from Antiquity to the Present*. Cambridge and New York: Cambridge University Press.

Tchernia, André. 2016. *The Romans and Trade*. Trans. James Grieve with Elizabeth Minchin. Oxford: Oxford University Press.

Temin, Peter. 2013. *The Roman Market Economy*. Princeton, NJ: Princeton University Press.

Thomas, Nicholas. 1991. *Entangled Objects: Exchange, Material Culture, and Colonialism in the Pacific*. Cambridge, MA: Harvard University Press.

Thompson, David L. 1982. *Mummy Portraits in the J. Paul Getty Museum*. Los Angeles, CA: The J. Paul Getty Museum.

Tilley, Christopher Y. 1999. *Metaphor and Material Culture*. Malden, MA: Blackwell.

Todd, Stephen C. 1993. *The Shape of Athenian Law*. Oxford: Clarendon Press.

Toner, Jerry, P. 2014. *A Cultural History of the Senses in Antiquity*. London: Bloomsbury Academic.

Torrence, Robin. 1986. *Production and Exchange of Stone Tools: Prehistoric Obsidian in the Aegean*. Cambridge: Cambridge University Press.

Trentmann, Frank. 2009. "Materiality in the Future of History. Things, Practices and Politics." *Journal of British Studies*, 48: 283–307.

Trimble, Jennifer. 2011. *Women and Visual Replication in Roman Imperial Art and Culture*. Cambridge: Cambridge University Press.

Trimble, Jennifer. 2018. "Beyond Surpise: Looking Again at the Sleeping Hermaphrodite in the Palazzo Massimo." In Brenda Longfellow and Ellen Perry (eds.), *Roman Artists, Patrons and Public Consumption*. Ann Arbor: University of Michigan Press, 13–37.

Tsakirgis, Barbara. 2007. "Fire and smoke: hearths, braziers and chimneys in the Greek house." In James Whitley and Ruth Westgate (eds.), *Building Communities: House, Settlement and Society in the Aegean and Beyond*. London: British School at Athens, 225–31.

Tybjerg, Karin. 2012. "'Senses and Hands to the Same Degree as Thought'—Ole Rømer's Mechanical Astronomy." *Centaurus*, 54(1): 77–102.

Ullucci, Daniel C. 2012. *The Christian Rejection of Animal Sacrifice*. Oxford: Oxford University Press.

Van Alfen, Peter (ed.). 2006. *Agoranomia: Studies in Money and Exchange Presented to John H. Kroll*. New York: American Numismatic Society.

Van Alphen, Ernst. 2016. "Exoticism or the translation of cultural difference." *Espacio, Tiempo y Forma*, 7(4): 159–70.

Van Eck, Caroline. 2015a. *Art, Agency and Living Presence: From the Animated Image to the Excessive Object*. Boston, MA, and Berlin: De Gruyter.

Van Eck, Caroline. 2015b. "Art Works that Refuse to Behave: Agency, Excess and Material Presence in Canova and Manet." *New Literary History*, 46: 409–34.

Van Eck, Caroline, Miguel John Versluys and Pieter Ter Keurs. 2015. "The biography of cultures: style, objects and agency. Proposal for an interdisciplinary approach." *Cahiers de l'École du Louvre. Recherches en histoire de l'art, histoire des civilisations, archéologie, anthropologie et muséologie* [en ligne], 7: 2–22.

Van Oyen, Astrid. 2016. *How Things Make History: The Roman Empire and Its Terra Sigillata Pottery*. Amsterdam: Amsterdam University Press.

Van Oyen, Astrid and Martin Pitts (eds.). 2017. *Materialising Roman Histories*. Oxford, Oxbow.

Varner, Eric. R. 2004. *Mutilation and Transformation: Damnatio Memoriae and Roman Imperial Potraiture*. Leiden: Brill.

Vera, Domenico. 1999. "Wine." In Glen W. Bowersock, Peter Brown and Oleg Grabar (eds.), *Late Antiquity: A Guide to the Postclassical World*. Cambridge, MA, and London: Harvard University Press.

Vernant, Jean-Pierre. 1983. "Hestia-Hermes: the religious expression of space and movement in ancient Greece." In *Myth and Thought among the Greeks*. London: Routledge & Kegan Paul, 127–96.

Versluys, Miguel John. 2010/11. "Archéologie classique et histoire de l'art aux Pays-Bas: des liaisons dangereuses." *Perspective*, 4: 687–701.

Versluys, Miguel John. 2014. "Understanding objects in motion. An archaeological dialogue on Romanisation." *Archaeological Dialogues*, 21(1): 1–20.

Versluys, Miguel John. 2015. "Haunting traditions. The (material) presence of Egypt in the Roman world." In D. Boschung, A. Busch and M. J. Versluys (eds.), *Reinventing* "The invention of tradition"; *Indigenous Pasts and the Roman Present*. Paderborn: Wilhelm Fink, 127–58.

Versluys, Miguel John. 2017a. *Visual Style and Constructing Identity in the Hellenistic World: Nemrud Dağ and Commagene under Antiochos I*. Cambridge: Cambridge University Press.

Versluys, Miguel John. 2017b. "Object-scapes. Towards a material constitution of Romaness?" In A. Van Oyen and M. Pitts (eds.), *Materialising Roman Histories*. Oxford: Oxbow, 191–9.

Versluys, Miguel John. 2017c. "Exploring Aegyptiaca and their material agency throughout global history." In T. Hodos with A. Geurds, P. Lane, I. Lilley, M. Pitts, G. Shelach, M. Stark and M. J. Versluys (eds.), *The Routledge Handbook of Globalisation and Archaeology*. London: Routledge, 74–89.

Versluys, Miguel John and Greg Woolf. Forthcoming. "Artefacts and their humans: materializing the history of Roman religion." In J. Rüpke (ed.), *Römische Religion* (Die Religionen der Menschheit). Stuttgart: Steiner.

Von Kaenel, H.-M. and F. Kemmers. (eds.). 2009. *Coins in Context: New Perspectives for the Interpretation of Coin Finds*. Mainz: Philipp Von Zabern.

Von Reden, Sitta. 1995. *Exchange in Ancient Greece*. London: Duckworth.

Von Reden, Sitta. 2010. *Money in Classical Antiquity*. Cambridge: Cambridge University Press.

Von Reden, Sitta and Walter Scheidel. 2002. *The Ancient Economy*. Edinburgh: Edinburgh University Press.

Vout, Caroline. 2012. "Putting the art into artifact." In S. Alcock and R. Osborne (eds.), *Classical Archaeology*, 2nd edn. Malden, MA: Wiley-Blackwell, 442–67.

Vout, Caroline. 2018. *Classical Art: A Life History from Antiquity to the Present*. Princeton, NJ: Princeton University Press.

Ward-Perkins, Brian. 2005. *The Fall of Rome and the End of Civilization*. Oxford: Oxford University Press.

Warren, James I. 2007. *Presocratics*. Stocksfield: Acumen.

Warren, Meredith J. C. 2017. "Tastes from Beyond: Persephone's Pomegranate and Otherworldly Consumption in Antiquity." In Kelli C. Rudolph (ed.), *Taste and the Ancient Senses: The Senses in Antiquity*. London and New York: Routledge.

Watkins, Trevor. 2004. "Architecture and 'Theatres of Memory' in the Neolithic of Southwest Asia." In Elizabeth DeMarrais, Chris Gosden and Colin Renfrew (eds.), *Rethinking Materiality: The Engagement of Mind with the Material World*. Cambridge: McDonald Institute for Archaeological Research, 97–106.

Watson, Andrew. 1999. "Foodstuffs." In Glen W. Bowersock, Peter Brown and Oleg Grabar (eds.), *Late Antiquity: A Guide to the Postclassical World*. Cambridge, MA, and London: Harvard University Press.

Webster, Jane. 2001. "Earth, fire and water: the making and marketing of Roman Samian ware." In N. J. Higham (ed.), *Archaeology of the Roman Empire: A Tribute to the Life and Works of Professor Barri Jones*. Oxford: Archaeopress, 289–302.

Weitzman, Kurt. 1979. *Age of Spirituality: Late Antique and Early Christian Art, Third to Seventh Century*. Princeton, NJ: Princeton University Press.

Wellington, I. 2006. "The role of Iron Age coinage in archaeological contexts." In P. de Jersey (ed.), *Celtic Coinage: New Discoveries, New Discussions*. Oxford: Archaeopress, 81–96.

Wells, Peter. (ed.). 2013. *Rome Beyond Its Frontiers: Imports, Attitudes and Practices*. Journal of Roman Archaeology Supplementary series, no. 94. Portsmouth, RI: Journal of Roman Archaeology.

Westermann, William. 1924. "Account of lamp oil from the estate of Apollonius." *Classical Philology*, 19: 229–60.

Wheeler, M. 2005. *Reconstructing the Cognitive World: The Next Step*. Cambridge, MA: MIT Press.

Willis, S. 2013. "Red from the green field: Samian ware at villas and other rural sites in Roman Britain. An examination of site evidence and general trends." In M. Fulford and E. Durham (eds.), *Seeing Red: New Economic and Social Perspectives on Terra Sigillata*. London: Institute of Classical Studies, 224–41.

Wilson, Andrew. 2002. "Machines, power and the ancient economy." *Journal of Roman Studies*, 92: 1–32.

Wilson, Andrew. 2008. "Machines in Greek and Roman technology." In J. P. Oleson (ed.), *The Oxford Handbook of Engineering and Technology in the Classical World*. Oxford: Oxford University Press, 337–66.

Wilson, Peter J. 2000. *The Athenian Institution of the* Khoregia: *The Chorus, the City, and the Stage*. Cambridge: Cambridge University Press.

Witcher, Robert. 2006. "Broken Pots and Meaningless Dots? Surveying the Rural Landscapes of Roman Italy." *Papers of the British School at Rome*, 74: 39–72.

Withington, Phillip. 2014. "Introduction: Cultures of Intoxication." *Past and Present*, 222 (Suppl. 9.1): 9–33.

Wolfsdorf, D. 2014. "Plato's epistemology." In J. Warren and F. Sheffield (ed.), *The Routledge Companion to Ancient Philosophy*. London: Routledge, 157–70.

Wolters, R. 2012. "The Julio-Claudians." In W. Metcalf (ed.), *The Oxford Handbook of Greek and Roman Coinage*. Oxford: Oxford University Press, 335–55.

Woolf, Greg. 1998. *Becoming Roman: The Origins of Provincial Civilization in Gaul*. Cambridge: Cambridge University Press.

Wright, M. T. 2001. "The Antikythera Mechanism." *Astronomy and Geophysics*, 42(3): 3.9-a-3.9.

Wright, M. T. 2003. "Epicyclic Gearing and the Antikythera Mechanism Part I." *Antiquarian Horology*, 27: 270–79.

Wright, M. T. 2005. "Epicyclic Gearing and the Antikythera Mechanism Part II." *Antiquarian Horology*, 29: 51–63.

Wright, M. T. 2007. "The Antikythera Mechanism reconsidered." *Interdisciplinary Science Reviews*, 32(1): 27–44.

Wright, M. T., A. Bromley and H. Magou. 1995. "Simple X-ray tomography and the Antikythera Mechanism." In I. Liritzis and G. N. Tsokas (eds.), *Archaeometry in South Eastern Europe: Second Conference in Delphi, 19–21st April 1991*. Rixensart: Council of Europe, 531–43.

Young, Rodney S. 1951. "An industrial district of ancient Athens." *Hesperia*, 20: 135–288.

Zanini, E. 1996. "Ricontando la Terra Sigillata Africana." *Archeologia Medievale*, 23: 677–88.

Zanker, Paul. 1988. *The Power of Images in the Age of Augustus*. Ann Arbor: University of Michigan Press.

Zimmer, Gerhard. 1982. *Römische Berufsdarstellungen*. Berlin: Gebr. Mann.

Zuiderhoek, Arjan J. 2009. *The Politics of Munificence in the Roman Empire: Citizens, Elites and Benefactors in Asia Minor*. Cambridge: Cambridge University Press.

Zuniga, G. 1999. "An ontology of economic objects." *American Journal of Economics and Sociology*, 58(2): 299–312.

NOTES ON CONTRIBUTORS

Lin Foxhall is Dean of the School of Histories, Languages, and Cultures and Rathbone Professor of Ancient History and Classical Archaeology at the University of Liverpool. She is on the editorial board of *World Archaeology*, has worked as an archaeologist in both Greece and Italy, and is the author of *Studying Gender in Classical Antiquity* (Cambridge, 2013) and *Olive Cultivation in Ancient Greece* (Oxford, 2007).

Jennifer Gates-Foster is Assistant Professor of Classical Archaeology at the University of North Carolina at Chapel Hill. Her interests range across the art and archaeology of the Near East and Egypt in the Hellenistic and Roman periods, but she has worked particularly in the eastern desert of Egypt. She is the author of a forthcoming monograph entitled *The Archaeology of Borderlands in Hellenistic Upper Egypt*.

Ann Kuttner is Associate Professor of the History of Art at the University of Pennsylvania. Her interests span the whole Hellenistic and Roman worlds. She was involved with the excavations at Villa Magna in Lazio and their publication, and she is the author of *Dynasty and Empire in the Age of Augustus: The Case of the Boscoreale Cups* (Berkeley, 1995).

Robin Osborne is Professor of Ancient History at the University of Cambridge and a Fellow of King's College Cambridge and of the British Academy. His work spreads over the archaeology, art history, and history of Greece, particularly between 800 and 300 BCE. His most recent books are *The Transformation of Athens: Painted Pottery and the Creation of Classical Greece* (Princeton, 2018) and, with P. J. Rhodes, *Greek Historical Inscriptions 478–404 BC* (Oxford, 2017).

Courtney Ann Roby is Associate Professor of Classics at Cornell University. Her interests focus upon scientific and technical texts from the ancient world and the interaction of verbal and visual elements in those texts. She is the author of *Technical Ekphrasis in Greek and Roman Science and Literature: The Written Machine between Alexandria and Rome* (Cambridge, 2016).

Rabun Taylor is Associate Professor of Classics at the University of Texas at Austin. His interests focus upon Greek and Roman architecture and urbanism. He has undertaken archaeological fieldwork in both Greece and Italy. His books include *Roman Builders: A Study in Architectural Process* (Cambridge, 2003) and *The Moral Mirror of Roman Art* (Cambridge, 2008).

Miguel John Versluys is Professor of Classical and Mediterranean Archaeology at the University of Leiden. His interests focus upon the Hellenistic world and the eastern Roman Empire. He heads a major research project "Innovating objects. The impact of global connections and the formation of the Roman Empire (ca. 200–30 BC)." His recent books include *Visual Style and Constructing Identity in the Hellenistic World: Nemrud Dağ and Commagene under Antiochos I* (Cambridge, 2017).

Caroline Vout is Professor of Classics at the University of Cambridge. Her work ranges widely across Greek and Roman art and its reception and the cultural history of the Greek and Roman worlds. Her most recent books are *Sex on Show: Seeing the Erotic in Greece and Rome* (British Museum Press and University of California Press, 2013) and *Classical Art: A Life History from Antiquity to the Present* (Princeton, 2018).

INDEX